Y0-BSF-757

Why Doesn't Russian Industry Work?

Already published

The Challenge: Economics of Perestroika
Abel Aganbegyan

Rural Russia Under the New Regime
Viktor Danilov

The Peoples of the Soviet Union
Viktor Kozlov

Five Days Which Transformed Russia
Sergei Mstislavskii

The Theory of Peasant Cooperatives
Alexander Chayanov

Universe of the Mind
Yuri M. Lotman

Why Doesn't Russian Industry Work?

LEONID KOSALS

Translated by
John Crowfoot, Igor Poluyan and Valeriya Sedova

I.B.TAURIS PUBLISHERS
LONDON • NEW YORK

Published in 1994 by
I.B.Tauris & Co Ltd
45 Bloomsbury Square
London WC1A 2HY

175 Fifth Avenue
New York
NY 10010

In the United States of America
and Canada distributed by
St Martin's Press
175 Fifth Avenue
New York
NY 10010

A full CIP record for this book is available from the British Library

Library of Congress Catalog card number: 93–61259
A full CIP record for this book is available from the Library of Congress

ISBN 1–85043–190–6

Typeset by Photoprint, Torquay, Devon
Printed and bound in Great Britain by
WBC Ltd, Bridgend, Mid Glamorgan

Contents

Tables and Figures

Tables

Figures

Preface

The End of the Ideology of Renovation

This book is dedicated to innovations made in the former USSR and in the present post-communist, post-Soviet Russia. All types of innovation are reviewed – not only technical and technological, but also socio-economic innovations, i.e. the changes in the types of property and power.

Russia is currently going through the next in a series of innovation booms. New political and economic structures, new types of social interrelation between the subjects of these cultures are being established. However, the majority of the population in the country hardly realizes at present what is going on around them and what changes are actually taking place. It is yet more difficult for Western readers to understand.

There are four reasons that make it difficult for the West to understand the innovations going on in Russia. The first is a result of their traditionally 'shadowy' meaning, a consequence of the duality in the Soviet elite's position, that of so-called 'nomenclature'. As the dominant class of the USSR/Russia, the élite used to wear the mask of the Soviet people, depicting itself as integral to them ('the party is one bone and one flesh of the people'). This gave rise to a latent element in the motivation behind innovations carried out by the dominant class. The second reason is connected with the first, in that the innovation became a part of the policy conducted by different dominant (or striving to become so) groups of society. Hence, the third reason: constantly changing innovations used by the authorities as an instrument to govern the people. And finally, the fourth reason – the existence in Russia of two levels in the development of the innovative processes: those coming from 'above' and those from 'below', initiated by ordinary workers, specialists and managers.

By taking these reasons into account it is possible to understand some specific features of the innovations in the former USSR and the Russia of today. These features are unprecedented; they occur in no other country in the world. Obviously the importance and scope of problems connected with innovations are different in different types of society. For example, under the conditions of ideologization of economies (as it took place in the USSR) and its politicization (as it used to be and still remains in Russia), the problems are changing from those comparatively limited to the sphere of science and technology, to global problems concerning all aspects of society – policy, legal regulation of economics, as well as its administrative management. Such globalization is explained by the monopolization of all serious innovations in Russia by the ruling élite: it is possible to achieve innovations of real importance in this country only for the political authorities in tandem with big managers; if an ordinary engineer, worker or scientist tries to elaborate and apply even an obviously useful innovation the innovator has to overcome the resistance of local and central élites. Their reaction to individual innovators is, as a rule, not to ban or prohibit their innovations, but to hinder and to slow them down, if possible. If an individual innovator starts to break through these obstacles, they can be seen to take the form of serious political, legal, economical and ideological barriers. Thus it becomes absolutely clear from this 'struggle with the system' that the innovations are really a complicated problem with roots in the former USSR.

It is not by chance, therefore, that while depicting innovative processes in Soviet economics the author has moved into a significantly broader field. As a result, the book provides comprehensive research into major social problems of Soviet economics during the agony period of totalitarianism.

The problem of innovations has been almost totally ignored by Soviet scientists. And this, to my mind, is not by chance. The problem was of specific and rather piquant importance to the authoritative power of Soviet economics and the Central Committee of the CPSU. In the 20th century, Russia has appeared to be an immense testing area for a grandiose 75-year Communist experiment, staged by History. This experiment was going on under the main slogan of renovating the traditional Russian socio-political and economic system (as they used to sing: 'We shall construct our own new world . . .'). Hence the entire USSR/CPSU 75-year history represented a chain of innovations conceived and fulfilled within the idea of constructing Communism. Such upheavals of the CPSU and Soviet state as industrialization, collectivization, solving national problems, nature transformations, great construction projects etc. were regarded by their authors and performers as grandiose innovations, fulfilled in accordance with the laws of building socialism and Communism in the USSR. And indeed, the systematic innovations did transform the economic relations and territorial structure of the country, the system of settling people in new places, transforming national relations.

The innovation policy has also influenced the culture: 'prolet-cult', Communist morals, Communist education, socialist realism in art – this is a list, far from complete, of revolutionary innovations in spiritual life. Absence of any control over the 'bosses' on high has made this field of social experiments and extending social and economic innovations practically unlimited.

Global, radical, macro-innovations 'from above' and 'cosmetic' micro-innovations 'from below' – this was the pattern of development of the innovation process during the 75-year Communist experiment in the former USSR.

Today, when it is known that the economic policy of the Central Committee of the CPSU cost the Soviet people 50–60 million lives, it is not appropriate to describe this policy as a chain of innovations. But the tragedy of Russian history does not exclude a theoretical analysis; on the contrary, the tragedy of history and that of the immediate present in Russia makes such analysis indispensable. Thus today one of the major purposes of a theoretical analysis of the innovations policy in the former USSR is to find the answer to the question: what was the function of innovations in this country? Were they really aimed at the creation of Communism, at the development of economics, at improvements in living standards for the population of the country? Or was there some other purpose?

In fact the ruling power of the CPSU did have its 'shadowy' purpose, and was successful in achieving it – a purpose that was neither written about nor spoken of in the USSR. And I think that probably only a few people guessed it. This purpose was the self-advancement and reinforcement of the power of the ruling authorities: the Party, the Soviet élite. Not only such actions as industrialization and collectivization, but also other more or less noticeable innovations as the Soviet trade unions, launching the Soviet satellite into space, the Kalashnikov submachine-gun, continuous steel-casting technology and whatever novelties were born and put into practice – everything was done on behalf and for the sake of praising the ruling and guiding force of all of this – the CPSU, or rather the power at its head. This power has managed to create and support the illusion of its supreme rightness for 75 years. The innovations it conducted were the major method of establishing this illusion and of maintaining this myth in the eyes of its own citizens and of the world public. This means that innovations in the USSR were not so much performing their direct economic functions as functions of an entirely different character – ideological and status-oriented. And it is for this reason that the several thousand ordinary economists who dared to protest against innovations carried out by the Central Committee of the CPSU were politically condemned as 'people's enemies' in the 1930s, or as 'thieves of socialist property' during Brezhnev's time, and subsequently died in prison.

Innovations in the USSR played the part of a specific mechanism for managing the behaviour of millions of people. They assisted in the mythologization of mass-consciousness and helped to educate 'the little screws' of the state machine.

What of the micro-innovations performed by the people from 'below', i.e. by the managers and specialists of enterprises, the workers and collective farmers? They also were performing a non-visible 'shadowy' function – they were pretending to improve quasi-progressive 'socialist productional relations', already established. For example, such 'micro-innovations' as the Communist labour teams of the 1950s or the team-contracting work in agriculture of the 1980s were assessed by the Central Committee of the CPSU as improving the mechanism of Soviet economics, as a method of increasing productivity of labour, of solving the food problem. These innovations used to appear in all branches of production all the time. And they used to appear always at similar periods, i.e. when a branch started to decay.

One more 'shadowy' function of micro-innovations has been revealed: they were aimed at finding potential reserves of the Soviet economics, reserves which could be used without changing the type of property, without weakening the leading role of the CPSU and of the state authorities. Therefore the micro-innovations of the 'lower strata' were allowed only within fixed and rather narrow limits, until these lower strata started seriously to improve the 'socialist productional relations'. To do it seriously, without sanction from above, was totally prohibited. Those who attempted genuinely to improve the Soviet economic system, thus encroaching upon the innovation monopoly of the 'upper strata', were immediately identified by the ruling authorities. Quite a lot of such serious innovators died during the USSR years.

These features, noted by myself and by many others, of innovations in the USSR and in post-communist Russia, are described in this book. L. Y. Kosals reveals that there were never, and could never exist, normal innovative processes in the USSR. Moreover, normal innovative processes are not possible in totalitarian systems at all in general, because they exist only in contradiction to these systems: a system in which political management is in co-operation with the administrative management of the economy is disastrous for real innovation. Only pseudo-innovations in the service of some latent purpose are possible under such a system.

I have pointed out some problems of a theoretical nature. They are important, of course. But now, another aspect of the innovations problem is far more important for Western countries – that is, an applied, practical one. Today's questions are as follows: Will Russia be able to adapt itself to the new forms of economic relations suggested by Western partners? Will the governing bodies of Russia be able to create favourable conditions for the normal activity of Western firms! Will Russian administrators, engineers and entrepreneurs be able to work at joint ventures, together with foreign specialists? Will Russian workers, specialists, administrators and employees be able to work the same way as their equivalents in foreign firms do? Will they be able to work in accordance with the norms of world civilization? The replies to these questions are of vital, practical importance for the Western entrepreneurs of today. The replies depend on the innovational potential of Russia. Nobody really knows the capacity and value of this potential. There are no books on it yet. My hope is that this book, depicting a vivid panorama of innovative processes in Russia and introducing the world to innovations in this country, will be a valuable aid for scientists as well as for those pragmatically interested in Russian economics.

R. V. Ryvkina
Professor of Sociology

Why Doesn't Russian Industry Work?

Introduction

Speaking about Russia, many people inside the country and in the West repeat that the reforms started by Gorbachev and continued by Yeltsin are irrevocable, and that Russia is steadily moving towards creating a market economy in a new democratic society. A number of old structures of the totalitarian system have indeed been destroyed in Russia. There is no longer an all-powerful Politburo or Central Committee of the CPSU; the KGB of the USSR has been liquidated; the old Gosplan of the USSR has been closed. Attempts are being made to establish a market economy, to liberate the individual from state dictates, to secure human rights, to form a multi-party political system.

But despite all this, words concerning the irreversibility of reforms in Russia resemble invocations pronounced for reassurance more than conclusions obtained as the result of analysis. In fact the newly born private enterprises and political parties are strikingly like former Soviet organizations in their behaviour, in the attitudes of their leaders and in the results of their activities. However, there now no longer exists a powerful supervisor, such as the previous totalitarian state used to be. Therefore the activities of newly appearing social actors are exacerbating the crisis of Russian society, rather than solving actual problems.

Now Russia is suffering from 'freedom-shock' and is trying to get used to it. People have not yet accustomed themselves to life under the conditions of freedom. Society has not yet elaborated institutions which provide guarantees against the abuses of freedom on behalf of individuals as well as of whole social groups. The principal question now is whether Russia has enough time at its disposal to set up these indispensable social institutions and to overcome its freedom-shock.

Meanwhile armed conflicts are gradually gathering force in outlying districts of the country. There are many potential hot-points in Central Asia, the Northern Caucasus and in national republics in Russia. The population is increasingly overwhelmed with disappointment in the transformations that are going on, and is losing confidence in their success. An era of social uncertainty has come, when the pendulum of changes may swing back to totalitarianism (most likely in the form of Russian facism) with almost the same probability as it may swing forth, to democracy and the market.

To understand the directions of and reasons for change in Russia it is necessary to study the mechanisms of social transformation which have been set up in the country during the last few decades and which continue operating in many ways up until now in various spheres of society. This book is dedicated to the analysis of these mechanisms. The main emphasis is given to a study of how actually the innovations took place in Soviet organizations, and how and why they were successful or they failed.

Three investigations in different spheres of society carried out with the participation of the author in 1985–92 provide the empirical basis of the book. The innovative behaviour of workers and its regulation mechanisms were studied in 1985 in a survey conducted in 47 collective and state farms of the Novosibirsk region. Three hundred managers and specialists involved with the innovations were polled, and statistical data on the socio-economic development of enterprises and their innovative activity were collected and processed. The attitude towards changes going on in the economy was analysed among 100 'RAPO' (administration of the Agro-Industrial Complex at the district level) managers in western Siberia in 1988. A study of the socio-economic problems of civil and defence research institutes in Moscow, Novosibirsk, Voronezh and Vladimir was carried out in 1992. This investigation was a part of the International Research Project 'R&D Management in Transition to Market Economy' (directors: Professor S. Glasiev from Russia and Professor R. Levin from the USA). There were 565 managers of research units surveyed in 21 institutes. Problems in the work of organizations, difficulties in the spreading of R&D results among the enterprises, as well as leaders' opinions concerning possible ways to solve the problems were investigated.

The book consists of three parts. In the first, possible ways of overcoming stagnation in innovative processes are analysed. Problems of stagnation in innovation at the level of the enterprises are discussed in the second part. In the third, stagnation causes in the innovative processes of Soviet society are analysed.

The author would like to express his profound gratitude to Professor R. V. Ryvkina, who supervised the first two studies on which this book is based.

Useful advice concerning the structure of the text was given by Professor T. Shanin, and was helpful in finalizing the book.

Valuable comments regarding manuscript preparation were given by Professors T. I. Zaslavskaya and V. P. Rassokhin.

Dr. B. D. Urlov and Dr. V. V. Valukov (the representative functionaries of the Russian Ministry of Science and Technical Policy) gave important assistance in the collection of data in research institutes.

The author is also grateful to his colleagues A. V. Ledeneva, V. A. Lisov, L. V. Potekhina, P. S. Rostovtsev and M. L. Sukhovskiy, who helped in collecting and processing the data.

I

From Stagnation to Transformation in Russia

1

Inadequacy and Hardships of Transformation

As innovative processes* depend on a vast circle of societal factors, in this first chapter we will look at the recent political and economic contexts of innovations in Russia. These contexts are determined by the transformation of Russian society into a democracy and market economy.

After the decades of slow social changes an epoch of stormy transformations has started in Russia. A flow of innovations in ideology, politics, the economy and culture is increasing, almost unstoppably. During the last five years the most noticeable innovations are the discreditation of Communist ideology; the disintegration of the USSR and a series of local wars in and between the former republics; the removal of the CPSU from power; the founding of multiple political organizations of various orientations; comparatively free elections; the opening of borders; and the collapse of the Central Planning System, allowing private property and creating a lot of non-state organizations. While many have found their own social niches, some people have hardly had time to become aware of the changes. They cannot completely use the new opportunities.

During the 'Brezhnev stagnation period' social changes were slow and gradual. Technological development was carried out unevenly, in jerks. Political drives and concentration of resources

*By innovative processes, we mean the totality of innovations carried out by an organization over a certain period of time. Thus the term can cover anything from a shift to new technology to a new way of organizing or remunerating the workforce.

in directions judged by the ruling powers as most important were the preconditions for movement. But over the last five years a technological degradation has taken place in almost all spheres of the economy. Equipment has been deteriorating, allocations for R&D reduced, the number of inventions fell.

Now the discrepancy between the rapid social changes and technological degradation has begun to be apparent. The people see that the promised political freedom has partially been achieved, that transition to the market (albeit at considerable cost) is being accomplished, but that life is getting steadily worse. Prices are going up at fantastic speed, the commodities available in shops are still scarce, the former deficits dominate now almost as much as then, and some new ones are being added. There have appeared the unemployed and refugees, groups not known in Russia since the time of the Second World War. Some social groups (pensioners without relatives, large families with many children, invalids) have found themselves on the brink of starvation. All this to a great extent is the consequence of a sharp recession of production, caused by the decrease of investments and the slowing down of technological innovations under the conditions of multiple changes in the political and economic system.

Although this discrepancy has only recently become apparent, its roots actually lie in the political and economic institutions of the Soviet totalitarian system. These have dominated Russia for more than 70 years – longer than in any other country of the Soviet bloc, and long enough to see the creation during this period of 'a new man' entirely ignorant of any norms of behaviour under the market and democracy. As a result, the attempt at transformation has turned out to be more painful and complicated in Russia than in any other country.

1.1 Democracy in Russia: *bellum omnium contra omnes*?

Russia has been living for more than five years in conditions of relative political freedom. The state is no longer persecuting its citizens for expressing their own opinion. Authorities have allowed the establishment of independent political organizations which now lay claim to political power in the country. The period of five years is sufficiently long to summarize some of the results of political freedom in the behaviour of Russian society.

The reforms in Russia started with Gorbachev's arrival in the Kremlin and the adoption of a new political line of the CPSU named 'perestroika' at the end of the 1980s. This was directed towards rapid modernization of the established system at the cost of its integration with the new political and economic institutions – democracy and the market. At the same time, and side by side with these institutions borrowed from the capitalist system, the foundations of socialism in the USSR were to be conserved throughout the assumed perestroika, i.e. the mono-party system, the leading role of the state sector in the economy, the preservation of state paternalism and centralized management for the main spheres of society. This conception was essentially contradictory in itself. It envisaged the possibility of achieving in a brief period of time what actually could have been attained during the decades of quiet evolution (to introduce the market while keeping the centrally managed state sector in the economy). Some directions of that strategy were not possible at all (to create democracy under the conditions of a mono-party system).

The changes in the ideology and political system took place very quickly in the USSR.[1] In 1989–90 Gorbachev had a feeling they were taking place too rapidly. Evidently he had been afraid that the power of the CPSU and the centralized management of the economy, as well as the entire union state, could collapse under the pressure of the liberal intelligentsia and national movements in the republics. Gorbachev tried to slow down the process of change and to make it more gradual. Some of his liberal counsellors retired from the scene. He also took a step back from 'Democratic Russia' and made some moves that were interpreted at that time as being in the right direction (in particular, evidently, in the second half of 1990, when operations in the Baltic area were prepared that were to be carried out at the beginning of 1991).

However, Gorbachev was not supported by those politically active groups that wished for quicker political and economic reforms, and they criticized him cruelly for the delays. Neither was he supported by the bureaucrats striving to stop the changes. His attempts to start up in Novo-Ogarevo a process of reconciling the contradictory interests of supporters and opponents of the economic and political reforms totally failed, and consequently led to an attempt to restore the old system in August 1991. The failure of this attempt provoked the sharp and chaotic disintegration of the traditional Soviet political and economic structures, based on CPSU control. In the shortest possible period of time – three or four months – the Union ministries and state committees right up to the statistics service were shut, the activity of the CPSU was suspended, the buildings of the district and regional committees of the CPSU were sealed up and their employees were dismissed. The activity of Party committees involved with enterprises was also halted.

The stoppage of the CPSU activity has entirely changed the political system in Russia. However, it has not led to the setting up of a democratic, multi-party political system, as many people expected. This was because of two factors.

The first factor is the population's lack of experience of democratic political life – the lack of any understanding of the idea of democracy and human rights. Previous experience under the Soviet system testified only to negative orientations (what should not be done). The majority of the Soviet people have never been abroad, in contrast to the citizens of East European countries. And living conditions in the former USSR are such that people cannot afford the time for any serious mass political activity, using it mainly for work and standing in queues.

The second factor leading to the non-establishment of a democratic political system in Russia concerns the favourable conditions enjoyed by the previous Soviet political élite. Paradoxical as it may seem, these conditions were to a great extent created by the removal of the CPSU from the political stage. This led, indirectly, to the total lifting of the previous restrictions for the activity of 'nomenclature'. A new system was created, in which many representatives of the old élite hold high positions.

In the previous Soviet system a nomenclature's functionary used to receive multiple favours that were not available to the ordinary citizen. However, the life of bureaucrats was strictly regulated by formal and informal norms restricting any possible tyranny of Communist officials under the mono-party system. For instance, professors at the highest Party schools had no powers to conclude contracts for research posts for professors in common universities.[2] Otherwise professors of the Party schools, owing to their informal contacts with high officials ('*blat*'), could have obtained very profitable contracts and as a result could earn more money than many professors of the common universities, executive bureaucrats in the system of education, and even Party leaders. It is obvious that such a situation could have provoked indignation among both the workers of the educational system and Party rulers.

As the Soviet political system evolved (over a period of more than half a century) specific standards of behaviour were elaborated. Party bosses had to be absolutely followed in those standards, for fear of a carefully developed system of punishments: from a Party reprimand up to dismissal from the nomenclature. This last meant social death for a representative of the Soviet élite. Of course, such restrictions of behaviour as developed for the Soviet élite had no democratic character, did not provide for the separation of powers and could not establish a system of checks and balances, vital for the existence of democracy. However, they certainly constrained the representatives of the ruling élite.

Gorbachev's perestroika shook the nomenclature system by removing a multitude of the old restrictions. For instance, the Party and state officials were permitted to be involved in private entrepreneurship, something that previously constituted a serious crime. It is necessary to point out that private entrepreneurship is also prohibited for state officials in most countries with a market economy, and, furthermore, that the active private entrepreneurship of bureaucrats has undoubtedly provoked hatred towards Gorbachev on the part of the population of the country. Most common people naturally had no such possibilities for private entrepreneurship as were available for the state and Party bosses in high places. This also aroused to some extent a wave of anti-market feeling among the people at the end of the perestroika period (in 1990–91), while in its first stage (1988–9) one could talk about a 'market enthusiasm' in the country. However, the market reforms would never have been possible without the possibility of entrepreneurship for the officials; they would have been stopped at the very beginning by the nomenclature, who hold real power in Russia. Gorbachev, on the contrary, made market reforms advantageous for the ruling élite, and thus started up the economic mechanism which finally assisted their transformation.

For all these reasons most of the population was actually cut off from establishing a new political system in Russia. Instead, it was built up mainly through the efforts of the old Soviet élite, joined by a number of 'new people' (these are mostly representatives of various professional groups of the intelligentsia – former engineers, physicians, economists, scientists). The 'new people' played an active part in new political movements and in elections to the legislative authorities. Many of them successfully became integrated into the Moscow and local political élites.

As a result, freedom in Russia has not yet led to democracy. At present several hundred political parties have appeared in the country. However, they do not exert any important influence upon the situation at the national level. One of these 'dwarfish' parties (made up of anything between several dozens to tens of thousands of members) may suddenly come to power at a time of destabilization, but under conditions of relative stability they do not play any significant role in the events going on in the country.

Up to October 1993 two forces determined the development of the situation in Russia. On the one hand, there was the Supreme

Soviet of Russia headed by Ruslan Khazbulatov, and on the other hand, the presidential–governmental bloc headed by Boris Yeltsin. The first of these forces was formally called legislative, the other one executive. Meanwhile, each of them was analogous to the abolished CPSU, in both their structure and their functions. Each was striving for total power, striving to issue legislative acts, to execute them and to control their execution as the CPSU used to do for over 70 years.

The legislative authorities of Russia, sometimes called 'Parliament' in the Western manner, had in their possession the Congress of the people's deputies as their superior organ (as previously the CPSU had its Congress as *its* superior organ). The Supreme Soviet operated at intervals between Congresses (the Communist Party had its Central Committee of the CPSU). The Supreme Soviet in its turn was managed by the Presidium of the Supreme Soviet (previously there was the Politburo of the Central Committee of the CPSU). The Presidium and sessions of the Supreme Soviet as well as the Congress sessions were supervised by one and the same person – Ruslan Khazbulatov – called 'Speaker of the Russian Parliament', also in the Western manner. However, he was closer to the General Secretary of the former CPSU in his real mode of behaviour and ambitions than to the Speaker of Parliament in a democratic state. Most deputies personally depended on him and his orders in getting apartments in Moscow, missions abroad, etc.

The Supreme Soviet did not only issue laws. Parallel with its legislative activity, it fulfilled the important function of an executive authority. For instance, it had under its direct subordination and control the pension fund of Russia, in which several hundred billion roubles had accumulated by 1992. The officials of this foundation amount to several hundred employees (equal to an average-size ministry). Its managers and professionals were appointed by the Supreme Soviet. The latter also supervised its current activity and directly influenced the distribution of colossal allocations outside the budget control system.

The Supreme Soviet replaced the Court authorities whenever it needs to and of its own accord. This happened, for example, in the well-known case with the newspaper *Izvestiya*, when the Supreme Soviet under Khazbulatov's pressure cancelled the Ministry of Information decision on registering the newspaper as an independent means of mass-media and subjected it to itself. And when the newspaper brought an action against Khazbulatov for damages resulting from this action, the Chairman of the Supreme Legislative simply did not appear before the Court, or even send his representative.

As far as the presidential–governmental bloc is concerned, there are no congresses within its frame of operations. There is still less 'glasnost', or openness, in its actions than in the activities of the Supreme Soviet. At the national level it consists of four parts: (1) the President's staff; (2) government and its staff; (3) the Security Council; (4) ministries and federal agencies (over 100). This bloc is almost totally controlled by President Yeltsin, who appoints and dismisses the leaders of all the institutions and approves the key decisions, while at the same time one of the main tasks of the presidential–governmental bloc is the fulfilment of economic reform – introduction of the market in Russia. In the sphere of economics the President even has the right of issuing legislative acts (edicts). Such acts often result in a violation of existing laws, which is justified by referring to a lack of correspondence between the old Russian constitution, new legislation and the task of transition to the market.

The Supreme Soviet and the presidential–governmental bloc both practically ignored the Court authorities, and the Court itself is now actually paralysed in Russia. The Court is thus unable to have a serious influence upon important decision-making, or to control the activity of the Supreme organs.

Although both the Supreme Soviet and the presidential–governmental bloc were aiming at total power in the country, they differed from each other in their structure and purposes. In the President's crew a new nomenclature is relatively predominant, being interested in greater freedom in the economy and in rapidly implementing economic reforms. It is oriented more towards the developed Western countries and towards closer contacts with them.

In the Supreme Soviet, an old nomenclature prevailed, being nationalist and pro-Communist-minded. This nomenclature wished to carry out the reforms at a slow pace, and actually to prevent them in certain spheres (for example, the Supreme Soviet was blocking full-value land reform). The Supreme Soviet had an 'oriental' attitude, relating more to the Russian provinces, to the agrarian lobby and representatives of the branches dealing with natural resources. The presidential-governmental bloc relates more to the ruling élite and to the mobile population of large cities.

There was a relative balance of forces in the struggle for power between the Supreme Soviet and the President and government up until the VIIth Congress (December 1992). Neither was dominant in the political life of the country. Their power struggles never resulted in victory, and in effect made it possible in 1992 for economic and political change to move at normal speed. The

President and the government were unable to speed up change: to conduct privatization rapidly, to introduce full-value private property for land in villages and cities, to introduce a bankruptcy law without delay etc. The executive authorities had to take into consideration the actual readiness of the population and the provincial élites for the laws initiated, thanks to hindrance from the Supreme Soviet. The Supreme Soviet in its turn could not stop changes that were going on spontaneously (free commerce, development of dealers' firms etc.), as these were prompted and protected by the President and government.

In 1992 a peculiar, quasi-two-party, system ruled Russia, with these two quasi-CPSU's competing for power. The balance between them could not provide the separation of authorities necessary for democracy. Both constantly usurped each other's functions, with no third power to control them (a consequence of the weakness of the Court authorities). However, they still constrained the authority of each other, and both were deprived of total control over the population and its economic activity. If one of these two authorities took a decision deviating too far from the law, human rights, or Russia's international obligations, it provoked a counter-action from their opponents which often led to the decision being blocked. Thus the actions of Yeltsin blocked the approval of the restrictions upon press activity demanded by the Supreme Soviet.

The conflict between these two leading political forces spread not only all over Moscow, but, in the form of antagonism between the Soviets of the people's deputies and the executive authorities, was typical for most Russian regions and districts. These regional conflicts also prevented the authorities from having political and economic life in their regions under total control. At the same time the constant conflicts in the ruling organs stirred up serious social tension, and provoked strikes in enterprises, demonstrations by various political groups, and harsh mutual accusations in the press.

Obviously, if either of these two authorities (whether, the Supreme Soviet or the President with the government) wins the final victory and removes its former opponent from the political stage it is quite possible that the winner will immediately try to establish an authoritarian regime in Russia. But the existence of the two quasi-CPSUs was the guarantee of stability in the country, as the ambitions of the one were restricted by the ambitions of the other, and nobody possessed absolute power as a result.

This balance was to some extent broken by the VIIth and particularly by the VIIIth and IXth Congresses of the people's deputies. The political course for market introduction was subjected to very sharp criticism at these Congresses. Gaidar failed by the overwhelming majority of votes to be elected to the post of Chairman of the government of Russia. Yeltsin was forced to suggest Victor Chernomyrdin supported by the Supreme Soviet for this post. The deputies also placed the appointments of the key ministers (of internal affairs, security, defence and foreign affairs) under the control of the Supreme Soviet. Yeltsin's power was restricted enormously.

These actions reflected certain changes in the mentality of the Russian population, whose living standards and social mood suffered greatly during the first year of the transition to the market. There is no doubt that after these Congresses economic reform will be delayed, but changes will not stop completely. Though the presidential-governmental bloc cannot implement economic reform freely, Congress cannot ban it and changes are going on spontaneously.

As a result of the events of 3–4 October 1993, the Supreme Soviet was abolished. Yeltsin, together with his team, has been trying to establish an authoritarian regime, creating a Federal Assembly (a new legislative body) under the control of a presidential–governmental bloc. If he succeeds Russia's social stability will be maintained, but at the cost of the decline of freedom.

In conclusion, then, political freedom in Russia has led to the reproduction of earlier stereotypes in the political behaviour of the population and the ruling élite. However, these stereotypes, under the new conditions of the collapse of the Soviet Empire and the dismantling of the Communist Party structure, have resulted in setting up two quasi-CPSUs and, probably, an authoritarian regime. Another important consequence of freedom in Russia caused by the old system is an upsurge of popular aggression which has brought an explosion of criminality and of conflict throughout the administration structures.

The totalitarian Communist system in Russia encouraged an inferiority complex in people, since any contact of an individual with the state (in the administrative bodies, in transport, in the sphere of public service, in the army etc.) demonstrated his or her total lack of rights and possibilities and the inability to solve individual problems independently.

Many problems which in a democratic society would be openly discussed and gradually solved were concealed in Russia, resulting in a constant hidden tension. Among the hundreds and thousands of problems of this kind that have accumulated through the decades are those of national movements (those of Tatars, Bashkirs,

Buryats, Tuvinians etc. in Russia), territorial claims of different peoples (among these claims in Russia are those of Ingushs for the Prigorodny district in northern Ossetya, the problem of border demarcation between the Ingush community and Chechnya etc.), poorly functioning public transport, poor services generally, and utter poverty in the field of education.

The freedom which has come as the result of perestroika has enabled everybody to fulfil more or less fully their own aspirations and system of values. At the same time, all the previously unsolved problems of previous decades have come into the open. The population is facing these alone, since the state will interfere only in extreme situations, when mass armed collisions require the intervention of military troops. All this has excited an upsurge of aggression in a population which has no experience of independent and democratic problem-solving. Impulses previously oppressed by the totalitarian system may now be freely revealed, and are exacerbated by the sharp decrease in living standards and the marginalization of some social groups. Criminality growth, as a result, has doubled over the last five years, according to the official data on registered crimes.[3] If under the Communist system the population had no weapons in their private property, nowadays in Russia they are openly trading weapons that are prohibited in many free democratic countries, i.e. gas canisters and pistols. There is an abundance of weapons available to the population, especially in and near the regions of armed conflict (e.g. in Chechnya, Prigorodny district of northern Ossetya). Thus in Chechnya a howitzer gun in excellent fighting condition with ammunition has recently been removed from one of the citizens.

Unfortunately, not many people have faced hardship with an appropriate reaction, but have instead turned on each other. Something like a war of all against all has started, which for the moment, fortunately has broken out in its utterly extreme form as armed conflict only in the smaller part of the territory of the former USSR.

Thus the changes in Russia are going on, though with conflicts that often develop into lawlessness. This also refers to the sphere of the economy.

1.2 Private property as a black market during the decay of the Central Planning System

At the end of the 1980s Gorbachev began the ideological rehabilitation of the words ‘market’ and ‘private property’, which had been repressed by the Soviet authorities. He wanted a 'socialist market' with state enterprises as entrepreneurs. The economic doctrine of perestroika envisaged private property within certain narrow limits; the passing over of land, natural resources and the property of large enterprises into private ownership was not intended. However, the Russian people soon looked beyond the narrow limits set by the leaders of the country. In 1991 demands to destroy completely the centralized economy management system, to introduce a capitalist market and to privatize the property of state enterprises, including land, were already quite common.

The position of central ministries began to change in 1988, after the adoption of the USSR Law of Co-operation, which allowed independent collective enterprises to be established. This law encouraged the appearance in the USSR of an economic sector relatively autonomous from direct state control, a move that was further encouraged during this period by the adoption of the Law on State Enterprise. In accordance with this law the property of state enterprises was passed over to the enterprise concerned, giving them total economic control. The state authorities had (and have) no right to interfere directly in the activities of state enterprises. The enterprises in their current economic activity have the right to dispose of funds, equipment and goods produced at their own discretion. They are free to conclude the agreements with suppliers and consumers most advantageous to do business with, and not with those prescribed by the ministry. They may decide to expand or to curtail the production, at what price to buy raw materials. But it should be noted that most state enterprises have remained monopolists in the production of their goods, now as previously.

An attempt by Gorbachev's colleagues to restore the old system in August 1991 was another landmark on the road leading to the decay of the centralized economic system. It was this attempt that finally led to the removal of Party control of the economy and to the disintegration of the centralized Union structure in the state economic management, which was succeeded by the Russian bureaucracy. This bureaucracy had taken under its control the property of the liquidated Union ministries and the abolished CPSU. The new Russian government headed by Gaidar arrived in the building of the Central Committee of the CPSU (on Staraya Ploschad) and used the entire infrastructure of the old authorities: communication system (ATS-1 and ATS-2), dachas in Arkhangelskoye, special hospitals etc. Other Russian supreme authorities acted the same way. For example, the Ministry of Economics received the property of the former USSR Gosplan.

However, Russian bureaucracy was unable to inherit the old administration methods together with the property, although many functionaries in the Staraya Ploschad, in the former USSR Gosplan and in other organizations were most willing to. The reason for this is that Russian ministries no longer exert the influence upon enterprises they once did.

The ministries have retained only two control-levers from all their former instruments of pressure: (1) the appointment of directors of the enterprises by contracts; and (2) overall economic information: on the branch, in the economy as a whole, as well as on the economic reforms planned by the supreme authorities (President, government, legislative body) and specific measures of their implementation which may concern the enterprises. These levers of influence allow the ministries to retain limited control, but not total regulation of the enterprises' activities.

The gradual decay of the centralized management system was accompanied by the growth of private activity in the population and by economic initiatives by officials outside the state sector. The liberalization has resulted in setting up a hybrid state–market system. Its nucleus consists of large state enterprises. These have founded a number of banks, private and semi-private organizations in the field of supplies, sales, small-scale production. These organizations depend greatly not only on their founders but also on the suppliers and buyers (monopolists as a rule) of state enterprises, as well as on local state administration. The economic dependence of the private sector on the state sector is further complicated by the fact that most directors of state enterprises, a number of executive officials of the management staff, as well as deputies are the leaders of various small joint ventures and joint-stock companies. Independent private enterprises in Russia are still scarce and lack the possibilities which quasi-private firms close to the state sector have at their disposal.

The process of decay in the state sector of the economy in Russia was quicker than that of the setting up of the private sector. As a result whole areas have appeared in which state enterprises are almost not functioning, and private firms are not yet available. The gap is especially large in those fields which were traditionally neglected by the Soviet administration, with allocations, equipment and hard currency distributed in the last priority. Above all, these affect the sphere of the population's needs – light and food industries, services, state restaurants etc. Many state shops for repairing footwear or clothes, and many cafés and canteens have closed for lack of financing from the state. However, they have not yet been replaced by private firms, and probably these firms will never be set up at all.

The setting up of a hybrid state–market system in the richly traditional wake of a shadow economy, with unfavourable conditions for legal private business, has resulted in the extraordinary expansion of the black market.[4]

Black-market activities in contemporary Russia are extremely diverse. The main types are as follows:

1 Hidden privatization of state enterprises by the managers and their misappropriation of some part of the income gained by these enterprises. This is most often accomplished at the cost of private firms set up within (or under) the enterprises managed by the directors or their relatives. Another method is to make unprofitable contracts on behalf of the enterprise for a bribe.
2 Bureaucratic entrepreneurship, i.e. making use of position and access to information concerning commercial operations by state officials. Entrepreneurship is prohibited to the executive members of the state staff by law. However, in reality, deputies as well as functionaries of ministries are widely involved in it.
3 Rendering services by state officials to private firms and state enterprises for bribes (for instance, for granting privileged state credits, for granting municipal real estate on lease at low rates, granting licences for the export of raw materials from Russia etc.). It is not uncommon for officials to claim payment for the simple fulfilment of their own direct duties, i.e. registration of enterprises, replying to requests for information etc.
4 Concealing some part of the profits of private firms to avoid paying tax. This activity has recently gained in scope, having involved an important number of private entrepreneurs. One of the businessmen interviewed by the author, who asked for his name not to be mentioned, said: 'My enterprise, according to the official documents, does not produce profits, and I do not pay taxes on profits. But in reality my profits were 15 million roubles in 1992, all of which were distributed over various expenditures. If I indicated officially these profits I should have had to pay about 11 million roubles in various taxes.'
5 Falsification of products; this is especially typical of consumer goods such as Kojak, vodka, designer clothes etc.
6 Illegal production and commercial operations – private production and trade in armaments, narcotics, illegal export of 'strategic materials' (such as uranium and rare earth elements and

some other metals and materials) without licences and escaping Customs control.

7 Large-scale financial machinations possible because of the incompletely formed financial system, indispensable for the market economy. The following two illegal operations are most common in Russia now. The first involves delays of money transfers by banks, which are making use of the money and transferring it only after deriving considerable profits. It is not uncommon for payments to take three or four months to be transferred within the same city, and five or six months between cities. The second group of these machinations involves receiving money by false financial documents. One of the most outrageous fraud transactions of this kind took place in 1992 – the so-called 'Chechenskiy avizo case', when 17 billion roubles were illegally received.

8 The activities of organized groups involved in rackets, forceful restriction of competition, removal of competitors and receiving debts on clients' orders by violent methods. These groups as a rule act in the most profitable spheres of private business. For example, a taxi drive in the evening from Moscow International Airport 'Sheremetzhevo – 2' costs at least $USA 20–30, which is 8–12 times higher than for the same distance in other Moscow districts. This gap is the result of the organized groups, which do not admit competitors to Sheremetzhevo and which also bloc the organization of regular evening bus trips. Another case is the result of Court paralysis. It is almost impossible to trust the Court to get money from an insolvent, and creditors are often compelled to employ groups of professional racketeers to enforce the payment, for a remuneration of 30–50% of the indebted sum. About 10% of inter-city commercial transactions are finished this way, according to V. Albert, an entrepreneur from Khabarovsk.

Almost all economic agents (directors of state enterprises, private entrepreneurs, state staff officials, politicians) are involved in black-market activity in one way or another, making it very difficult in practice to distinguish the legal market from the black. This is due to incomplete economic reform, which is making numerous, absolutely indispensable, market operations illegal. For example, up to the end of 1993 selling and buying land in villages and cities is illegal as is trading real estate. And because of the close entanglement of the legal and black markets it is difficult to assess the scope of the shadow activity, except to point out its very wide and constantly growing prevalence.

Moreover, large stable social groups have recently started setting up in Russia, with black-market operations as their main activity.

In the opinion of many experts they are modelled upon the old (existing in Brezhnev's time) criminal organized groups. Now they are beginning to want political power, and may seize it in the conditions of destabilization that now prevail in the country. Thus V. Savostzhanov, head of the Moscow department of the Ministry of Security in Russia (and Deputy Minister), wrote at the end of 1992: 'A confidential meeting of a number of authoritative persons of the criminal world was held in order to co-ordinate actions in case of instability and inability of the administration to control the situation. When the legal bosses start fighting each other not for life but for death, they said, then the shops will be ours, the houses will be ours, the streets will be ours.'[5]

The black market has set up in Russia as a stable social institution. Its gradual decrease in power may be expected only under the conditions of further liberalization of the economy and in the long term.

A legal private market of insignificant size has emerged in Russia, though without many of the attributes of a modern market (for example, the market of capital is not available). At the same time the old economic institutions are partially destroyed, partially decaying, and are no longer important for the Russian economy.

1.3 Technological degradation as a result of political and economic changes

The important, though not pre-planned, consequence of the political and economic changes in Russia was the destruction of the old institutions which had provided for the implementation of technological and socio-economic innovations in Soviet enterprises. These institutions, and how they differed from the market mechanisms designed to encourage innovations, are described in subsequent chapters of the book. It is important to state now that such destruction has led to the technological degradation of the Russian economy.[6]

The technological degradation is expressed in three main forms: (1) in the transition to more primitive and simple technologies (enterprises rejecting complicated 'high technology'); (2) in the decrease of innovative activity in the Russian economy; (3) in cutting down state expenditures for science, and in the actual disintegration of many research organizations.

Let us discuss these manifestations of technological degradation in more detail.

Before the disintegration of the USSR almost all large Russian industrial enterprises (the industrial production of the country is mostly concentrated in the large enterprises) had partners in various republics – Ukraine, Belorus, Kazakhstan, Baltiya. Many of these partners were practically the only producers of their products. For example, some component units for television sets were produced only in Lithuania, and 90% of the component units for the Russian engine-building enterprises were produced in Ukraine.[7]

After the Union disintegration a considerable part of the old relations went too. Worst affected are the complicated branches, which had many highly specialized suppliers. This refers first of all to the military enterprises and household machinery production, which is also concentrated mostly in these enterprises in Russia. Thus, according to a survey data of 312 managers of large heavy-industry enterprises (90% of which are those of the military–industrial complex) conducted in January 1992, the most difficult problem for the directors in their work was the rupture of traditional economic relations. This was pointed out by 80% of respondents (as compared to only 18% of directors, who complained about the curtailment of the state order).

The adaptation to this situation took place in the second half of 1992, when complaints about the breaking of traditional economic bonds ceased. This adaptation was possible because they actually stopped producing complicated types of industrial articles and rejected high technology, transferring to more primitive technologies requiring few partners and simpler components. This ensured better inner stability and steadiness of production. The achievement of inner steadiness is one of the key factors for the survival of enterprises under the general political and economic instability in the country.

Another method of Russian economic adaptation to this instability was the decrease in innovative activity. The number and scope of newly introduced technologies and products, as well as issued patents and author certificates for inventions and discoveries, declined. Thus the data on the inventions, used in the production, testify to the steady decrease of innovative activity in Russia during the 1980s by 1.5 times (Table 1).

Since during this period (starting from the beginning of the 1980s) the population growth and the increase of the scale of the Russian economy were taking place, specific data on innovative activity dropped still more. However, the sharpest downfall against the background of this decrease was in 1991. The decline was apparently even greater in 1992, according to preliminary

Table 1 *Number of inventions used in the Russian economy (in thousands)*

	1980	*1985*	*1986*	*1987*	*1988*	*1989*	*1990*	*1991*
Inventions	45.0	37.2	37.1	35.8	32.2	30.7	29.2	8.9

Sources: 'Scientific-technical progress in RSFSR in 1990', Statistics manual, Moscow, Republican Informational Editing Centre, State Committee of RSFSR on Statistics, (1991), 48 [data on 1980–90] and 'Inventions and rationalization proposals: Main indicators', Working Paper of Russian Society for Inventors (Moscow 1992), 1.

data from the author's interviews with officials of the Russian Society for Inventors.

The decrease in innovative activity in the Russian economy should not be assessed as only negative. It reflects in many aspects the refusal of enterprises to accept innovations imposed from above. This process results from the first attempts at transition to the market economy, when the directors began looking for real advantages for themselves and their organizations, and gave up what was not profitable for them.

A vivid illustration of technological degradation can be seen in the gradual decay and transformation of Russian science.

Soviet science was part of the totalitarian state, and made a real contribution to its security.[8] Science as a part of the totalitarian system was fulfilling, in our opinion, four main functions.

Firstly, science was ensuring military–strategic aims in the country's development.

Secondly, it was providing a functioning ideology, and its introduction and extension into various strata of Soviet society supported the myth about its scientific management.

Thirdly, science was serving the requirements of the branch ministries, providing for their status. The symbiosis that developed between the research institutes and the ministries was profitable to both sides: the ministries were implementing the guaranteed financing of the institutes and 'protecting' them from competition; they were demanding research 'output', while the research institutes made the ministries' projects look 'scientific'.

Fourthly, R&D units developed innovations for production requirements agreed by the ministries and participated in the drives for their extension.

The transformed and transforming Russian society no longer needs these functions of science, and the state, having exhausted its material and financial resources, is no longer able to keep and support more than 1 million scientists in more than 1500 institutes,[9] most of which were busy with military R&D. Therefore science has found itself facing the inevitability of change.

Changes occurred in two stages:

First stage: freedom-shock

After the euphoria about freedom achieved as the result of perestroika, the institutes became aware that real state support had considerably decreased.[10] Orders were being curtailed on behalf of enterprises, which no longer received funds for R&D from their ministries.

Qualified scientists who could earn tens and hundreds times more in the private sector started leaving the research units. The social climate, the attitude towards one's own work, has changed in the R&D centres: a number of researchers have started using the institutes only as their 'registration place', fulfilling their main work outside the organization.

The influx of capable university graduates into science decreased as they also left for business appointments.

An actual decay started in research institutes. Thus (according to the data of the survey, held in 1992, among the 565 heads of 21 research units in Moscow, Novosibirsk, Voronezh and Vladimir), in answer to the question asked in 1992, 'What is the situation in your institute?' the managers replied:

The situation is good	2
The situation is hard, but the main research potential has been retained	82
The research potential is lost, the organization has actually collapsed	14
Other replies	2

One may draw the conclusion from these data that several dozens of research organizations in Russia in 1992 were in a good position, about 200 had practically disintegrated, and the other over 1000 institutes were in a hard position, although they retained their research potential on the whole.

One sector of military R&D is in a critical position, with a share of decaying research units more than 10 times higher than that in civil institutes. This is not by chance. It may be explained by the fact that up until recently institutes involved in defence were closed not only to foreign visitors, but also to penetration by whatever changes were taking place in the country. However, after the

August 1991 events the situation was sharply changed, and the military order considerably decreased. The privileged conditions regarding specific financing and material supplies for military R&D centres were cancelled. The effects of freedom-shock following this were powerful. As a result they lost a number of researchers and many researches were curtailed. Thus in one of the defence institutes in Moscow the number of researchers has more than halved, as compared with 1985 and this is the common situation in institutes studied.[11]

However, in the early 1990s other tendencies also became evident.

Second stage: renewing the inner structure and changing the status of research units

The institutes started looking for their own niches in the changing Russian society. Many of them began to change the themes of their researches, adapting them to the requirements of a market economy. They started mastering new types of activities in which they were never involved previously and which were bound up with the commercialization of their R&D results, and set up new branches on this basis. New private research firms started emerging. Thus in reply to the question 'Do you wish to establish a private research organization?' 26% heads of research units in state institutes in 1992 indicated their desire to start their own business. Considering that the number of research units in Russia is about 50,000, the number of potential entrepreneurs, taking into account only the heads of units, is over 10,000.

Almost all state R&D organizations in Russia started up some activity that was unrelated to science. For instance, the institutes began buying brokers' places in stock exchanges, founding trade firms to sell construction materials, opening fashion shops where some of their employees could find jobs to avoid being dismissed.

The changes in Russian science are not simple. The questions whether R&D units will manage to renovate themselves enough to pull the Russian economy out of its impasse, or prefer to press the government and squeeze more and more money out of the state budget remain to be answered.

Neither is there any precise reply to the question of whether the technological degradation of the Russian economy is a natural temporary consequence of the transition to the market. If this is so it means that this degradation will gradually be overcome as market mechanisms start functioning. If, on the other hand, the process of decay and degradation cannot be stopped until almost the whole economy inherited from the old system is totally destroyed, then the market transition will soon be blocked and a Communist system of one form or another will be restored in Russia.

It would be appropriate to discuss the mechanisms regulating social transformations which have taken place in Russian/Soviet society. This will make it clearer what should be changed, and how, what reactions to the required changes may be expected, and where the limits lie of possible changes in Russia.

NOTES

1 We may explain the high rate of these changes using M. Olson's concept of the logic of collective action. As he argues: 'How can autocratic regimes that appear to have such awesome power over their citizens collapse so quickly? The fragility of autocracies grows out of the perceptions of the government's civil and military officials. If a government's operatives, and especially those in the police and the military, believe that they will be punished if they fail to carry out their orders and rewarded if they do, an autocracy is secure. If the cadre perceive that a dictatorship is invincible, it cannot be overthrown by its subjects.' See M. Olson, 'The logic of collective action in Soviet-type societies', *Journal of Soviet Nationalities*, i/2 (1990), 16.

2 These schools trained the future representatives of the local and central élites and were supervised by the Central Committee of the CPSU. The contracts for holding researches were concluded by the scientists with the enterprises without strict direct control by the state, a small island of relatively free economy under the strictly regulated system.

3 See 'Statistical data on criminality in Russia', *Rossiyskaya gazeta*, 5 February 1993.

4 The economic policy of the Yeltsin–Gaidar government (and Chernomyrdin's government too) also made a contribution to the development of the black market in Russia. It has introduced extremely high taxes, consuming actually over 60–80% of the profits. Some politicians and journalists wrote that these high taxes were introduced under the slogan of the necessity to reach financial stabilization. Without such a slogan, they asserted, Russia would not be able to receive aid and credits from the International Currency Foundation.

5 See V. Savostyanov, 'Is a coup threatening us?' *Vecherniya Moskva*, 18 November 1992. The events of 3–4 October demonstrated that the situation had progressed beyond mere words. During the night, near Ostankino, where militants from Russian National Unity had attacked the TV centre, groups of gangsters tried to steal the more expensive cars such as Mercedes and engaged in fist-fights with the private security guards who were guarding the carparks.

6 The actual reason for technological degradation was lack of long-term

incentives for the development of production. The lack of such incentives, in its turn, is caused by the abolition of private property. One can only hope that the current depression of production is temporary and will be revived if a normally functioning market system is set up in Russia.

7 See S. Leskov, 'Leaders of defence branches in Russia and Ukraine are pushing the politicians closer to each other', *Izvestiya*, 15 January 1993.

8 Science in the USSR was certainly never just a part of the totalitarian system: prominent scientists worked, discussions were held and other processes all went on despite the official bans. But all this was possible only because science played an important supporting role in the totalitarian system.

9 See 'Scientific-technical progress in RSFSR in 1990', Statistics manual, Moscow, Republican Informational Editing Centre State Committee of RSFSR on Statistics (1991), 35.

10 According to U. Osipov's (President of the Russian Academy of Science) evaluations, the share of R&D expenses in the national income decreased from 5.6% to 2% during 1990–92. See S. Leskov, 'Prime Minister troubled by the fate of science', *Izvestiya*, 20 January 1993.

11 For more detail on freedom-shock in Russian research units, see L. Kosals, 'R&D organizations in Russia: freedom-shock', in *Research and development in the transition to a market economy*, ed. S. Glaziev and C. M. Schneider, Laxenburg, International Institute for Applied Systems Analysis (1993).

2

Restructuring the Social Mechanism of Innovative Processes: Variants and dilemmas

To discuss the reorganization of the way in which Russian society deals with innovation, we must look at the restructuring of Soviet society as a whole. First we shall examine the conceivable variants of transition and then consider the possible changes in the mechanism of innovative processes.

2.1 The labyrinth of the future

Following the recent break-up of the Soviet Union, many variants of the development of Russian society are conceivable, and progress towards one or another will give us different versions of transition. There are two polar extremes of such development, between which lie all the remaining variants. The first is a centralized command society based on socialist monopolism. The second is a self-administering society based on pluralism.[1] These differ in the range of social institutions and procedures they encompass, the range of social groups and roles they include, and in the forms of activity people pursue within them. For example, the command economy has the following characteristics: a single dominant subject in all spheres, the dependence of all social institutions on politics and ideology, standardized forms of organization, social paternalism, manipulation of individual behaviour and an imprecision of social norms.

These will be discussed more fully later, but here they help to provide a contrast with the self-administering society which must be founded on democratic forms of administration. To a considerable extent its development depends on activity and enterprise from below; the people act independently while the state (indirectly) regulates society, and political institutions express the democratic will of the people.

The social institutions capable of ensuring the functioning of a self-administering society should be organized as follows:

1 In each area of public life there must be a great number of relatively independent and autonomous subjects. They must be able (i.e. have the means) to carry on their independent activities. These must include elements of competition for the attention of the consumer. (Here we mean consumption in the broadest sense, not just in the sense of economic goods and services.)
2 There must be mechanisms for ensuring the democratic co-ordination of the interests of different subjects. In this way the perpetual dominance of a single subject will be avoided.
3 Social institutions must be autonomous and not be dependent on politics or ideology. This means that activities in a particular sphere (science, scholarship or culture, for example) and the norms that govern them must develop from, and be based upon, criteria specific to that particular sphere. Institutions must not become ideological. Legal guarantees must defend them from external and incompetent interference, or from 'improvements' being made to their naturally arising norms of conduct to fit someone else's idea of how things should be done.
4 These social institutions must be assured of a variety of organizational forms in which they may function. Organizations, whether formal or informal, must come into being, grow and then die in a natural fashion in accordance with the demands of the particular institution's development. The establishment, development and demise of such organizations will then be the result of their natural social selection. Then organizational forms do not ossify or become self-sufficient; they do not take priority over the needs of development or hold it back.
5 There must be a minimizing of social guarantees within the self-administering society, and equal exchange must be ensured between individuals and between society and the individual. Market principles (the principles of economic freedom) must develop not only in the economy but also in those social institutions where this is both possible and reasonable (for example, in part of science and scholarship). This also implies the assurance of more rational relations, in the family for instance, so that responsibility and reliability are developed, providing precise moral guidelines, and excluding parasitic and dependent attitudes.

6 Such a society presupposes the existence of clear and absolute moral and legal norms which even the highest leader cannot infringe. These norms make certain methods unacceptable within the framework of all social institutions, even for attaining the most 'enlightened' aims. Among such unacceptable methods we may mention restrictions of the individual's freedom of behaviour (economic, political and other) or of movement, and the use of coercion.

Taken as a whole, the complex of social institutions based on these principles (in economics, politics, law, teaching, research etc.) will ensure the formation of a self-administering society.

Intermediary types of society between these polar extremes can also exist. They are distinguished by particular organizational features of separate social institutions, perhaps of the economy and/or culture.

The different variants of transition are based on movement towards one of these types of society. Such movement consists of the implementation of a great many different changes in the main spheres of public life: reform of various economic institutions, transformation of the political system, the law, education, and so on. Moreover, these changes may vary in their depth, speed and degree, being either radical, evolutionary or revolutionary. Change may take different directions and be democratic, conservative or reactionary.

Democratic changes

Movement towards a self-governing society is founded on pluralism, and this presupposes using democratic methods to effect a profound overhaul of the main institutions. Public life must be demonopolized and conditions established in which independent activity from below can find expression; this activity will be limited by norms that have been discussed and legally approved. To achieve this in Russia, some of the existing institutions must be broken up, particularly the ministerial system of administration and the domicile registration system (*propiska*). A number of new, chiefly market-oriented, institutions must be founded. For example, if non-state firms are to develop their economic activities all of the following are necessary: institutions governing the interaction between supply organizations and non-state firms; sales outlets for goods made by the non-state sector; advertising; credit for the economic activities of non-state organizations. At present, some of these requirements are hardly met at all (e.g.

advertising) while others are only in an embryonic state (e.g. interaction with supply organizations). The setting up and smooth operation of these essential institutions may therefore demand considerable efforts from managers at various levels and from the population as a whole. They will have to devote much 'social expenditure' (time and effort) to the design and implementation of these democratic mechanisms and then to their supervision and to the elimination of any difficulties and disruptions that occur.

Conservative changes, (or 'running on the spot')

In this case, special measures would be taken to galvanize and revitalize the activities of existing institutions and mechanisms, *without fundamentally changing them.* Of course, this might lead to changes in the forms of public life, but they would be of a superficial and cosmetic character. In essence, this would mean changing everything, without changing anything, by making better use of existing mechanisms. This approach creates the illusion of change and emasculates the democratic forms in the economy and public affairs: nothing is left but a verbal shell. Take, for example, the non-state firms; they might be allowed to continue to exist, but would be given a plan to fulfil (whether it would be called such is of no importance). By subjecting them to stricter accountability than state enterprises, only the label 'private enterprise' would remain to counter accusations of anti-democratic behaviour. The coup in Moscow of August 1991 represented an attempt at conservative change in Russia, when the party of the ruling élite tried to effect a return to the orthodox Soviet system.

Reactionary changes

The third and final tendency consists of a clamp-down on every sphere of public life. Monopoly in all social institutions would be strengthened, the economy militarized, and the individual's choice of economic and other forms of activity severely limited (e.g. the residence registration system would be made stricter, and opportunities to move from one enterprise to another restricted). Existing market and democratic institutions, such as commercial banks, and private firms, and the election of leaders, would all be abolished. Strict sanctions and punishments would be applied to those who infringed labour discipline, held divergent opinions, and to all who 'deviated' in one way or another. In these circumstances, all manifestations of independent activity without higher approval would begin to be treated as deviations. An important constituent element of these reactionary methods is the attempt to supervise all spheres of the population's life and activities and to set up machinery to exercise that supervision. In its most extreme form the reactionary approach would lead to 'neo-Stalinism', though at a higher level of public awareness and economic development than in the 1930s and in different historical and cultural circumstances. It would involve the forcible installation of the institutions of a powerful authoritarian regime led by a dictator or a ruling oligarchy.

Each of these trends may in theory take a revolutionary or evolutionary form, and as such there are six theoretical variants of transition (Table 2).

Table 2 *Variants of transition*

Degree of restructuring	*Trend of change*		
	Democratic	*Conservative*	*Reactionary*
Revolutionary	1 Democratic revolution	2 Conservative revolution	3 Reactionary revolution
Evolutionary	4 Democratic evolution	5 Conservative evolution	6 Reactionary evolution

In practice, transition can only follow one of these paths, and in the countries which made up the former Soviet Union the societal choice has still not finally been made. There has been no painstaking and rigorous comparison of the versions followed by selection of the optimal variant. But such a public choice should amount to the attainment of a consensus between the basic groups of society that will, or may, be affected by such changes, and not be an order passed down from above by those who knew what is needed to the mob, which does not know. All must be conscious of this choice, through open and public discussion of the different variants of transition. Moreover, everyone who wants to state an opinion must be given the opportunity to do so, so that a generalized view of the proposed changes could evolve as a result of discussions in the press, on television, in public debates, meetings and rallies. Moreover, the greater the 'social literacy' of society and the more, as a consequence, representatives of different groups know about one another (and the better they understand each other's interests and aspirations), the more quickly consensus will be reached – so long as all other circumstances remain the same. As of yet, no such process has been clearly established.

Making this choice, as we have said, means putting the value system of society into practice. If you like, it is culture in action, solving various dilemmas. For example, is the market, and the openly unequal incomes it brings, preferable to directive planning and the inequality that hides behind an outwardly insignificant differentiation in incomes? Do people prefer political freedoms and the opportunities they offer for the expression of all public moods, including extremist opinions? Or would they feel happier with limitations on democracy and the repression of extreme points of view? Is the danger of unemployment a price worth paying for far-reaching technical progress, or is it better to have guaranteed full employment and a slow rate of technical change? This list can be considerably extended.

In the former Soviet Union, the press and academic discussion did a great deal to describe the range of possible dilemmas created by transition. It cannot be said, however, that this field has been described and conceptualized in sufficient detail and thoroughness. This is because no serious analysis of the possible results and consequences for Russian society of implementing different variants of transition has yet been made. We do not know what will be the gains and losses for different social groups, nor how far they themselves are prepared to go.

Charting these unfamiliar waters is extremely important; we must try to identify the underwater obstacles before they damage or even sink our ship. One of the main dangers arises from the intertwining of the different variants of transition. We may set out to pursue the democratic version only to find ourselves following a conservative or even a reactionary course. To find our way through the labyrinth of the future, we must analyse various scenarios for the future development of Russian society. With the help of such a compass, we may be able to take a different turning, abandoning a path that, though it seems preferable, promises to lead to serious losses.

Such an analysis may expose the limitations of each particular variant and make society's choice a more conscious and well-founded one. The most active part of our society, on the other hand, has already made its choice. A polarization of views has become apparent. While one part of the political and economic administration and the intelligentsia is working towards a democratic revolution, another is tending towards neo-Stalinism or national socialism.

Two general forces are established in Russia now: that of

President Yeltsin and the government;[2] and that of the Communist and nationalist opposition. The President and his team attempt to carry out privatization and other market economic changes while the Communist and nationalist opposition tries to stop it. Their struggle has reached the point of armed force.

Thus there are two diametrically opposed views, but for the time being no intermediate or third approach. This last, in our view, would be a democratic evolution of Russian society. Such an approach would not promise immediate and significant achievements, but has the advantage that it would ensure an 'evenly applied perestroika' – one that preserved social stability and avoided sharp disproportions and contradictions. This in turn means that, compared to democratic revolution, it is less likely to end up on a conservative or even reactionary course – a pattern that is already familiar in Soviet history, according to our hypothesis about the cyclical pattern of development of society in the former Soviet Union.

2.2 The cycles of development of society in the Soviet Union

If we exclude the 1980s, we may distinguish at least four turning-points in the history of Soviet society. In the early and late 1920s, and in the mid-1950s and mid-1960s, society chose a particular course of development. The results of these choices are schematically shown as follows (Table 3):

Table 3 *Turning points in the development of society in the Soviet Union*

Liberalization	*Reactionary coup*	*Liberalization*	*Conservative coup*	*Liberalization*	*Reactionary coup?*
early 1920s	early 1930s	late 1950s	late 1960s	mid-1980s	mid-1990s?

On Lenin's initiative there was a liberalization in the early 1920s which involved the introduction of the New Economic Policy (NEP) and a certain democratization of all areas of public life. Stalin and his supporters then staged a reactionary coup. As a result the command economy came into existence and society was placed under the total supervision of Stalin's administration, a body that ruled by manipulating people's enthusiasm and fear. It was then that socialist monopolism took shape.

The liberalization initiated by Khrushchev in order to overcome

Stalin's 'cult of personality' led to the Thaw of the late 1950s. However, this was interrupted by Brezhnev's conservative coup.

Gorbachev himself was slowing down the process of perestroika – liberalization in the mid-1980s – by early 1990, and he was stopped in August 1991. The coup of August 1991 was provoked by the disintegration of the USSR and the liberalization of the economy and political system. After that, in some new independent states, civil war broke out (as in Tadzhikistan and Georgia). In others (e.g. Russia and the Ukraine) nationalist reaction emerged in opposition to liberalization. In most new states it is likely that reactionary nationalist regimes will be able to establish themselves in the mid-1990s.

Taking these turning-points into account, our analysis leads us to the following hypothetical diagram of the cycles of development of Soviet society (Fig. 1):

Stagnation → choice → liberalization → choice → Conservative
(crisis) (reactionary)
← ← ← ← ← ← ←coup

Figure 1: Cycles of development in Soviet society

A state of stagnation and crisis stimulates the carrying out of democratic reforms in the economy and other areas of public life. New forms emerge and experiments are conducted. The most varied groups of the employed and the population as a whole become more active. Innovators are able to put their ideas into practice and their efforts find support. Innovations from below increase in number and become more rapidly widespread. Economic indicators improve and the richness and variety of public life grows. The reforms stimulate development, but also undermine the system of socialist monopolism created by Stalin and his supporters. Independent subjects begin to emerge: co-operators and private producers in the economy, and dissidents in politics. New schools and trends also arise in the arts and sciences which are tangential to the 'general line'. This leads in turn to a consolidation of conservative forces in the administrative apparatus, which then conducts counter-reforms. Under their influence, new forms are either abolished, or they are emasculated and old ideas accommodated within them. Innovators are slapped down and repressive measures are taken against independent subjects in politics, economics, science, scholarship and the arts. Socialist monopolism is restored and calm once again reigns; all the noisy opportunists, renegades and anti-Marxists have been silenced. After a certain time, stagnation follows this calm. Since people cannot fulfil their desires, their level of activity declines. Innovators find support neither from below nor from above. Alienation from work, political institutions and society as a whole becomes widespread, and an underworld second economy develops. Economic indicators worsen, life in society becomes monotonous and dull, and innovative activity declines in all fields. This leads to a consolidation in the apparatus of supporters of democratic change. They then carry out democratic reforms and the cycle resumes.

There have been two such cycles in the development of Soviet society since the early 1920s. In both, periods of democratic reform lasted about 8 to 10 years, while periods of stagnation lasted 15 to 20 years (not including wars and periods of post-war recovery). Although the periods of stagnation were prolonged, the impetus generated during democratic reforms was sufficient to ensure the forward movement of Soviet society. If this pattern continues, the period of liberalization will terminate in 1993–4.

These 'long waves' in Soviet history derive from the political institutions of socialist monopolism. This system has an inner tendency to stagnation and immobility. It has no institutions that ensure constant development, and instead relies on 'campaigns'. Therefore, it depresses the rate of activity of innovators and any centres of development that spontaneously emerge from below.

The 'revolutions' carried out from above were certainly large-scale actions. Yet of necessity they were limited both in time and in the extent to which they involved various different social groups and strata. Furthermore, any revolution lays stress not so much on creating new institutions as on destroying the old ones. The democratic changes these past revolutions introduced were insufficiently deep and consistent and did not put down roots into the popular culture. The decision in favour of democracy was reached after political in-fighting at the top. Therefore it did not become the conscious and responsible choice of broad strata of the population.

Yet this choice should be made responsibly. Democracy presupposes considerable social expenditure, both by leaders whose task of administering the economy and society would be made more difficult, and by ordinary citizens, who would be required to take independent action.

An initial impulse is essential. If the system of socialist monopolism is really to be dismantled in Russia and other former Soviet states, however, there must be a long and gradual assimilation of the democratic institutions that might serve as a foundation for a well-established, self-administering society. A long period of democratic evolution is needed in order for democracy to put down deep roots and form a part of the cultural tradition shaping everyday behaviour. Only then will the former Soviet states avoid a repetition of the cycles of Soviet society; only then will thèir growth be dynamic and forward-moving.

The first impulse has already been given by the changes that have taken place since the mid-1980s. There must now follow a de-monopolization that will create the conditions for pluralism and thus permit the social mechanism of innovative processes to be restructured.

2.3 Pluralism and innovation

Such a restructuring must have the following effects. It must draw broad strata of the population and those in employment into innovative processes. It must make efficient and useful innovation a permanent part of their activities, and free them at the same time from various pseudo-innovations. The way to achieve this is through a democratic re-organization of the social mechanism of innovative processes which may be achieved as progress is made towards pluralism. In turn, pluralism presupposes a steady widening of the freedom of individuals and groups in all fields of public life and the creation of institutions that defend this freedom and enable it to be put into practice.

Three principles, at the very least, must be recognized if Russian society is to advance towards pluralism. They should form the basis on which economic and social institutions are organized.

The free establishment of associations

This means that each individual or group of persons may set up any type of organization without seeking permission from higher authority. All that is needed is registration for the carrying out of any activities that are not contrary to law, and, moreover, this applies to any field whatsoever (politics, economics, education etc.). This applies to both commercial and non-profit-making organizations, and the latter may embrace political, ideological and charitable bodies.

This principle must have a juridical basis so that an individual or a group of persons are able to appeal to the law if the organization they wish to set up is forbidden. The conditions that enable a great number of independent subjects to emerge in different fields of public life depend on implementing the above principle. Demonopolization will be impossible without it.

A number of laws directed against monopolies are also essential to the right freely to set up associations. These should limit the creation of monopolistic organizations by the state (with the exception of particular sectors like defence and energy supplies) and also forbid non-state monopolies. If this principle is put into practice a great many more organizations may come into existence; so many, in fact, that it becomes simply impossible to supervise them from above, as now happens.

Economic, political and ideological self-determination for subjects

The above voluntary associations must have the right to be internally autonomous and sovereign and to choose the form of organization that best suits their aims and needs. They must be free from external interference by superior bodies (with the exception of specified instances such as external auditing). This principle also requires confirmation in law. It will enable rational ways of organizing activities to be applied corresponding to the specific nature of the enterprise (whether in politics, education, economics or another field). It will ensure the variety in organizational forms that is required for rapid and dynamic development.

The free formation of links and relations between subjects

No one has the right to impose suppliers and consumers on people, or to force them to provide sponsorship, unpaid services and so on. Free negotiated relations, voluntarily entered into by the different agents, would seem to be most suitable for putting this principle into practice. It is essential, of course, to ensure the social equality of the agents in these economic, political and other relations.

The implementation of these principles may help to bring about a new situation in Russian society where there is healthy social competition and dynamic development. By 'healthy social competition' we do not mean elbowing each other aside in the struggle to distribute resources, but the equal right of each to do what they wish in their chosen sphere of activity without the dictatorial impositions of various authorities. It means that the consumer can choose the best product or service, and yet the unsuccessful can still have definite guarantees of their survival. Under socialist monopolism competition cannot be healthy because it is almost entirely unregulated and hidden from public scrutiny; it chiefly amounts to a struggle between various monopolists for 'unearned' resources. Competition can only be healthy when it is open and legal, and has developed ethics and rules that enable the individual to determine what is acceptable and what is not. Naturally, such rules cannot be written down in some ministerial office and then passed down as instructions. They can only develop, like all genuinely organic social norms, through practical activity; and they must arise from below as a result of the social consensus reached between free partners.

Such a new situation under conditions of pluralism must lead to change in the way the mechanism of social selection operates. Under socialist monopolism, it is obedient officials who get promoted. In a pluralist society, on the other hand, the enterprising and innovative individuals who transform society will chiefly be able to achieve success. If this happens, society can move ahead and develop dynamically without any zones or periods of stagnation and immobility.

The political system must be the starting-point in implementing these principles. It binds together and unites all spheres of society, and therefore changes in the political system are a global condition for major changes in every other field.

If the principles of pluralism are put into practice, it will be possible to implement the democratic variant of transition as far as the social mechanism of innovative processes is concerned. Such a restructuring must ensure that enterprises feel an economic need to innovate, that a climate favourable to innovation is established in the enterprises, and that a market for innovations is created. When the enterprises feel this need, and a market for innovations is in operation, giving them the freedom to choose the form and means of innovative activity, they will develop an inner compulsion to innovate themselves. In other words, incentives to greater activity in renewing production methods will be created. A climate favouring innovation will in turn establish the social conditions in which this activity may effectively be applied.

The following measures are prerequisites if enterprises are to feel an economic need for innovation:

The legal privatization of state enterprises

The process of latent privatization is now spreading in Russia, with informal private owners receiving the profits and the state bearing the expense.

After legal privatization state economic bodies cease to determine the entire economic life of the country and become just one of a great many economic subjects, with the particular function of expressing the interests of the state in the economy. The property of non-state enterprises must be separated from that of these state bodies, and the latter must be prohibited from exercising distributive functions over the property of the non-state enterprises.

The economic role of owner of the means of production must be established

This is primarily necessary to ensure that enough economic responsibility is carried for administering an enterprise's property after it has been separated from the state. Under socialist monopolism, the managers of enterprises typically bear an administrative responsibility. Economic responsibility, by contrast, in its extreme form may mean bankruptcy and loss of property.

Moreover, the owners draw up the long-term goals of the enterprise's activities and do not allow day-to-day interference by state bodies. This system forms the basis for elaborating the enterprise's innovational development strategy, which supposes that there will be an intensive development and application of innovations. In this way a demand arises for the services of the innovator, and hence the necessity to provide him or her with normal conditions of work.

The role of entrepreneur must be created

The property-owner's role is to establish the stable working of the enterprise, which is essential for developing and applying innovations. The entrepreneur has to provide the other elements of innovational activity, flexibility and risk-taking. The entrepreneur must be able to justify the economic risks involved in innovation; he must likewise know how to organize innovative activity by creating all the social, organizational, material and financial conditions it demands.

Formation of a precise and rapidly functioning mechanism for setting up organizations from below

Innovative activity is highly complex and involves many people; large numbers of new economic ties must be established. This requires quick reactions and carries many risks. Therefore, to be successful, innovation often demands the rapid creation of new organizations. If this is not feasible, the risks and complexity of innovation will be too great (at least if we are talking of large-scale innovation).

The setting up of new enterprises must be supported and stimulated and promoted from below, primarily on the initiative of groups of innovators and of individual innovators. Recent Russian laws give definite opportunities for this. They must be used to stimulate competition to attract the consumer and to establish conditions of work for the innovator.

Competition between producers for the attention of the consumer

Competition not only allows the consumer to demand an improvement in the quality of goods; he or she can now refuse old models and instead buy new commodities that better meet their needs. In this way the consumer stimulates the producers.

If there are no superior bodies to turn to for help, competition between producers makes an innovating strategy the only possible way of avoiding losses. This ensures there is an economic selection of those people and organizations that are intensively innovating. Those enterprises which implement innovations are then enabled to develop and expand. Under these conditions, large organizations emerge on a sound basis as a result of their directors' and workers' readiness to innovate, rather than accepting bureaucratic decisions from above. Naturally this helps increase receptivity towards innovation in the economy as a whole.

The formation of an economic need in enterprises for innovations should provide real grounds for the creation of a favourable climate for innovation. Without special measures, however, it will only arise accidentally, where there are especially capable directors. In theory, such a climate could be created in almost any enterprise if the following measures are introduced. (Of course, we are assuming that the global, institutional conditions mentioned above are already in existence.)

The formation of an innovative community

To make successful use of major innovations, personnel must be carefully selected. This ensures that the enterprise has a stable nucleus of innovating managers and specialists who know well the specific features of production at that particular factory, and who strongly identify with its interests and aims. They must work in close practical contact with each other and rely on a core of skilled rank-and-file employees. To form such a community, the management of the enterprise should be able to pursue an independent personnel policy and have effective means of attracting skilled specialists.

The passing on to new generations of values and models of behaviour elaborated within this innovative community is a very important part of its preservation and reproduction. Thus it is important to develop something like an apprentice relationship that ensures the acceptance and adaptation by young specialists and manual workers of the norms and habits of active participation in innovation. Here we do not mean a formalized apprenticeship, but the existence of informal and friendly contacts between employees of different generations. Older colleagues must be able to inspire respect and a striving to emulate them; they must possess the features of charismatic leaders and have informal authority. Too wide a generation gap in the innovative community must be avoided and the young must be sure they will be given sufficiently important and independent work when they, in their own opinion, are ready for it; they must also get the support and attention of their older colleagues when they need it. The older staff will support the young in new undertakings, and the young in turn will not simply wait for the former to vacate, and therefore release, the more responsible positions.

Norms of active participation by employees in implementing innovations

This presupposes the obligatory fostering, in both material and non-material respects, of active participation. It is desirable, moreover, that this fostering (at least of a non-material kind) should already be in place at the stage of innovation. It is essential that personnel feel confident that their efforts to renovate production will be noted and rewarded with the minimum possible delay. As well as active support, there must also be an atmosphere of disapproval for passivity in attitudes to innovation.

It is very important that people are not chiefly oriented towards minimizing social expenditure in renewing production. The dominant attitude should be in favour of achieving success in this field, which should be seen as one of the major forms of success in life.

The special status of the active innovator in the enterprise

There must be a transition from the dependent status of supplicant to something more like a 'cult of the innovator', seen as one who ensures the development of the enterprise and its success in competition. This must be linked in all minds with a growth in the well-being of employees, including the directors. The managers, in turn, must create special conditions for the innovator and the essential patronage which he or she requires. For example, workshops could be set aside at all large enterprises which, on a temporary or permanent basis, conduct experiments and investigations of new technical and technological solutions. Practical innovators could be put in charge of such workshops.

It is essential that the management of the enterprise shows confidence in those of their employees who take the risks involved in devising such innovations. There must therefore be no detailed interference but, on the other hand, constant support and help in these undertakings. The employee, for his or her part, must of course earn this confidence.

The right to make mistakes is very important – or, more precisely, the right to be creative and imaginative. If individuals fear they may be punished for each mistake or failure, their imagination, energy and initiative will be inhibited and they will be less inclined to run the risks inevitably involved in innovation. Of course, this should not absolve innovators from responsibility for their actions. The final assessment, however, should be made after a sufficiently long period has elapsed and must be oriented towards the end results.

Drawing in employees from various social groups (specialist and ordinary workers) and of different ages

It is essential that conditions be created under which different social and age groups can work together in an unrestricted atmosphere and without the pressure or assertion of authority. New, unconventional and efficient solutions may then be found to problems facing the enterprise, and the adoption of innovations thus be eased.

The formation of a confidence in long-term goals

The management of the enterprise must have a goal-oriented development strategy. It must be actively striving to attain major long-term goals and be prepared to set up an elaborate programme for their achievement. Then a creative atmosphere will emerge and people will find their work interesting; they will not spare their efforts for the 'general good', including innovation.

We believe that if these measures were implemented, favourable conditions would be created for a sharp rise in innovative activity. The necessity to conduct a large number of innovative drives from above would then disappear, since there would already be activity from below.

There would then no longer be a need for going through the stages of acceptance and institutionalization of innovations, where numerous fiats of superior bodies are required. With the chance to break away from the bureaucrat, each can be engaged in his or her own affairs: the innovator will innovate; the bureaucrat will maintain the organizational order that facilitates the activities of the innovator and eases, rather than hinders, the introduction of innovations.

These measures must lead to a considerable raising of the status of the innovator, within the enterprise, in the economy, and in society as a whole. Innovating as an activity would become prestigious and attractive in the eyes of the workforce and the general population. In other words, there would be a change in the values and culture of our society in favour of innovation. Naturally, such a change cannot take place quickly, although any move in that direction is important.

The demand for high skills should also increase, both among manual occupations and among technical specialists. If there is no interference from outside, conditions will emerge for the establishment of professional associations that have a genuinely high status, with concomitant rewards for their work.

Once there are no longer superior bodies capable of interfering in the activities of enterprises carrying out innovative drives, enterprises will independently set their own targets and develop programmes for their attainment. They will then avoid the periods of 'hibernation' and 'storming',[3] that mark the beginning and end of plan periods, and instead develop a steady work tempo.

If the demand for innovations does rise substantially, and social conditions emerge that favour their implementation, then a market for innovations will become essential. This must form a part of the overall market economy coming into existence as a result of economic reforms. We consider that the creation of the market institutions essential for the implementation of all the abovementioned measures will constitute one of the major difficulties of these reforms. Perhaps they will become a bottleneck that holds up everything else. Accordingly, we shall look separately at the ways in which these institutions might be formed.

NOTES

1 These two kinds of society are 'ideal types'. They are abstractions embodying the principal features of societies that differ in the principles according to which their social institutions are organized and in the forms of activity pursued by the population.

2 President Yeltsin's team (as was Khazbulatov's group) is however very heterogenous. For example, the economic division of the government (headed by E. Gaidar), including Goscomimushzestvo etc., opposes the Security Council (headed by Oleg Lobov); and the economic division of the government is itself divided in Moscow, St Petersburg, etc.

3 As a rule, Soviet enterprises were prevented from working for up to two-thirds of business hours during the initial period of a project, because of shortages of materials. To complete the project on target, enterprises had to work hard, or 'storm', towards the end. This resulted in managers suffering nervous breakdowns and in social tensions among personnel, and was a serious obstacle to innovation.

3

The Market as a Precondition for Stimulating Innovation

By the end of the 1980s the view among Russian economists was that it was essential to create a 'socialist market economy'.[1] Among those who wrote on this subject were Oleg Bogomolov (1987), Gavriil Popov (1987) and Nikolai Shmelev (1987). When Leonid Abalkin discussed economic reform he asserted that it was essential to 'shift to direct dealing and wholesale trade; we must, finally, set up a socialist market and enable it to exercise its own distinctive means of influencing the level of production and the quality of output'. I do not know what such writers mean by a 'socialist market economy' and suspect that nobody knows. Therefore I shall hereafter refer simply to the 'market economy'.

At the same time, many of these authors considered it would be relatively easy to set up such a market – once other obstacles had been removed. In a discussion of the way in which the economy should be structurally reorganized, Popov wrote that:

> The central authorities must take an active part if the fundamental breakthrough and complete re-equipping of industry required by the second level of structural reorganization is to succeed. Considering the successes and tragedy of our past history I think such active involvement is problematic. The formation of a market is by contrast relatively straightforward.[2]

I disagree with Popov's last statement: I believe it will be very difficult to create a market economy in the states of the former Soviet Union. The main problem in setting up a market does not lie in the economic or organizational difficulties it will involve. Rather, it lies in the social tension and conflicts that will arise during the transition from the command economy to the market. These tensions demand that the market also be examined from the viewpoint of sociology or, more exactly, of economic sociology. We must examine the market as one among many social mechanisms that will inevitably affect other existing institutions and also the individual.

3.1 The market as a social mechanism

Popov and Shmelev, in my view, gave a sufficiently full definition of the market in *economic* terms in their 1988 article:

> The conception of 'the market' includes three elements: unregulated supply or freedom of production, unregulated demand or freedom of acquisition, and unregulated prices that balance supply and demand. If only one of these three is absent then there cannot be a market in the full sense and its characteristic self-organization and automatic regulation cannot then come into play.[3]

Economic sociology adds to this by examining how individuals can and must function within the market. It considers how their behaviour should be assessed and what attitudes they need to have. It determines how social institutions (politics, ideology, the law, morality etc.) influence the individual and what particular features those institutions must possess if they are to shape individuals who are market-oriented in attitudes and behaviour.

So first we must analyse whether the preconditions for the emergence of such a market mechanism exist in the states of the former Soviet Union. If we conclude that some of them are absent, we must discuss how they might be introduced and the consequences of doing this.

The main social conditions required for the formation of a market can, I believe, be summarized as follows.

Diversity in each sector of the economy

There must be many independent agents in each sector of the economy and in each type of product (by 'agents', we refer to producers and buyers and those who service their needs). The main roles these agents must play are as owners of the means of production, as specialists in its management, and as manual workers engaged in production. To enable them freely and fully to play these roles, the necessary institutions must be set up along with corresponding organizations such as a stock exchange. Other important roles are those of entrepreneur and innovator. In fact there are dozens, even hundreds, of economic roles in developed market institutions: stockbrokers, advertising agents, salesmen, tax inspectors and so on.

In the market system these economic agents have distinctive values and motivations. Among the most fundamental of these we may mention rationalism, an orientation towards economic expediency, and a striving to maximize results. At the same time each role also, of course, has its own distinctive system of values and behavioural motivations. Thus the property-owner is geared towards management, the specialist towards his professional vocation, and so on. Most of these roles were absent in the USSR: consequently, so were the behaviour and consciousness corresponding to them. The Soviet economy had a quite different role structure from that of the market economy, being dominated by politicians and administrators.

In a market system these agents are extremely flexible, rapidly appearing and disappearing in response to the current economic climate. One of the important institutions that assures this flexibility is the right each person or group of individuals has freely and legally to set up an economic organization as long as its activities do not infringe any law. They equally have the right to disband such an organization.

Freedom to enter into direct economic ties

The economic ties made in a market economy are distinguished by their competitive nature. They are based on exchange, for the most part through the medium of monetary equivalence, and not on barter. The establishment of equivalent exchange reflects their voluntary nature.

A very important feature of market interaction is that the producer is not tied to a particular buyer, or vice versa. This contrasts markedly with the Soviet system, where enterprises were provided with suppliers by orders from above. Freedom is limited in the market system by a strict form of economic responsibility, where economic agents are answerable for their actions and pay out of their own pocket without the direct aid of government bodies.

A last important feature is that the norms governing these ties (e.g. prices, tariffs, wage levels) are formed from the bottom upwards. They arise out of a social consensus found between juridically equal partners. This permits an enormous variety: there are as many prices as there are deals; two employees doing the same job at the same factory may receive very different salaries; and so on. As a result, all the varied conditions under which economic activities take place (climatic, economic and political) can be very precisely reflected in these norms, creating favourable conditions for these activities at each particular moment in time.

Economic activities are objectively assessed

Such assessment is based on the norms mentioned above; these result from a consensus reached by a great many agents, none of whom may individually and arbitrarily change these norms. In the market system, this assessment is objectively reached without the extraneous criteria that characterized the Soviet system. It is not the individual who is being assessed, but his or her work, and it does not matter whether he or she is a Party member, works for a private or a state enterprise, and so on. Each therefore has the same right to self-expression, but it is the most capable, hard-working and energetic individuals who will succeed.

The market system is thus a social mechanism which rapidly responds to economic demand and effectively directs human energy and efforts to those spheres where the demand arises.

Other social institutions need to be specially organized to enable the market to work effectively in the economy and to facilitate its dynamic development.

Politics must be relatively segregated from the economy, and politicians and political forces must not be able to interfere directly in economic activities. The state and other political institutions must be organized on democratic lines. They must guarantee the equal rights of those who participate in economic affairs and not permit them to flout the obligations they have undertaken: such behaviour must be subject to legal sanctions. Moreover, political institutions must ensure that when consensus is reached by free economic agents about the norms and regulations governing economic activities these will be legalized and also given the force of law.

Precise legal norms that define and regulate the different fields of activity are essential. They must be impartial in character, making even the most highly placed government and Party officials and leaders liable to punishment for their infringement. This is possible in a law-governed, constitutional state where political figures do not have the right to interfere in the work of the police and the courts. In turn this assures the individual of his liberties and the independent status of economic agents.

Religious and cultural institutions must help to shape a particular type of personality – one who puts a high value on individual self-expression through work and the individual attainment of success. In the absence of such personal qualities as independence, responsibility, honesty and punctuality, it will be impossible to maintain enduring and stable economic relations without state regulation.

3.2 Is a market system possible in Russia?

Before we can answer this question, we must examine how far the social preconditions for the formation of a market exist in the Russian economy.

The passing and implementation of the 1988 Law of Co-operation enabled independent economic agents to begin to appear. For the time being they are very few and they produce only a tiny proportion of the country's GNP. Their numbers are, however, increasing.

State enterprises themselves are beginning to transform themselves into non-state firms according to the government's programme of privatization. These innovations are currently not so widespread.

Russian enterprises have received the right of more or less free access to foreign markets. Joint ventures with foreign firms are also being established, and by 1992 their numbers were in the thousands.

Public attitudes have been shifting in favour of the development of market institutions. This can be traced in society's attitudes to competition, a very important feature of the market. As recently as 1985–6, the word 'competition' was derogatory, since it was considered exclusively the attribute of the capitalist economy; it led to anarchy in production, to economic crises and the destruction of the forces of production. The necessity for competition was openly discussed on the radio and television and in the press at the end of the 1980s. A survey of directors of district agro-industrial associations (DAA) in mid-1988, for example, found that 76% were in favour of direct competition between co-operatives and the state enterprises of the Agro-Industrial Complex, with only 10% opposed. Moreover, 22% of those interviewed believed that such competition should be actively encouraged. Only 12% considered competition should be limited, while 38% favoured allowing it to whatever degree it arose. Thus the directors of these DAAs were inclined not only to permit competition between co-operatives and state enterprises but even to speak in favour of encouraging it. The great majority of them (66%) expected this to lead, first and foremost, to an improvement in the functioning of state enterprises. Now nobody in Russia doubts the necessity for competition in a market economy.

All this suggests that there has been definite progress towards the formation of market institutions. However, we may doubt that they will lead, in the foreseeable future, to such a development unless more profound changes occur. If the system of socialist monopolism is preserved, if enterprises continue depend on ministries and government departments, or the controlling packet of shares is held by the state in large joint-stock companies, then there seems little hope for the market. The same may be said for the various forms of state interference in pricing and the determination of other economic regulators, and the lack of legally recognized owners of the means of production. In brief, is it possible for wide state interference and the market to co-exist?

In my view, two quite different issues are involved here. First, can a market emerge when the state exercises economic dictatorship? Second, can the state successfully regulate the workings of the market once that market is already in existence?

The answers to these two different questions seem to contradict one another. No, the market cannot emerge when the state and other political institutions intervene and interfere so deeply in the running of the economy. However, the state *can* successfully regulate the market once it is already in existence.

At this point, a general statement as to how the market arose in Western countries will be useful, since it is there that it has reached its highest level of development.

In the West, the formation of the market took several hundred years and was influenced and shaped by major historical events such as the Reformation and the Enlightenment. The former encouraged such human qualities as rationalism, honesty and punctuality in business relations, and a conscientious and thorough attitude. The Enlightenment contributed political democracy and constitutional, law-governed states which hardly interfered, at least not directly, in the economic activities of free citizens. These influences resulted both in people with particular human qualities, plus hundreds and thousands of written and unwritten laws and regulations guiding their conduct, with a host of organizations to guarantee that these regulations were observed. Consequently, both a mechanism existed, and the people capable of using it. Yet in spite of this, the market still experiences serious disruptions at times, even to this day.

In Russia, by contrast, the market is beginning to be formed under quite different conditions. The system is profoundly and deeply disfigured by the command economy that was created by Stalin and his supporters. The most obvious and important manifestation of these defects is that the individual is almost totally unprepared for work in market conditions. It is inconceivable that stable and voluntary relations between juridically equal economic partners could be established without the qualities of honesty and punctuality, for example. Yet how could such qualities have developed in the Soviet command economy? Relations in a market economy depend on trust and the conviction that a business partner will keep to his or her word and deliver goods on time. In the command economy, directors of enterprises continually failed to do this, even after reaching an agreement, because they were forced by orders from above to sell their output to another consumer. In these circumstances, what kind of confidence could develop in business relations?

The values surrounding entrepreneurial behaviour are equally determined by the society in which it has developed. Under a market system such activity is allowed, and even encouraged, and entrepreneurs act openly in accordance with precise legal norms. In the command economy, on the other hand, legal entrepreneurial activity aimed at production was almost entirely absent, but so-called 'redistributive' entrepreneurial activities were, on the contrary, very common. The latter involved the legal extraction of resources from higher bodies, and embezzlement and pilfering. These particular forms of entrepreneurial activity were sufficiently widespread in Soviet society to leave a distinct impression on its members. They encouraged wiliness, dishonesty, and lack of respect for, and ignorance of, the law. They also bred cynicism about the possibility of showing one's abilities in any legally permitted organization.

The lack of appropriate qualities and patterns of behaviour among the Russian population is matched by the absence of any developed market institutions and the organizations necessary for their functioning. If restrictions are suddenly removed from above in a particular part of the economy, the response may be an improvement in the quality of work, thus responding to demand. Yet this still does not lead to any marked improvement in the meeting of demand but, on the contrary, gives rise to new shortages. One example is that of subscriptions to major Soviet journals and newspapers in 1989. With the coming of glasnost, the latter began to attract large numbers of new readers by satisfying their demand for information, but immediately came up against the limitations of a printing industry beset by outdated technology and a shortage of paper.

In these conditions, continued state intervention in the economy prevents market institutions from attaining the 'critical mass' necessary before they can begin to function in any real sense.[4] Neither does it permit the population to acquire the necessary attitudes and qualities. The conclusion is evident. If such radical change is to take place in the foreseeable future, state direction must be removed from the running of the economy and the population must be rapidly introduced to market conditions set up by Gaidar in 1992.

However, the formation, acquisition and internalization of hundreds of norms and patterns of behaviour requires a long period of time. In essence, the acquisition and mastery of this new economic culture will take at least one generation, or around 25–30 years. Even within such a long period of time, moreover, the transition from the command economy to the market will mean vast changes in the lives of many millions of people. They will have to change their way of life to become much more mobile, since the system of compulsory domicile registration (*propiska*) must be abolished if the market is to function normally. They must be prepared to change their work and to re-train, and become used to much wider and openly acknowledged differences in income levels and living standards. They must appreciate that to earn an average income they must work hard, and that they must be quite highly qualified in order to find work.

A large part of our population is not ready for this. The danger therefore arises that, when such a market reform sweeps through the economy, an entire stratum of people will emerge who cannot find their place in the market system. Furthermore, they will not just be temporarily unemployed or unwilling to find suitable work for themselves; such people – and there will be many of them – will simply be unable to adjust to the new conditions. This will primarily affect poorly qualified and older employees, a certain part of the clerical and executive levels of the administrative bureaucracies, and research workers and teachers in further and higher education. They have no future at all in the market system. A new 'marginal' stratum may come into existence.

There has long existed a traditional Soviet marginal stratum of alcoholics, *bichi* and *bomzhi* (those with no fixed place of abode), who voluntarily ceased to participate in established institutions. Now that market reform is rapidly introduced in Russia, a quite new and much more socially threatening marginal stratum has come into existence, composed of those who formerly enjoyed a comparatively high social status.

Over the years, the Soviet forces of law and order developed methods for combating and regulating the 'anti-social' behaviour of the traditional marginal stratum. The legal code, the incarceration of the most aggressive and insubordinate in camps and prisons, and enforced work-cures for alcoholics were sufficient to deal with them. The new marginal stratum uses new forms of social protest, including actions of a political nature. They are the social base for Communist and fascist parties in the former USSR. In contrast to traditional marginals, the new marginal stratum represents a serious threat to social stability. Such people provide support for various extremist tendencies, reactionary movements and crime (including mafia-style organized crime). This development could threaten to negate all reforms and lead to neo-Stalinism.

Another specific aspect of Russian society that is leading to social tension as a result of market reforms can be seen in the large number of small and medium-sized Soviet towns that arose around a single or at most two or three large factories. This was quite natural under the regime of socialist monopolism, when decisions about the building of factories and the location of towns were taken from above. Market reforms may lead to the bankruptcy of many such enterprises and, consequently, to long-term mass unemployment in these small and medium-sized urban centres. This threatens mass spontaneous action by workers, especially in provincial areas.

Given these concerns, it might seem preferable to establish market structures initially in individual sectors of the economy. To achieve this, the structures must relate to almost all of a particular technological chain in order to minimize disruption and lack of co-ordination. Most suitable for such treatment seem to be the agro-industrial complex and branches dealing with other consumer goods. The second stage in the formation of a market would be to involve those branches of the economy that directly supply these two economic complexes. The third stage would then draw the majority of sectors of the economy into such market relations.

With this gradual but steadily expanding introduction of the market a democratic evolution could be maintained and the risks of destabilization reduced to a minimum.

This plan might be possible if the situation in Russia were that of a rational democratic evolutionary process. Instead, it was an irrational revolutionary process, and now we have an almost spontaneous and unmanaged market transition.

A developed market mechanism should contain at least five different markets: goods for consumption, labour, capital goods, stocks and shares, and inventions and innovations. Each has its own distinctive features. We shall look in detail only at the last of them.

3.3 The market for innovations as a precondition for stimulating innovators

The formation of market structures (including competition) should make innovations economically attractive to enterprises and hence create a market for innovations.

As an activity, innovation is characterized by the considerable uncertainty and risk involved. This should be recognized in the forms and level of incentive offered to its initiators.

If such incentives are to have a long-term effect, the innovator must have the legal right of ownership of the fruits of his efforts. Thus the Soviet practice of not paying for inventions and innovations but only for physical labour must be abandoned. It must be recognized that only a few people are capable of such original contributions and that their work is no less valuable than mass production in the factory. Only the administrators in charge of research and other fields derive any benefit from the present system, not infrequently putting their own signatures under the results of another's work.

A network of innovative organizations must thus be set up in which the most favourable conditions for inventing, publicizing and introducing new practices and technologies are provided for innovators. These must operate according to quite different criteria from those applying in factories engaged in well-established forms of production. Allowance must be made for the frequent miscalculations, mistakes and failures that arise from the uncertain and risky nature of innovation. Consequently, the permitted rate of profit for such an enterprise's output when successful must be considerably higher than elsewhere, to compensate for the less steady rate of income. Taxes on the profits from innovative activities must accordingly also be lower.

It is very important that contracts for such work be freely concluded and voluntary. This must form the basis on which innovative organizations function; the main role of the state will be to act as guarantor that contracts are honoured and to supervise their implementation.

The following eight types of innovative organization are needed, none of which at present exist in Russia:

1 Advertising and information-providing firms that gather information and publicize all innovations. They may specialize in servicing specific industries and technologies, and their services must, of course, be paid for.

2 Organizations that specialize in producing non-standard equipment to order. These small but technically well-equipped organizations with qualified staff meet the needs of innovators for small runs or even 'one-off' models of equipment, instruments, computer programmes and so on.

3 Banks for technical development that finance the creation, testing and dissemination of innovations. These may issue stocks or shares and operate at various levels, in cities or entire regions. Naturally, the bank must have the right to buy and sell innovations, and to commission and carry out new projects as well.

4 Firms that do nothing more than study the prospects for introducing and selling innovations to enterprises.

5 A variety of intermediary 'brokers' commissioned by innovators and innovating enterprises to find customers for their inventions.

6 Employment agencies that find highly qualified specialists (of working or pensionable age) to work full or part-time in such enterprises.

7 Legal firms that specialize in the defence of innovators' rights and provide legal advice (e.g. on setting up in business, loans etc.).

8 Finally, specialized non-commercial and non-profit-making foundations that help to finance and implement promising, long-term research and development. Although such work offers no immediate financial return, it is essential if innovations of commercial value are to be produced. Depending on their earnings and profit levels, all innovative organizations should pay part of their takings into such foundations.

These eight types of organization should form a self-sufficient system, providing all the services enterprises need to develop and implement innovations.

The setting up of such a network of bodies would make it much easier to develop innovations. However, it cannot, and must not, be set up in the traditional Soviet bureaucratic fashion: at one sweep and throughout the country. It must develop naturally, taking account of the distinctive needs and conditions of an area's different cities, regions and republics, and in response to genuine demand from a specific organization.

It is very important that Western experience in the renewal of production be drawn from, and to this end it would make sense to set up a number of joint ventures with Western consultative firms. On the Russian side, the partners might be the handful of existing consultative agencies, certain research institutes, institutes of higher education and research firms. Such joint ventures could considerably speed up and facilitate the setting up of market institutions in our country. By preparing our directors, technicians and workers for contacts with Western partners, they would help overcome the existing barrier of economic skills and values that now separates them.

In the first part of this book we have sketched out several scenarios for the country's future development. In particular we have described that complex of institutions and conditions that are necessary if our economy is to lift itself out of its present degradation and encourage innovation.

Some may ask, however, why we insist on one particular scenario. Why do we need these forms of entrepreneurial activity? Are all the innovative organizations we have listed really essential? It may even be questioned why we need a market for innovations, or this entire complex of socio-economic measures.

The answer is that any cure must affect the primary cause of infection and not merely treat its symptoms. In our view, the measures suggested will partially remove the chief obstacle to innovation in the Soviet Union: political intervention and the bureaucratic management and direction of the economy.

We shall return to a more detailed and substantiated discussion of the causes of stagnation in Part III of this book. First, however, we must provide a much more concrete account of how innovative processes are hindered and discouraged at the level of the enterprise. This will form the subject of Part II.

NOTES

1 L. M. Abalkin, 'The new economic thinking, a need of the day', *Nauka i Zhizn*, vii (1988), 6.
2 G. Popov, 'Aims and machinery', *Znamya*, vii (1988), 173.
3 V. Popov and N. Shmelev, 'The anatomy of deficit', *Znamya*, v (1988), 172.

4 In this sense, 'M. Popkova' (pseudonym of Larisa Piyasheva) is surely right in her assertion that the plan and the market are incompatible, even though we disagree with her when she says the market is *always* incompatible with the plan. (See M. Popkova, 'Who bakes better pies?', *Novy Mir*, v (1988).) Her article made a serious and constructive polemical contribution to the debate, but nowhere in the press or the academic world was it appreciated. On the contrary, she was accused of attacking the idea of perestroika itself.

II

Innovations and Innovators in Soviet and Russian Enterprises

4

Renewal of Methods of Production in Enterprises

4.1 Types of innovation in enterprises

The innovative process is the accumulated result of the activities of people engaged in implementation of innovations over a certain period of time. The most important indicators of this process are: the number and exact type of innovations introduced; the economic and social costs and the results of their implementation; and the overall consequences of such change.

We must again emphasize the inherent unpredictability of any innovative process. It is difficult, and at times impossible, to foresee what its results and consequences may be; they lie months, and even years, in the future. One dramatic example from recent Soviet history is Khrushchev's Virgin Lands campaign in the 1950s. This marginal region of Kazakhstan at first produced bumper crops and then, five years later, suffered a degree of soil erosion that was almost without precedent in the USSR. More recently, in the 1970s, there was a drive to improve living conditions for those working on the land by bringing them together in new centralized settlements with all modern conveniences. In practice, this condemned many small villages to extinction and adversely affected production by locating agricultural workers far away from the land.

Unexpected difficulties and obstacles are thus always encountered when putting a suggested innovation into practice.

The term 'innovative processes' does not cover all the changes happening in society; it is limited to those with a conscious aim, implemented to attain particular beneficial results. Underlying all innovative processes is the implementation of innovations and, specifically, of those forms of activity which are new for the economic organization concerned, be it an enterprise, a region, a branch of production, or the entire economy.[1] The larger and more complex the economic organization, the greater the uncertainty and the larger the number of people who participate. Such innovations are correspondingly more difficult to direct and control.

Before we can describe innovative processes, we must have a practical classification of innovations. The specialist literature distinguishes two types: those that are socio-economic, and those that concern technology and equipment.[2] The latter may be further subdivided into:

1 rationalization of production;
2 the development of new machinery and equipment and the mechanization of production;
3 improvement in the existing production technology;
4 implementation of new technology either with or without the transition to the output of new commodities;
5 the implementation of new systems of technology.

Table 4 shows the type of innovation and the level at which it is implemented.

At any moment all the types of innovative process listed in Table 4 may be taking place in the Russian economy. Together they represent that part of the country's economic development which is the result of the deliberate efforts of various economic agencies. As a result, new types of product are developed, levels of production rise, structural changes take place, and the efficiency of the economy improves. If innovative processes do not proceed at a rapid pace and their role declines over an extended period, then stagnation in production or even regression may set in.

4.2 Innovation in agricultural enterprises

In our 1985 study of innovation in collective and state farms in the Novosibirsk region, we used two types of information: official statistics and sociological survey material. These sources of information were only partially comparable. The survey responses primarily referred to the results of participation in implementing innovation as assessed by directors and specialists; it proved

Table 4 *The structure of innovations in the Russian economy*

	Level of implementation			
	Enterprise	*Region*	*Branch*	*Economy*
Type of innovation				
1 Rationalization of production	Proposal	–	–	–
2 New equipment	×	×	Development of new equipment	Technical progress
3 Improvement in technology	×	×	×	×
4 New technologies	Transition to low-till ploughing	×	×	Technological progress
5 New technological systems	Industrial technologies for preparing land	×	×	×
6 Innovations in administration and management	Sub-contracting work teams	Setting up regional AICs	×	Economic reform
7 Organizational innovation in the use of equipment	Automatic system control	×	×	×
8 Social innovations	New working regimes	×	×	Changes in labour code and pension laws

– absence of given type of innovation
× presence of given type of innovation

impossible to avoid some double-counting. By contrast, the official statistics mainly dealt with the quantity and nature of innovations annually introduced at a given enterprise, the expenditure involved, their productivity, and so on.

So far as the implementation of innovations is concerned, we must admit that the quality of such statistical information was generally poor. Firstly, it was incomplete, and by no means included all the innovations made at the enterprise. Experts have estimated that no more than half of all the rationalization proposals were recorded. Certain enterprises provided no reports at all about the introduction of innovations. In this sense, the sociological data were fuller. Secondly, many aspects of innovations that are important for an analysis of innovative processes were not provided by enterprises in their obligatory reports to the State Committee for Statistics. For example, we cannot learn from this source how much time was spent on implementing a particular innovation, how difficult its application proved for the body concerned, and so on. For this type of information we had to rely entirely on sociological studies. Thirdly, it was almost impossible to assess the proportion of different types of innovation in the total figures since the enterprise used different statistical forms for its reports that were not comparable. Lastly, the statistical sources also included implementation of innovations that existed only on paper; sociological methods proved more reliable in exposing these fictitious achievements.[3]

Thus each of the types of information used had shortcomings not found in the other. But despite being defective and difficult to compare, we believe that the use of different sources of information, as in all social research, allowed us to give a fuller and truer picture of the innovative process.

The majority of innovations introduced in agricultural enterprises had to do with equipment and technology (71.8%).[4] Among them we distinguished rationalizing proposals (11.7%), mechanization of production and creation of new equipment (7%), the improvement of the existing technologies used in agriculture (29.3%), and the adoption of new technologies (23.8%).

The number of innovations adopted overall in agriculture in the 1980s was extremely modest. Each enterprise on average adopted only 1.3 rationalizing proposals and less than one invention (0.5) each year. Even if most rationalizing proposals were not statistically recorded, this still means that there was no more than one rationalizing proposal for every 50–100 employees each year. If we compare this to rates in industry, the difference is even more striking. The rate for agriculture was 5–10 times less than in industrial production, while the latter was itself perhaps 100 times less than in Japanese industry.[5]

A 1986 study of the Altai Territory in western Siberia suggested that only 15% of manual workers in agriculture ever made a single rationalizing proposal during their lifetime. (This conclusion covered unreported as well as statistically recorded proposals.) Within the category of innovations in equipment and technology, rationalizing proposals also formed a low proportion of the total. This contrasts with the experience of developed countries:

> the volume of inventiveness by manual workers in the total of adopted innovations is very high in the industrially developed countries. For example, in the USA available assessments put the proportion at half of the total.[6]

The great majority of workers employed in Russian agricultural enterprises in the 1980s therefore did not manifest an independent and active involvement in innovation.

Each enterprise on average spent 335 roubles a year on inventions and rationalization of production. Of this sum, 122 roubles were paid to those proposing such innovations. At the same time, the most successful enterprises from the technical point of view (11% of the total) differed markedly in both respects; they introduced 3–4 times more rationalizing proposals and inventions, and they spent nine to ten times more on their implementation.

By the end of 1992, economic crises and increasing shortages of money and material resources led to a reduction in innovative activity in enterprises by up to and over a half.

When we looked at different branches of production within collective and state farms, we found a marked difference between grain and vegetable production and animal husbandry. In a single enterprise, the former attracted 1.4 new technologies each year, the latter only 0.3. Yet the former innovations provided an annual average of 22,000 roubles, while the latter yielded over twice as much, at 55,000 roubles. The most successful farms adopted 2–3 times more than the average of new technologies in grain production, and paid out 9–10 times more, while in animal husbandry the figures were correspondingly higher: 6–7 times more technologies, and 18–20 times more money.

Thus, though the overall levels of innovation in agriculture were very modest, there was a great disparity between the most advanced enterprises and all of the others.

Could the current shortages of agricultural produce and meat be eliminated, then, by raising all enterprises to the level of the most advanced and innovative farms? We calculated what such a hypothetical improvement would achieve if each enterprise on average attained the same rates of innovation as the 'leaders'.[7] The gross output proved to be approximately 11 million roubles more, giving a total for the Novosibirsk region of 112 million roubles, or roughly a 10% increase.[8]

The prospects for achieving a radical improvement by raising the backward enterprises to the level of the 'leaders' are therefore not very great. This is because of the nature of the innovations adopted even in advanced enterprises. Usually they include elementary and routine advances (the use of chemicals to preserve feedstuffs etc.) that have long been known and used throughout the world, and, though new for the enterprises, are quite familiar to Russian research on inventions and innovations. While an increase in the numbers of such 'innovations' is a necessary condition for expanding and developing production, it is by no means sufficient in itself.

The overwhelming majority of enterprises do not pursue an active and purposeful policy of innovation. They prefer not to take risks and simply rely on routine adoption of progressive technology. In order radically to change the situation it is necessary for enterprises to shift to a new type of scientific and technical progress that some have termed 'revolutionary'.[9] In agriculture, this means the application of bio-technology, genetic engineering, and so on. However, the deployment of a revolutionary form of technical progress requires that not only technological and economic but also social preconditions are met. These social requirements are discussed later in the book; see Chapters 5–7.

At the same time, there is no indissoluble barrier between 'revolutionary' and 'non-revolutionary' forms of technical progress:

> Even the most fundamental innovations undergo extremely far-reaching modification before they can be fully applied in practice. New technology does not spring like Minerva, fully-armed from the head of Jove; as a rule, it is the result of innumerable improvements introduced through the accumulation of practical experience, which have widened the scope of already existing but less specialized systems . . . . What at first sight seems to be a spontaneous technological shift is in most cases the result of a prolonged and consistent line of development.[10]

This connection between two types of technological progress

makes it essential to seek out the forms of management and administration that will ensure their combination.

Socio-economic innovations

Socio-economic innovations are goal-oriented changes in the social and economic structures of the enterprise that have been implemented by the producers. During the period in question their proportion of the total number of innovations was 28.2%. They involve innovations made in three different areas: in the system of administration and management, in the technical procedures of organization, and in social interaction.

Within this broad category of innovations, those affecting the system of management and administration accounted for 24.7% of the total. When we conducted our survey in 1985, there was very little variety in these measures: mainly they affected the workforce and, to a lesser extent, the workshop structure of management. Neither did the forms of change in management practices within a particular enterprise reach very deeply. Models of workforce organization which left much of the former organizational structure intact gained wide application; the principles of incentives and of relations between the workforce and the administration did not lead to any practical increase in the rights and opportunities of employees.[11]

Among the organizational and managerial innovations that were implemented at a higher level, but that proved to have a major influence on the management of agricultural enterprises and their general position, we should mention the setting up of District Agro-Industrial Associations (hereafter DAA) in 1983. Their primary purpose was to deal with the problems in administering the Agro-Industrial Complex (AIC) at the district level, which by then had become quite acute; in particular they were intended to break down the ministerial barriers that still existed within the AIC. A survey of those in charge of such associations carried out in 1988 suggested that they had failed in this task. At least, that was the opinion of 50% of those interviewed, while only 42% felt that the DAA had managed to co-ordinate the various interests at the district level.

The limited prospects of success might have been foreseen and predicted from the very beginning. In 1983, Professor Ryvkina and the author sent a questionnaire to about 100 Party district committee secretaries in western Siberia. Only a third of them then thought that the new DAAs would be able to carry out their allotted functions. Obviously, with such a negative attitude from the leading political figures at this level, successful innovation could hardly have been expected. Moreover, other studies came to similar conclusions. On the basis of such findings, an active dialogue should immediately have begun between the central Moscow authorities, the district level of administration and management, and the workforces of the enterprises concerned. In this way, the main deficiencies in the reforms of the administrative structure could have been exposed and eliminated. This did not happen. Furthermore, we were forbidden from making the findings of this survey public. Thus, instead of the timely exposure and solution of these problems, we now face a great many new difficulties which could have been avoided.

By the late 1980s, the situation was changing markedly, primarily because enterprises were beginning to transfer to full cost accounting (*khozraschet*) and self-financing. New forms of organization within the enterprise were appearing, or rather re-appearing, since co-operatives and leasehold contracts once worked well in Russia and the USSR. There was lively discussion about shareholding enterprises and state-co-operative organizations, and these were already being set up.

The second type of socio-economic innovation, concerning the technical procedures of organization, accounted for a mere 3.3% of the innovations adopted. By this term, we mean progressive changes in particular levels of the administration or organization of production. The distinctive feature of this type of innovation is that it is a consequence of innovations in the system of management and administration. These lead to a sharp rise in demand for new forms of clerical work, accounting etc. If a radical reform of the administrative system continues and intensifies, we may therefore predict a great boost in demand for new technical procedures of organization. The consequent rise in the number and variety of such innovations will in turn raise demand for properly trained specialists able to facilitate their development and application. Many more computers and other modern office equipment will be required. The necessity will then also arise for a wide and de-centralized network of organizations providing consultancy and other services to the consumers of these new and complex forms of equipment. Perhaps the basic infra-structure of production (communications systems, heat and electricity supplies etc.) will also require major restructuring. It is possible that innovations in the administrative system may lead to the most varied changes in the way we live and work in our country.

The third and final major group of socio-economic innovations is concerned with social interactions in enterprises, improving the working and living conditions of all employees. These 'social' innovations may involve more progressive patterns of work and leisure, improving canteen facilities, and so on. They are very few in number and before 1985 accounted for only a tiny percentage of the total, at 0.2%. Yet they are of prime importance for the proper functioning of any enterprise; otherwise the number of conflicts at work, dissatisfaction with the work itself, and poor relations between manual workers and executive staff will become counter-productive. Perestroika has emphasized the importance of the human factor in the economy, and attention to such innovations has therefore greatly risen in recent years.

Transition in Russia changed the structure of innovative activity. Now it consists for the most part of socio-economic innovations: the establishing of small businesses under state enterprises, the reorganization of state enterprises into joint-stock companies and so on. Technological innovations are dramatically down, but the two types of innovation are closely inter-related.[12] The implementation of social innovations can help speed up the introduction of scientific and technical advances by giving employees an incentive to innovate (see Table 5).

Table 5 shows that the overwhelming majority (67%) of enterprises classified as backward in terms of socio-economic innovation in the 1980s also fell into this category in terms of technological innovation. There are no technological leaders among them. In contrast, among those that led on socio-economic indicators, hardly any were technically and technologically backward (a mere 9%). Thus, socio-economic innovations such as new systems of payment which aimed at improving employee attitudes to work achieved real results. In turn, they also helped to improve attitudes towards the introduction of new types of equipment and technology.

4.3 The influence of innovations on enterprise development

We examined two aspects of this influence in our 1985 study. Firstly, we evaluated the influence of innovations on economic results. Secondly, we considered how they affected the socio-economic position and activities of different groups of employees. Twelve indicators were taken to measure the economic results, and may be grouped into four categories:

1 volume of output;
2 efficiency of production;

Table 5 *The link between types of enterprises and their implementation of socio-economic, technical and technological innovations (%)*

Type of enterprise making socio-economic innovations	*Type of enterprise making technological innovations*			
	Leaders	*Average*	*Backward*	*Total*
Leaders	18	73	9	100
Average	18	53	29	100
Backward	0	33	67	100

Based on data collected for all the enterprises studied in 1985. The introduction of innovation in equipment and technology was quantified in terms of roubles spent and the results of introducing the new technologies in animal husbandry and agriculture. Socio-economic innovations here refer to the proportion of employees working on a team contract in both animal husbandry and agriculture.

3 quality of output;
4 economic efficiency.

Innovative processes were defined by 33 indicators grouped in three categories: introduction of new technologies, invention and rationalization, and socio-economic innovations.

We may calculate the contribution made to the enterprises by these new technologies by measuring the growth in profits resulting from their introduction. In livestock farming, this amounted to an annual average of 7800 roubles, and in agriculture, of 3900 roubles.

The effectiveness of expenditure on the introduction of new technologies also differed between these two branches of agriculture. For every rouble spent on grain production the profit was 2.31 roubles, but in animal husbandry it was only 67 kopeks (i.e. almost three and a half times less).

The proportion of profit that could be attributed to the introduction of new technologies in the studied enterprises amounted on average to 5% of the total.

Each enterprise annually received, on average, 41,200 roubles from inventions and rationalization. Of this total, 37,300 roubles or 91% was derived from the application of inventions, although the latter accounted for less than a third (28%) of all proposals. Thus, the introduction of one invention was 25 times more effective than the adoption of a single rationalization proposal. Naturally, however, the implementation of inventions entails far more expenditure of time and effort by employees.

Soviet enterprises traditionally increased the volume of production by consuming more resources, primarily capital stock. We attempted to measure whether an alternative innovating strategy was more favourable to the enterprise's development than this traditional method. As we have already mentioned, a 10% growth in output would result if all enterprises reached the average level of innovations of the leading enterprises. In contrast, if the volume of capital stock were raised to the maximum possible, following the traditional method of Soviet enterprises to increase the volume of production, output would quadruple, but costs would increase sevenfold.[13] It is therefore obviously more profitable for the economy as a whole to introduce innovations, since it works out twice as cheap per unit-output as the traditional method.

It would not be profitable for the enterprise, however, under the old conditions of management. A system that favoured the more expensive items of output would make it unprofitable for the enterprise to adopt an innovative strategy. Such an enterprise would do better to take hand-outs from the state, in the form of increased capital stock.

This situation remains unchanged in the state sector. In the tiny private sector some ambitious businessman try to innovate and to make money using new technology. But these are isolated cases, because the main obstacles to innovation in the new Russian economy are much as those in the old Soviet *narodnom hoziastve* (people's economy).

The conclusion we drew regarding traditional versus innovative methods may be supported and illustrated by the analysis that the directors of the enterprises in the study themselves made of the results of innovation (see Table 6).

Table 6 *The expert assessment of the results of introducing innovations according to directors and leading specialists*

Detail of improvement	*Assessment (%)**
Growth in economic efficiency	50
Improvement in quality of work and output and in standards of production	31
Growth in output	21
Improvement in employee working conditions	15
Growth in labour discipline and active involvement	8
Improvement in organization of production	8
Reduction in time spent on certain agricultural tasks	8
Fulfilment of production plan and sales to state	4
Improvement in functioning of equipment	3
Independence from weather conditions	2
Improvement in relations within the workforce	2

*Since each expert could refer to more than one result, the total sum of assessments amounts to more than 100%.

As we can see from Table 6, half of the innovations adopted led to a growth in efficiency. Just under a third of all innovations facilitated an improvement in the qualitative indicators of production. Only a fifth, however, led to an increase in output. And fulfilment of the plans for production and for sale of output to the state was only facilitated by 4% of all innovations! In these circumstances it is hardly surprising that enterprises shun innovations – very few of them help to attain the aims of the old system of production. Indeed, this growth in efficiency might even have led to a worsening of the enterprise's position (increases in plan targets, decreases in subsidies previously allocated because of low profitability etc). The economic reasons for the extreme caution of Russian enterprises in this field are quite clear. As we shall see in subsequent chapters, there are also more profound causes for this restraint on innovative processes.

A more subtle analysis of the influence of particular innovative processes on enterprise development made it possible to support and expand these conclusions.[14] Analysis of the matrix of correlations showed that innovative indicators were on the whole positively linked with the results of production: volume of gross output, labour productivity, profitability, and others. Yet there was one indicator of development with which all innovative indicators were negatively linked. This was the provision of capital stock. The majority of innovations were aimed primarily at saving labour instead of using capital stock. Under the old conditions, the enterprises were trying to implement the more expensive innovations to obtain more equipment, machinery and other resources from the state.

Another interesting indicator is the level of bonus that was awarded to directors and specialists who adopted and applied new equipment. Here we observed a weakly negative correlation with the indicators of output. The material incentives were not properly organized and, in their then form, did not fulfil their supposed function of encouraging the implementation of highly effective innovations. In practice, the levels of bonus were not related at all to the actual result obtained by implementing an innovation or to the efforts that a director spent on introducing it. The lapse in time between implementation and payment of the bonus also played a role.

There were varying degrees of correlation between indicators of innovative implementation at enterprises and various production development indicators. The most positive influence on gross output, for instance, was the adoption of small-scale innovations and rationalizing proposals (measured by number of rationalizers, quantity of applied rationalizing proposals etc). Small-scale innovations had a markedly lesser effect on indicators of efficiency and productivity, though, than did large-scale innovations. This in part is one reason why so few new technologies and other large-scale innovations were implemented.

We may conclude that, in the past, innovations played an infinitesimal role in the development of output of Soviet enterprises. The routine introduction of progressive technology and cosmetic socio-economic innovations did not ensure profound changes in the system of management. Enterprises attained their goals by following the traditional development strategy, the attraction of additional productive resources from the state. It was therefore only to be expected that stagnation and immobility became increasingly widespread as these resources were exhausted.

This process could have been restrained or avoided altogether had employees been much more actively involved in innovating. They would thereby have compensated for the exhaustion of these more traditional resources. The direct social causes of stagnation in production and output are therefore the shortcomings in the level of innovative activities undertaken by employees.

NOTES

1 E. E. Hagen emphasizes that the concept 'innovation' does not exist in the abstract: an innovation is always implemented in a specific field of human endeavour and in a specific context. See E. E. Hagen, *On the theory of social change*, Homewood, Dorsey Press (1962), 87.

2 Among Soviet writing on the classification of innovations, see N. I. Lapin et al., 'Innovations in organizations', in *The structure of the innovative process*, Moscow (1981). The classification we use here and throughout the book is primarily based on these ideas. (A third type is also mentioned, the composite innovation; since this is a combination of the other two we do not list it separately here.)

There are many classifications of innovations in the specialist literature, each applied for different purposes to a variety of economic and sociological studies. See for instance Zaltman, Duncan and Holbek, *Innovations and organizations*. New York, J. Wiley & Co. (1973). Roman and Puett distinguished six types of innovation in their *International business and technological innovation*, New York, Elsevier (1983), 254–8: these are social, economic, product, procedural, process and managerial.

3 Moreover, as has already been mentioned, innovative processes are inherently difficult to quantify statistically.

4 Calculated from our research findings.

5 Calculated from data taken from A. Radov, 'Inventors and bureaucrats', *Ogonek*, xviii (1988).

6 J. Kalisiak, *Badane efectywnosci ekonomicznej postepu techniczno-organizacyjnego*, Warsaw (1973), 18.

7 These calculations employed a regression equation in which the number of innovations adopted in the enterprise and a number of other characteristics were independent factorial indicators, while the volume of gross product was the dependent output variable.

8 Calculated from data included in *Narodnoe khozyistvo Novoibirskoi oblasti* (1987), 25.

9 See V. S. Muchnik and E. B. Golland, *Economic problems of contemporary scientific and technical progress*, Novosibirsk, Nauka (1984).

10 D. Sahal, *Patterns of technological innovation*, Reading, MA, Addison-Wesley (1981), 135.

11 See Ryvkina, Kosals, Kosals and Narukov, 'On the socio-economic reasons why traditional types of workforce in the early 1980s do not give very satisfactory results', Novosibirsk, Siberian section of AS USSR (1985).

12 Writing about the development of agricultural production, Ermishin states that 'progress here advances in three organically inter-related spheres: equipment and economics, nature and biology, and finally the organization and management of production. The first is linked to the development and improvement of the technical means of labour, the second to the preservation and increase of soil fertility, yields, and improvements in plant varieties and stock breeding.' This interconnection between the different types of innovation has hardly been studied at all at the empirical level. See P. G. Ermishin, *Scientific and technical progress in agriculture*, Kiev-Odessa, Vyshaya Shkola (1981), 17.

13 Calculations made using the regression equation mentioned in note 7, above.

14 It was carried out using the 'spot-stripe' algorithm developed by P. S. Rostovtsev.

5
The Level of Innovative Activity Among Employees

5.1 The protagonists of innovation

It is very important to clarify who initiates an innovative process. Once we know this, we can ascertain the width of the social base of these innovative processes, which social groups are involved and which do not take any part. Then we may determine whether this base is wide enough and, if not, which other groups might be involved.

The innovators in Russian society do not constitute a homogeneous social group made up of individuals of equal status. The different positions they occupy predetermine to a great extent their capacity to implement their ideas.

The 'independent' innovators are the most frustrated and form the very lowest level. It is the lack of support for their efforts by any organization that distinguishes their position. Among them, as a rule, are to be found those specialists, technicians and manual workers who have made a discovery or an invention that is not related to the formal activities of their employing organization. For example, a young worker may invent a press for attaching labels to jeans although he is officially employed in building equipment for atomic power stations, or a physicist may devise a new and more effective method of treating an illness, not only are these innovations of no interest to their immediate employers, they are also invisible to other research institutes, design bureaus and factories. Innovators who are already pensioners or do not work in any fixed place also fall into this category.

Another group is made up of innovators 'in spirit', whose

official posts do not give them the opportunity to put their ideas into practice. Among them are white-collar workers, specialists in the Academy's research institutes, and others who show an interest in innovation but lack the material and technical means to put it into practice.

Finally, there are those who are officially recognized as innovators, who can be divided into different groups. First, there are the technical specialists and directors of enterprises who, among their other duties, are obliged to apply advances in science and technology to their production methods. Then there are technical specialists and directors of a variety of organizations that specialize in the development and application of innovations: science and production combines; industrial research institutes; design bureaus; scientific labour centres; and now innovative firms developing and providing consultations about innovations. In the past heads of ministerial departments and leaders of party bodies also came under this heading.

The transition to a new line of production, and the introduction of new technologies is often a purely formal decision by the 'official' innovators. When they do not actually obstruct and hinder innovation (and this frequently occurs) they are more concerned to avoid punishment for not carrying out instructions to innovate passed down from above.[1] Strictly speaking, therefore, they are not agents of innovation at all. We were obliged to include all those who participated in implementing such innovations in our study, but then differentiated those who were genuinely and actively engaged in innovation in our analysis of these findings: those who might be termed innovators 'in spirit'. These individuals were distinguished from other employees by a number of characteristics.

We paid particular attention to the innovative activities of the directors and technical specialists of enterprises, since we considered their attitudes decisive for innovation in the economy as a whole. No efforts by the specialists of research institutes and design bureaus, or by worker-innovators, could make up for the passivity of enterprise directors. If the latter did not participate in, or wish to introduce, technological change, nothing could be done.

5.2 Stages of innovative activity

To be successful, innovative activities require the performance of certain specified actions which together make up the technology of development and implementation. If this sequence is not followed, and stages are omitted or sloppily performed, then the output of these innovations will be correspondingly lower. The accurate observation of all these procedures, on the other hand, will deliver the full effect of the innovation.

Each stage in this complex process is distinctive in content and results, and has a particular function. The specialist literature on the subject usually distinguishes three stages: the creation or elaboration of the innovation, its wider promotion, and its implementation directly in production.[2]

These distinctions, in our view, are necessary but still inadequate. The centralized Soviet command economy forced the innovator to carry out a great many other activities that did not easily fit into these three categories. Most important of all was to obtain official recognition for the innovation: permission had to be granted at various levels for it to be included in the plans, for tests to be carried out, and so on.

The Soviet press and specialist literature often discussed this aspect of innovation. Yet it remains insufficiently explained, particularly from a social point of view. We possess isolated facts that illustrate this problem. A single technological system involving only 10–15 engines and pieces of machinery, for example, required 400–500 official letters of approval. Moreover, the time lost in transferring the documentation from one organization to another was as much as the time spent on the entire development of the innovation.[3] In order to get a small electronic unit for domestic radios into production, the agreement of up to 12 levels of officialdom and 160 signatures had to be obtained. By way of experiment, a number of ministries agreed with the State Standards Committee to reduce the number of official agreements from 12 to four.[4] As a result, new equipment was introduced twice as quickly.

The necessity of obtaining these numerous permissions and approvals proved an insuperable barrier for many. It was openly described as long ago as 1956 in Vladimir Dudinstev's *Not by Bread Alone*.

The independent innovators were the most severely affected. Without official representation and support, their inventions were neglected for years in certain cases. A device that would protect workers from industrial injuries suffered just such a fate. In late 1987, its creator, L. Solodovnikov, wrote that this 'was the usual fate of the isolated innovator who is simply not capable of breaking through such bureaucratic barriers'.[5]

A great many real difficulties were clearly involved in obtaining official permission. Since this is crucial in delaying innovations we believe that a further, fourth, stage be identified in the Soviet, and now Russian, context: the institutionalization of innovations. This stage precedes that of wider promotion. Unless innovations had already been written into the planning system, they are not guaranteed the necessary material, technical and financial resources which enable them to be implemented in practice.

In the market economy, basic decisions about the introduction of innovations are taken by individual firms. In the command economy, innovators are obliged to apply to higher authority for permission to innovate. As a result, the innovator in the Soviet Union became dependent on the more or less arbitrary decisions of the bureaucrat. To explain how this arose, and what its immediate and long-term consequences will be, we must carry out a separate theoretical and empirical analysis. Otherwise, we shall not be able to develop the basic remedies for such obstruction.

5.3 The structure of innovative activities

While each stage in innovative activity has distinctive features, there are also common structural elements.[6]

The aim

The aim of an innovation is to resolve some problem facing the enterprise (raising production efficiency, increasing output, improving product quality etc.). The context in which the need for innovation is seen is not limited to only local conditions of economic management. The global criteria of enterprise functioning, the state of supplies of materials and equipment, and the degree of independence in economic decision-making are all important as well. The aim, in other words, depends on the particular features of the economic system.

As already noted, innovations may be imposed from above. In this case, the aim is to avoid punishment and demonstrate loyalty to higher authority. Others may innovate solely in order to catch the attention of their superiors and thereby advance their own careers. In these cases, innovation not only fails to solve any problem faced by the enterprise; it may exacerbate those that already exist, or even create new ones.

The content

This refers to the actions the agent of innovation must carry out: planning of implementation; organization of such processes; work with personnel; formation of the means for implementing the innovation (application of material resources, procedural materials etc.).

The variety, complexity and magnitude of the difficulties involved in implementing innovative activities are important distinguishing features of this process.

The means of implementation

This covers both the resources of raw materials, equipment and finance, and also the organizational and procedural provision for innovation. The specific conditions under which an innovation is implemented, and therefore its very success, depend on the availability of these means.

Expenditure of various types of resources is involved in implementing an innovation. Some may be expressed in monetary terms as *economic costs*. In addition, the agent also contributes various forms of *social expenditure*. The latter are linked to the expenditure of time and effort by certain groups; the decisions demanded of those in official positions, who must accept additional responsibility and risk; the loss of status or socio-economic position that certain employees face when their posts lose a degree of importance; complications in managing both production and the workforce, which may result in conflict; less access to important information; and fewer opportunities to obtain illegal or unearned income from unofficial economic activities[7].

The social expenditure involved in implementing innovations is not at present taken into account in Russia, either in studies on the subject or in design and planning calculations. Yet in practice it is a major factor for people who are deciding whether or not to implement an innovation, or whether to participate in its implementation.[8]

The situation is quite understandable. A particular employee will bear the weight of social expenditure, while the economic expenditures seem to him or her to be *gratis*, a present from the state. As a result, employees consider these economic costs very little, if at all. The shift to cost-accounting is changing this situation, but only very slowly. It is because we do not take social expenditure into account that we are unable to offer well-substantiated explanations for the difficulties hindering the promotion of innovations in the Russian economy. We cannot explain why people are often passive or even opposed to innovations at every level of the administrative system. Yet if we take *all* types of expenditure into account, we shall find that economically cheap innovations are socially very expensive, and vice versa. Such a total assessment could theoretically enable us to predict how easily and how widely a particular innovation will be implemented.

The results and consequences

When employees decide to implement an innovation, of course, they consider not only the expenditure it involves, but also its results and consequences. By 'results', we mean those socio-economic effects desired by the proponent of the innovation. By 'consequences', we mean those unplanned effects of innovation that may, in the proponent's view, be important or not. These consequences arise, first of all, because innovative processes are inherently open-ended. Secondly, they arise because the enterprise is a totality of several interrelated (technical, economic and social) structures that also interact with their external environment. An innovation aimed at changing one of these structures leads to a number of changes in the others that may then in turn, reflexively, affect the original structure. The positive effect of this innovation may be either negated or reinforced by these consequences. This is one of the reasons why it is important to have some idea of the possible consequences of an innovation when it is first implemented, so as to reduce the chance of indirectly negating the desired changes.

5.4 The centralized planning of innovations and the degree of employee activity

The great majority (82.7%) of directors and chief specialists who were interviewed said that they did engage in innovative activities.

Of those who answered in the affirmative, the annual average number of innovations they implemented amounted to less than one (0.8). If we take all those interviewed this figure was even lower (0.6). Furthermore, innovation is not a continuous activity, since only 22% of those interviewed implemented more than one innovation in a year. The application of the advances of science and technology is only of episodic importance to directors and specialists, and is, in the main, subordinate to the demands of everyday management of production.

On average these directors and specialists will spend six months, and a quarter of their working time, on the implementation of a single innovation. The activity is collective in character and involves an average of 16 people, usually from all the main social groups: manual workers, middle-ranking managers and specialists, and chief specialists.

The literature on innovation notes that it differs from traditional activities in the following ways. The operations involved are less standardized, and there is a greater element of creativity, variability and uncertainty. At the same time, it is an administrative activity for the director and therefore includes the same range of procedures as any other type of administrative activity: planning and developing the innovation; organizing its implementation; liaising with employees; and providing the necessary buildings, transport, equipment etc. to support this innovative activity and its organizational and procedural back-up.

The activities of directors and specialists in planning the implementation of scientific advances in their enterprises come under certain influences. On the one hand, the enterprise has its own requirements for a particular type of innovation which, in theory, the directors should always reflect.[9] However, these activities also form part of the system of centralized directive planning, the established organizational principles and procedures of which determined how the directors and senior specialists approach scientific innovation. A plan for implementing scientific advances constituted part of the overall production and financial plan for the enterprise, which, in practice, was passed down from above and contained a list of the innovations that the enterprise had to implement. Moreover, this indicated the volume of innovation (the number of hectares to be ploughed using the new technology, the volume of milk output, and so on). Finally, it also determined the scale of the planned expenditure, the expected profit, the number of employees to be redeployed, and any other indicators, depending on the type of innovation (see Table 7).

However, this plan passed down from above did very little to resolve the most acute problem enterprise directors faced: how to assure the materials and equipment required for innovation. Neither did the majority of directors and chief specialists feel any demand for the plan to be fulfilled. Many of them asserted that the plan from above was merely a formality, and according to one:

> By sending down such plans higher authorities pretend that they are aiding technical progress. We pretend that these plans guide our activities and that we are engaged in carrying them out. Yet sometimes we are given plans that entrust us with

Table 7 *The main functions of the implementation plan for scientific advances as part of the innovative activities of directors and chief specialists (as % of those participating in implementation).*

Implementation plan	*(%)*
Helps to organize work in introducing innovation into the enterprise	40
Lays down moral obligations for implementing certain innovations	39
Makes it possible to demand that subordinates participate in innovations	30
Helps to provide the necessary resources for this innovation	27
Lays down administrative obligations	20

implementing one and the same innovation over a period of years when we have long ago already adopted it.

Indeed, the greater part of innovations adopted by these enterprises are made outside of the officially confirmed plans. Our survey found these to make up 54% of the total innovations, while only 46% had been included in the centralized plan.

The plans passed down to enterprises from above thus reflected their actual needs only to a limited extent. There is nothing surprising in this, since only the workforce of a particular enterprise can determine whether it requires a certain innovation and then draw in the necessary specialists from outside. These requirements for innovations are situational; they are determined by the specific production conditions and circumstances of each agricultural enterprise. Even two agricultural enterprises which are immediate neighbours, and therefore share almost the same type of soil and climatic conditions, can still require quite different innovations.

Economic conditions are changing in Russia and the former Soviet Union. Previously, plans were passed down from above, and enterprises had to report back on plan fulfilment – which meant that the implementation of most innovations remained outside the plan requirements. As a result, innovative processes were determined not by the plan but by other regulators. In a planned economy this made provision of the necessary material, equipment and other resources extremely complicated. Furthermore, it led many directors and chief specialists to look on innovation as an activity of secondary importance which was not demanded of them.

Now, however, under the dissolved Central Planning System, state enterprises have no plans to implement innovations. The government provides no special funding for this purpose. State enterprises, as before, have no sense of their own need for innovation. Therefore the spread of new technology in the state sector of the Russian economy has declined.

Only a little over a third of those participating in implementing innovations (36%) considered the implementation plan to have a significant influence on their innovative activities. The rest regarded this influence as insignificant (31%) or non-existent (11%), or they simply 'didn't know' (22%).

This situation was the natural consequence of the Soviet system of planning. Plans for implementing innovations were drawn up according to almost the same procedures as for other traditional enterprise activities. If this system had frequently shown its unsuitability for routine activities, it was wholly inappropriate for innovative activities, if only because of the situational nature of the demand for innovations at individual enterprises.

Organizing the implementation of innovations at enterprises is the second part of the innovative activities of directors and specialists. A total of 72% of those engaged in innovation were also engaged in organizing its implementation.

We may break this activity down into the day-to-day organization of implementation and the organizational restructuring of the administrative structure. The latter causes the greatest difficulties when implementing innovations and led to problems in 55% of applied innovations. On examining this organizational restructuring, we found that in 35% of cases additional, permanently functioning subdivisions (workteams, groups, sections etc.) had to be set up. Other problems and modifications cited were: changes in the functions and obligations of certain employees (18%); the introduction of additional tasks for manual workers and engineers (15%); the setting up of temporary work groups of manual workers and engineers for implementing this innovation (6%); a change in the overall structure of administration (3%); and the introduction of other alterations (6%).[10]

Work with personnel is the third component of the innovative activities of directors and chief specialists. Almost all those who were interviewed and who took part in implementing innovations were engaged in this activity. This involves selecting those who will carry out innovations, distributing the innovating roles between them, and liaising with various groups of employees in connection with their implementation.

We focused our attention on certain types of interaction involved in innovation: (1) discussion of innovations with employees (73% of those implementing innovations); (2) promoting the necessity of innovation and convincing employees of this (again 73%); and (3) teaching them new approaches to work that are essential for the implementation and subsequent functioning of these innovations (40%).

Since innovative activity is complex and unpredictable, the skill, educational level, responsibility and reliability of the executants are particularly important. Success depends to a great extent on the appropriate choice of executants, and the correct distribution of roles between them. By nature, innovative activities are collective. Many people from different occupational groups and holding various positions of authority must participate, and their joint efforts must be co-ordinated. Therefore, the management of innovations in enterprises may largely be concerned with the problem of effectively regulating relations between groups and particular employees. The vertical (managerial) relations between different occupational groups depend on their interests, their position in production and administration, and are particularly important.

The functions of those in different occupational groups and holding various positions of authority differed.

The directors and chief specialists were the main initiators and organizers of the innovation process. They ensured the overall direction and decided whether a given innovation should be implemented or not. They directed the innovation process, oversee the quality of innovative activity of all the other participants, and determined when to finish it (the degree of its completion). They bore most responsibility for the fate of the innovation in the enterprise and for its yield.

Middle-ranking managers and specialists were directly involved in organizing the implementation of innovation. They carried out the instructions of the enterprise director and chief specialist, designated the rank and file executants, allotted them to their place of work, and gave the necessary instructions. In a word, they organized and ensured observation of the technology of implementation. Rank and file employees were usually the executants of implementation. Implementation demands skill and an original approach, so highly skilled and experienced employees who have shown an interest in innovations are chosen to carry it out.

Each group adopts a definite position in these innovative interactions, as expressed in one or another attitude to innovation. These may ease or obstruct the innovation.

The attitudes of these participant groups form the innovative climate at the enterprise, which then influences the activities of individual employees. Therefore, the administration of innovative processes at enterprises amounts to the regulation of inter-group relations. The aim of such regulation is to create a favourable innovative climate that will facilitate the successful implementation of innovations and achieve its maximum effect.

Middle-ranking management constituted the most problematic group here. As we shall show in quantitative terms, innovation added most of all to their workload. All the difficulties and disruption linked to innovation affected middle management first of all, since they control the day-to-day management and organization of production.

The next component of innovative activity is the creation of the conditions for its implementation. A comparatively small proportion of directors and chief specialists were involved in providing both the necessary equipment and material resources (37%) and the information and procedural methodology (29%). Yet this is where the greatest difficulties lay. Almost all directors and chief specialists engaged in innovation (94%) had problems with the material and technical back-up for these innovations. By comparison, 69% had difficulty in persuading their employees of the necessity for implementing this innovation, while only 31% mentioned difficulties in organizing the process of implementation itself. Other components of innovative activity accounted for even fewer difficulties. The problem of material back-up was acute, and yet, as we see, directors were weakly involved in its resolution. The explanation is that this depended, to a great extent, on conditions that were beyond the control of the enterprise.

This provision depended on the AIC system of planning and of material and technical supplies. Of the difficulties in providing this material back-up, 70% were directly linked to their absence at the enterprise and the necessity of applying to other organizations for their provision. Expert assessments by directors and chief specialists suggested that innovations were on average guaranteed only 51% of their necessary material back-up. The missing resources were obtained by displaying 'socialist entrepreneurship' (in a number of cases, moreover, only partially). This led to a worsening of quality of innovations, the implementation of unfinished innovations, and a failure to realize their full potential.

From this description of the four components of innovative activity, we can see that the structure of innovative activity is complex and varied. It interlocks with many sub-systems of the management mechanism. At the same time, it is implemented through the specific actions and deeds of individuals; i.e., through their behaviour.

5.5 Types of innovative behaviour

The majority of directors and chief specialists we interviewed implemented innovations but did not display a very high degree of initiative in doing so. This is clear if we look at the proportions of innovations that they implemented on their own initiative. In 1986 these accounted for roughly three-quarters of all rationalizing proposals, a half of new technologies, and rather more than a third of new forms of organization and payment for work. At the same time, there was a significant variation in levels of activity in implementing innovations among employees.

We may distinguish several possible lines or strategies of innovative behaviour according to their results and consequences. This behaviour represents a choice of a particular strategy made by an employee in accordance with his innovative consciousness, and the implementation of this strategy in a real production situation. By studying data obtained from interviews, surveys, analysis, the press and specialist literature, we identified five main strategies of innovative behaviour. Each has its distinctive features for the different social groups.

The independent elaboration of innovations and their active implementation

This strategy is the highest form of innovative behaviour and, as a rule, involves great expenditure of time, effort and energy. It demands particular qualities of the employee, who must be a creative individual (this is true of the majority of innovators). In fact, the innovator, in the content of his or her actions, comes close to the activities of those engaged in the creative and artistic professions. Therefore, these actions cannot be completely formalized or reduced to a particular technology. At the same time, however, many successful innovators have also been entrepreneurs (one example is Edison). They could assess the demand for a certain invention and aimed to produce objects that were valuable for people. This, of course, does not mean that all inventions must give an immediate benefit and otherwise do not have the right to exist. If society laid down such a condition, and innovators' efforts were assessed in these terms, it would paralyse their imaginations by inducing the fear of making a mistake.

When the author participates in the implementation of an innovation this gives, in general, the greatest socio-economic results and minimizes the negative consequences. Better than anyone else, the author can ensure that an innovation is adjusted to the specific conditions of a particular enterprise. Therefore, it would improve both the quality of implementation and increase the rate of socio-economic development if mechanisms facilitating the participation of the author were introduced. However, only a very small number of employees followed this strategy: less than 1% of all those participating in implementation. The figures were rather higher (6.3%) among directors and chief specialists.

Independent activity in implementing innovations

This strategy presupposes certain elements of creativity and is characteristic of innovative activities that are implemented with high quality. As a rule, the result of this strategy is the implementation of a finished innovation with a relatively high socio-economic effect. About 20% of all employees participating in the implementation of innovations pursued this strategy. Among directors and chief specialists they amount to roughly 50%, among middle-ranking managers and specialists 25%, and among ordinary employees about 10%.[11]

Participation in the implementation of innovations without manifestation of independent activity

This strategy presupposes that the executants show a moderate degree of active involvement, but as soon as any difficulties are encountered this level of activity may disappear entirely. Under normal circumstances, this strategy leads to the implementation of an innovation that provides a certain socio-economic result. If difficulties arise, however, it may also lead to the implementation of an unfinished innovation, and be rather similar to the strategy described under the next heading. The threshold of difficulties is evidently defined, above all else, by the very widespread situation of a lack of material and technical resources and a low level of initiative among the individual participants.

Of those involved in implementing innovations, this strategy affected the largest group of employees, at 55%. This covered almost half of the directors and chief specialists, three-quarters of the middle-ranking managers and specialists, and more than 90% of ordinary employees.

Passivity in implementing innovations

This strategy presupposes a refusal to act, to take the necessary decisions or accept the responsibility that innovations demand. However, there is no active opposition to their implementation.

Passive employees among those surveyed accounted for 21% of the total, with ordinary employees and middle managers predominating.

Active opposition to the implementation of innovations

This can take the most varied forms. Its proponents may criticize a valuable innovation as unnecessary, ineffective and even harmful. They may accuse innovators of pursuing their own selfish goals or of opportunism, or praise the existing and familiar order as having advantages over the proposed innovation when the reverse is the case. They may also take decisions that hinder implementation, or even forbid it: a refusal to permit existing resources to be used, prohibition of tests, burdening the innovator or rationalizer with routine tasks, and so on. We know of a case in which the director of a *sovkhoz* forbade the testing of a new hay-stacker invented by one of his workers. Instead, it was tested more than 100 kilometres away from the enterprise where the inventor worked.

Roughly 4% of employees involved in the implementation of an innovation actively resisted it. All types and levels of occupation and responsibility were included, but ordinary employees and middle management predominate.

The last two strategies of innovative behaviour described above lead to the negative consequences of non-implementation[12] and to unfinished innovations which give only a partial effect in relation to their potential.

Our research findings show that the greater part of non-implemented innovations were to do with organization and management (collective sub-contracting accounted for 36.6% of all non-implemented innovations) and with new technologies in animal husbandry (24%). When asked for the main reasons for this failure to implement innovations, those surveyed replied: shortage of material and equipment (32%); unwillingness of employees and lack of initiative among specialists (28%); shortage of trained staff (9.9%); and the unpreparedness of the enterprise for implementation (10%). Only in 5% of cases did directors and chief specialists consider that the innovation was not actually required by the enterprise. The shortage of material and equipment was indeed the main explanation offered, but had employees themselves shown a higher degree of activity in providing material and equipment this could have been compensated for. In turn, this of course had led to a more labour-intensive form of implementation.

The failure to implement effective innovations, and the absence of conditions for the self-realization of innovators, leads to a vast squandering of potential benefits. These are the socio-economic consequences of passivity and resistance. A quite typical case is what happened to the multi-stream technology for producing lupin seeds developed in the late 1950s by V. A. Vasiliev.[13] Lupins are a crop with a high protein content (up to 46%, while wheat offers only up to 25%). Increased lupin production could therefore help to improve the protein balance of feed in animal husbandry, a major problem in the former Soviet Union. Moreover, if industrial technologies are to be effectively mastered in agriculture, obtaining high-quality seeds is very important, and the multi-stream technology could also be used for other crops, such as buckwheat. However, three to four times more lupin seeds are still sown than necessary because of their low quality, leading to losses that amount to 10 million roubles per annum in Belorussia alone. If the new technology were applied, these losses could be avoided and the harvest yield would rise by up to 25%.

The proposal put forward by Vasiliev consisted of a mechanism that could sort out the higher quality seeds, which were denser than others. However, the administration of the research institute where Vasiliev worked and his immediate superior did not support his idea. Instead, the laboratory in which he worked was merged in the early 1960s with another, and his associates were transferred to work on other subjects. The inventor did not have the appropriate conditions in which to work; the apparatus and machinery which took him a great deal of trouble to obtain were handed over to other sections of the institute. In the late 1960s Vasiliev was entirely taken off work on lupins and had to continue in his spare time. His superior, who had previously ignored this crop, now proposed his own technology for seed production which was a simplified version of Vasiliev's. Nevertheless, at the end of the 1970s, the Belorussian Ministry of Agriculture supported the building of a plant for the multi-stream technology. Soon, however, the institute administration took Vasiliev off work on implementing the new technology and he was forced, in the early 1980s, to set up his experimental apparatus in an unsuitable barn and conduct experiments with the help of the collective farm workers.

In the 1970s, plants based on the idea put forward by Vasiliev began to be built abroad. Yet in the Soviet Union multi-stream technology has still not been introduced. For 20 years Vasiliev has vainly tried to circumvent the passivity and opposition of official figures and been branded as a trouble-maker for his pains. The Belorussian Ministry of Agriculture gave very feeble support to the idea of multi-stream technology, quite insufficient to gain its implementation. In practice, only the inventor and a small group of enthusiasts were actively involved in its promotion.

Even when inventions were registered, passivity and resistance to their implementation had resulted in vast losses. Only every seventh invention registered in the Soviet Union had been implemented,[14] and many valuable innovations are not applied for decades. For example, some 20 years ago the first electric engine without manifold traction was made in the USSR, but it still has not been brought into production in any of the regions of the old Soviet Union. As a result of this and other shortcomings, experts consider that our rail system:

> is fated to work with outdated technology for at least another decade. Even if a miracle takes place, and the Soviet engineering industry increases its rate of work on new equipment many times over, it is only after the year 2000 that our rail system and the economy as a whole will feel the benefit. Before that, much time will have to be spent on reconstructing many plants and providing thousands of new engines, hundreds of thousands of wagons and carriages, and so on.[15]

NOTES

1 See, for example, R. L. Lebedev and G. M. Poleshchuk, 'About the attitude of the manager to the launching of new products', in *Proceedings of the Siberian branch of the USSR Academy of Sciences*, Economics and Applied Sociology Series, issue 3 (1984).

2 Innovation, according to the well-known authors on this subject Lapin, Prigozhin, Sazonov and Tolstoy, is: 'the organizational form of innovative activity. This is a complex process of creation, wider promotion and practical application of this innovation to better satisfy an existing need or meet an entirely new need.' See N. I. Lapin, A. I.

Prigozhin, B. V. Sazonov and V. S. Tolstoy, 'Innovations in organizations', in *The structure of the innovative process*, Moscow, All-Union Institute for System Analysis AS, USSR Academy of Science (1981), 9.

3 See V. M. Dominov, *The implementation of scientific advances in the agro-industrial complex*, Kishinev, Institute for AIC Problems, All-Union Academy of Agriculture (Moldavian branch) (1983), 18.

4 See *Literaturnaya gazeta*, xi, September 1985.

5 See *Sovetskaya rossiya*, 12 December 1987.

6 We here follow the approach of R. V. Ryvkina, *The rural population's way of life*, Novosibirsk, Nauka (1979) 88–9.

7 According to Zaltman, Duncan and Holbek, the social expenditure of innovation may take the form of ridicule, ostracism and even expulsion from the reference group. See G. Zaltman, R. Duncan and J. Holbek, *Innovations and organizations*, New York, J. Wiley & Co. (1973), 34.

8 Fliegel, Kivlin and Sekhon consider the decision to adopt or reject an innovation in developing countries (but not in developed countries) to be guided by assessment of its social expenditure. See F. C. Fliegel, J. E. Kivlin and G. S. Sekhon, 'A cross-cultural comparison of farmers' perception of innovations as related to adoptions behaviour', *Rural sociology*, xxxiii (1968).

9 The idea that innovations arise and are then diffused as a reaction to a definite social need is developed in a number of works by modern researchers. See, among others, J. Schmookler, 'Economic sources of inventive activity', *Journal of Economic History*, xxii (1962); J. P. Martino, *Technological forecasting for decision-making*, New York, Elsevier (1972; Russian trans. 1977).

10 Since those interviewed could name more than one type of change, the total amounts to more than 55%.

11 These and all subsequent assessments in this chapter were reached with the expert help of the directors and specialists.

12 The problem of non-implementation has been studied in the specialist literature, though not from the sociological viewpoint. See V. P. Rassokhin, 'How to solve the problem of non-implementation', *Khozaistvo i pravo*, x (1978).

13 See A. Kozlovich, 'The technology of "non-management"', *Literaturnaya gazeta*, 23 August 1985.

14 See A. Zinoviev, 'Prokopov's invention', *Izvestiya*, 15 February 1988.

15 Y. Fedorov and N. Fufryansky, 'Accelerating the reconstruction of our railways', *Izvestiya*, 4 April 1988.

6

The Innovative Consciousness

6.1 The value of innovating activity

The innovative consciousness is shaped by participation in implementing innovations and the experience the individual thereby acquires. At the same time, it is also formed by the dominant social norms in the group where the employee is working. There is therefore the possibility that the two will come into conflict, and the innovative consciousness of the individual will clash with the group norms. An active innovator may work in a group where innovation is not accepted, or a passive employee may be hired by a group that is actively involved in reforming its production methods. We can only understand how people react in such circumstances by studying their innovative consciousness.

First and foremost, the innovative consciousness values innovation above traditional and routine tasks. Those with a highly developed innovative consciousness set a high value on innovative activities. At present, the great majority of Russian employees do not rank this attribute highly. In a study carried out in 1985, even directors and chief specialists placed it only fifth (level with 'Ensuring steady delivery of supplies'), while 'Timely preparation of reports to higher authorities' came third (see Table 8).

The importance allocated by employees to one or another responsibility determines, to a great extent, the amount of time and effort they devote to their fulfilment. The low value attributed to innovative activities in particular leads to a low level of activity

Table 8 *The comparative importance of duties carried out by directors and chief specialists in their own assessment (proportion indicating one or another obligation among their three main obligations in %).*

Rating	*Obligation*	*Proportion*
1	Ensuring that the plan is met on time	47
2	Ensuring that work is well organized	42
3	Timely preparation of reports for higher authority	41
4	Supervision to ensure observance of production technology	37
5	Ensuring steady delivery of supplies Implementing scientific advances and advanced experience in production	34
6	Maintaining order and discipline at work	32
7	Ensuring a healthy psychological climate at work	16
8	Raising one's level of skill	13

on the part of directors and chief specialists and thus lowers the numbers of implemented innovations. Those who rated innovative activities more highly and placed it third on average each implemented 2.1 innovations over three years. Those who rated them even lower, in seventh place, implemented only 1.3 innovations over the same period of time.

There are innovators who regard their own efforts to ensure the implementation of their ideas as the most important activity in their lives. Such people *are* encountered in the Russian economy, if only rarely. One of their distinguishing traits is altruism and a commitment to the public welfare. As an example of this we may take B. I. Shuvalov, who invented a quite new method of attaching artificial limbs. He turns out to be, in the words of *Izvestiya*:

> the kind of eccentric who without any particular effort can achieve miracles. The press made him famous and he received hundreds of letters begging for help. So he did what he could, advising, sending designs and even going back to his own

workbench . . . He did not take a kopek from anyone, not even from those who offered him money, and even themselves brought him his 'fee'.[1]

6.2 The motivation of innovative behaviour

The directors and chief specialists are aware that too little effort is put into innovation in their enterprises. The number of innovations introduced into the production process to ensure its rapid and dynamic development was considered insufficient by 61% of those interviewed. Only 25% considered that they were sufficient. A further 3% even asserted that these innovations were too numerous, while 11% could give no answer. This assessment is a reflection of the dissatisfaction the directors feel with the existing situation. Yet this dissatisfaction is not transformed into an incentive for boosting these activities, since innovative activities are not highly valued by employees and the objective conditions for the intensive implementation of innovations is lacking.

This raises questions about the motivation for innovative behaviour: the reasons why employees wish to innovate. In response to this question, the most frequent motives cited were:

1 to improve the economic position of the enterprise (63%);
2 to make one's work more varied and interesting (50%);
3 the better to carry out one's occupational responsibilities (29%);
4 for occupational improvement with the help of innovations (25%);
5 one's work easier in the future (24%);
6 to strengthen one's reputation as a director or specialist (10%);
7 to carry out the instructions of higher authority (8%).

Economic motivation, such as raising one's income by innovating, was extremely insignificant, with only 4% of those interviewed mentioning it. This is hardly surprising, since the implementation of innovations does not generally have a marked effect on bonuses (only 33% of those interviewed received a reward for their innovation) and even less on basic salary.

The motivations of active innovators and passive employees are very differently structured. Two types of motivation are more strongly expressed among the active innovators: occupational self-improvement, and the striving to make work more varied and interesting through innovation. There is much less striving among such employees to use innovations to make their work easier in the future. Active innovators aim to achieve the maximum in their sphere, irrespective of the time and effort they must expend in doing so.

Passive employees, on the other hand, try to minimize the social expenditure and costs involved in innovation (risk; the loss of time, effort and status). They usually take part in innovations when the situation becomes critical; when there is a demand for them to do so from above, or when production may halt altogether if an innovation is not implemented.

It is perhaps helpful to think of 'innovation needs' – the psychological demands that prompt people to make improvements to their work environment. Among active innovators such needs seem to be highly developed. They are very responsive in detecting new problems, and the actual process of innovation is interesting to them. They may therefore participate in innovations even if they do not receive any reward for their work.[2]

The shortage of people with such developed needs is a source of the social difficulties in implementing innovations. Directors and chief specialists consider that in a quarter of the cases where the implementation of innovations met with social difficulties it was the lack of interested persons that was the cause.

Active innovators usually have a great many innovative suggestions for improving specific parts of the production process. These ideas, of course, may not correspond to the immediate needs of the enterprise. In this case, they have little chance of being implemented. When such ideas coincide with the real needs of the enterprise, however, the objective possibility of implementing them arises. The totality of these innovative ideas constitutes the enterprise's 'bank' of innovative ideas. If innovative processes are to proceed normally, this bank must hold all the existing needs of the enterprise for innovations, and also a certain surplus (i.e. all the innovative ideas that do not reflect the formulated need for particular innovations, but which can be used in the future).

The totality of innovations that an employee would like to implement can be termed an 'innovation plan'. It is important that any such plans are independent. If employees have developed innovation needs and possess a rich store of innovative ideas, they will be able independently to form their own innovation plans. If, on the other hand, their innovative consciousness is only weakly developed, their innovation plans will be shaped primarily by the administration (at district or regional level) and bear much less relation to the real needs of the enterprise.

Four-fifths of directors and chief specialists said they had innovation plans. Of these, 67% planned to implement only one innovation, 21% to implement two, 9% to implement three, and only 3% to implement four. The majority of those interviewed did not therefore have elaborate innovation plans, indicating that their innovation consciousness was weakly developed.

We analysed the composition of the innovation plans of directors and chief specialists and compared these to the structure of innovations implemented at the time of the interview. This enabled us to draw certain conclusions about the possible tendencies of these innovative processes (see Table 9).

From Table 9 we can see that the structure of proposed innovations (and the relation between their various types) is, in the main, similar to the structure of previously implemented innovations. Also characteristic is the predominance of technical and technological over socio-economic innovations. Existing technologies are more frequently improved than replaced by the introduction of new technologies, and purely social innovations are almost entirely non-existent. Nevertheless, there are still certain discrepancies in these findings that permit us to conclude that change is possible. One of the main potential areas for change lies in greater stress on socio-economic innovations: future plans to implement these exceed past implementations by 11.4%. One of the main explanations for this is the current heightened interest on the part of administrative bodies in implementing new forms of economic management. This is shown, in particular, by the 7.7% difference between future plans and past practice in administrative and organizational innovations.

Another major shift that may take place in the future will be towards the more active implementation of large-scale innovations which bring comparatively high returns to the enterprise and to society. This is reflected in a number of indicators here. The implementation of rationalizing proposals is assigned a lesser importance than it played in recently implemented innovations (8.4% less); likewise the improvement of existing technology (1.8% less). The implementation of new technology, on the other hand, shows an increase (3.1%) in importance.

This comparison between the structure of proposed innovations and that of those actually implemented gives grounds for concluding that directors and chief specialists were moderately progressive in their intention to renew production methods. It could not be claimed that they intended radically to overhaul their production methods, but there is a certain positive shift away from the present structure of innovative proposals.

Table 9 *Innovation plans of directors and chief specialists and the structure of innovations planned and of those actually implemented in the recent past (%)*

	Future plans	*Recently implemented*	*Difference between future plan and recent practice*
TECHNICAL AND TECHNOLOGICAL INNOVATIONS	60.4	71.8	−11.4
1 Implementation of rationalizing proposals	3.3	11.7	−8.4
2 Mechanization, new engines and machinery	2.7	7.0	−4.3
3 Improvement of existing technology, including:	27.5	29.3	−1.8
agriculture	9.4	11.4	−2.0
animal husbandry	18.1	17.9	+0.2
4 Implementation of new technology, including:	26.9	23.8	+3.1
agriculture	14.8	14.1	+0.7
animal husbandry	12.1	9.7	+2.4
SOCIO-ECONOMIC INNOVATIONS	39.6	28.2	+11.4
1 Organizational and administrative	31.9	24.7	+7.2
2 Equipment and organization	7.0	3.3	+3.7
3 Social	0.7	0.2	+0.5
TOTAL	100.0	100.0	

Our examination of the structure of innovative consciousness in Russian agricultural enterprises revealed that this consciousness was not very highly developed. Innovative activities were not valued and there was a negative attitude to participation in such activities. The innovation needs of employees were weakly developed while their innovation plans were insignificant. The structure of future innovation plans differed comparatively little from the current practice of innovation, and was therefore unlikely radically to change it.

There were some changes regarding innovation in the consciousness of employees in 1987–93. Many planned to become farmers, to start their own businesses, including businesses of their own invention. The value they put on innovations was higher than it had been. One cause was the possibility of increasing living standards with the support of innovations in private firms. And there was and is increasingly the intention to innovate, in spite of the declining innovative activity in state enterprises.

We have studied the innovative consciousness of employees. Yet we are still unable to predict their innovative behaviour. The reason is that such behaviour is situational and depends to a great extent on how an employee assesses each particular innovation. Even one who is favourably inclined in general towards innovations may reach a negative evaluation of a particular innovation, and vice versa. Therefore we must examine what guides employees in shaping their attitude to the implementation of a particular new innovation, and what leads them to facilitate, or to refuse to participate in, its implementation.

NOTES

1 M. Kruglinsky, 'A sore point', *Izvestiya*, 22 December 1986.

2 Such an employee need not have reached a high level of formal education. Similarly someone who is educated may have no need to innovate. Such needs depend on the creative potential of the individual and not on the quantity of facts and theories he or she possesses. The innovator is creative rather than academic or theoretical.

7

The Climate of Innovation in Enterprises

The group innovative consciousness or outlook of a workforce – what may be termed the climate of innovation of an enterprise – is formed from the individual innovative consciousnesses of all its employees. This is part of the organizational climate of the enterprise and reflects the traditions, norms and behavioural stereotypes in renewal of production that have taken shape there. These are what guide the behaviour of individual workers.[1]

In its influence on the individual level of activity of employees, the climate of innovation is the resultant of all the regulators of innovative processes. If this resultant is aimed at their acceleration, a favourable climate of innovation arises; if it leads instead to their obstruction, the climate proves unfavourable. In this chapter, we shall examine the differences between enterprises that have favourable and those that have unfavourable climates of innovation. Those enterprises that led the way in renewing production were shown to have a favourable climate of innovation, while those that lagged behind had an unfavourable climate. Therefore, we shall examine the differences in their group innovating consciousnesses. These differences are also linked to differences in behaviour and, eventually, to the results of implementing innovations, which will also be examined in this chapter.

The climate of innovation plays an extremely important role in the social mechanism whereby production is renewed. Therefore we shall first look at the functions of the climate of innovation in this mechanism.

7.1 The functions of the climate of innovation

First of all, the climate of innovation must ensure a rapid reaction to difficulties and problems that arise in the work of the enterprise. It must help to identify on this basis the need for innovations. We may call this function *reflexive*. If it is to be properly fulfilled, employees must be oriented towards the independent solution of problems and not towards help from superior bodies. The present state of affairs in the Russian countryside is quite different, as the well-known commentator I. Vasiliev has written:

> If one wanted to express in an aphorism the essence of the present relations between the inhabitants of rural society and the administrative bodies and individuals they have elected, then I can think of nothing better than the following lines from the poet Nekrasov: 'When the squire comes, he'll settle our dispute for us . . .'[2]

For a favourable climate of innovation in which these functions are properly carried out, another situation is typical:

> When we begin an experiment we do not ask anything more of the state . . . We want to achieve something impressive in our capital construction with our existing means, only making small changes in the system of planning and accounting or, more accurately, of management. All we ask is that no one prevent us from testing out our proposals. We can't force new contents into old forms.[3]

A second function of the climate of innovation is *regulatory*. Its purpose is to make the active participation of employees in innovations the social norm. If such a norm exists, it means that a stable tradition of constant implementation of innovations has been established. When employees decide whether to participate in implementing an innovation, they take this tradition into account. There must be rewards for observing this social norm if it is to become a stable tradition. These are usually both material (monetary bonuses for participation) and non-material (increase in prestige within the workforce). There must also be social sanctions for infringing this norm; those who are passive and refuse to participate in innovations must be condemned.

When such a norm is established, it acts as a powerful means for the group regulation of people's behaviour and changes the innovative behaviour of the workforce as a whole. An illustration is provided by V. P. Serkov, in his description of his work group (he made a successful career in the old bureaucratic system as deputy director of the USSR Ministry of Heavy Industry's centre for the scientific organization of work; the centre no longer exists):

> Certain managers consider our work group to be too restless. Indeed, its members seem to work well and earn good salaries but are somehow dissatisfied and always searching for something more. Yet isn't the constant quest for improvement a norm of our code of ethics?[4]

The third function of the climate of innovation is *translation*, or the 'relay effect'. When an individual enters a different workforce, he or she must adapt to its accepted norms of behaviour, altering his or her own system of values if this proves possible and necessary. The fulfilment of this function therefore implies that the individual is taught to accept the collective system of values. If a norm of active participation in innovations is accepted in a workforce, the individual must agree to participate in the renewal of production, learn to work in a different way, and may, in the end, come to place a high value on innovative activity. If, on the other hand, such a norm is absent and the tradition is to avoid participation in innovations, then the individual is obliged to suppress his or her urge to renew production and becomes accustomed to passivity. Vasiliev repeats the story of a land-improvement specialist who could not gain recognition for his right to work in a new way:

> For the first time in my life, I acted against my inclinations. I couldn't get used to this but simply put up with it. I learnt to say one thing and do another. Every time we held a meeting I would speak out and persuade everyone that we should first put the old ploughlands in order . . . I appealed for reasonable management. This was sincere and quite intentional. I suffered. They couldn't help but hear me, I thought. But no, they didn't hear nor did they understand. To this day they have not understood. Meanwhile I understood very well: 'You won't win! . . . You can say as much as you like about being independent. They won't stop you, but you will only be allowed to sow as much as they order you to.[5]

The fourth and final function of the climate of innovation is *selection*. Those people whose value-system corresponds to that of the workforce are selected. Not all employees agree to conform to the dominant values of the given enterprise. If the disagreement is acute, the individual feels this conflict of values and is forced to leave the enterprise and find another job. The workforce deters those whose views and principles do not correspond to its traditions. This pressure may take various forms: condemnation of the non-conformist's behaviour; psychological isolation of the individual; deterioration of his or her work conditions; and so on.

In a favourable climate of innovation, those employees who respond passively to, or even resist, innovations are forced to find other jobs. At the moment, this happens most frequently in non-state firms and not in state enterprises. Fedorov, the chairman of one of the first non-state co-operative cafés, on Kropotkin street in Moscow, was asked if he had any employees who worked badly: 'Sometimes,' he replied, 'but the following day they find themselves working somewhere else.'[6]

An unfavourable climate of innovation will weed out the active innovators, or even those who simply regard innovations in a favourable light. In this atmosphere of passivity, the efforts of active innovators are suppressed and lack any support. The innovators therefore come into conflict with the workforce and are forced to find other employment.

The favourable climate of innovation – one which carries out these functions well – is distinguished by the following features. It reacts rapidly to the innovation needs of the enterprise. It establishes a social norm of active participation in innovations by its employees and inculcates in new employees the same norm, selecting those who are active innovators. In such a climate, valuable innovations meet a positive response from the majority of the workforce. There are also innovations for which the enterprise is not yet ready, or which it does not need at all, or which may have serious negative consequences for a large number of the workforce. These meet with a negative response.

In an unfavourable climate of innovation, employees acquire an insensitivity to the innovation needs of the enterprise. Typically, there is a lack of norms and traditions of strong involvement in innovation. In this situation, the decision whether to participate in implementing an innovation is made by the employees themselves in accordance with their individual preferences and attitudes towards innovation. As a result, there is a striving to cut the social expenditure involved in the renewal of production.

The unfavourable climate of innovation inculcates an avoidance of innovations in those who come to work at such an enterprise. As a result, active innovators cannot flourish there. As a matter of course, they demand help from those around them to put their ideas into practice; the successful implementation of an innovation usually requires the involvement of a comparatively large number of people with different occupational skills. This, however, conflicts with the workforce and management orientation towards minimizing social expenditure. The energy of the active innovator is very likely to be insufficient in itself to overcome all difficulties if the necessary helpers cannot be found (or are not active enough) and if the management is passive or even hostile in attitude. The innovation is then not implemented and the attitude to the innovator usually worsens in the workforce. He or she is consequently forced to find another job; if this process is continually repeated, it may entirely extinguish the initiative of that individual.

7.2 The climate of innovation at progressive and backward enterprises

Since the climate of innovation is formed by the group innovative consciousness of the workforce, we shall compare the progressive and backward enterprises with regard to those elements of the innovative consciousness that were distinguished in Chapter 6. In this section, we shall look only at the main components of the innovative consciousness: the value attached to innovative activities and the structure of behavioural motivations.

We may classify enterprises according to their implementation of new technologies. Three types of enterprise can be distinguished: progressive, average and backward. Using the findings of our survey, we compared the directors and specialists of these three types. Since, in every respect, the average enterprises were found to occupy an intermediate position between the two extremes, the differences between them will be used in order to present a full picture.

The directors and chief specialists of progressive enterprises attached a relatively high value to the implementation of innovations, 46% of them considering this to be among their main duties, as opposed to only 29% of the management of backward enterprises. For those employed in the most advanced enterprises, innovative activity was considered one of their most basic duties, ranking third in importance. Only 'Ensuring that work was well organized' and 'Supervision to ensure the observance of the production technology' rated more highly, and these by very little.

The importance which directors attach to these values serves as a behavioural guide for their workforce. *Izvestiya* gave the following example of the Bratsk plant for manufacturing heating equipment:

> In spring 1981, the new director, P. Samusenko, made a strange declaration at a meeting of section heads and chief specialists. 'Don't think about the plan. Worry about the way in which we work. That is your chief task.' ... But what did they do to the plan? ... Although alterations to plans after their inception are condemned, the plan for the Bratsk factory was altered several times – they were told to produce more. Even with these additions, however, the Bratsk workers will meet their five-year plan obligations in many indicators in September to November ...[7]

Backward enterprises present a different picture. Application of scientific advances to production ranked among the least important tasks, occupying seventh place. For backward enterprises, plan-fulfilment and timely preparation of reports to superior bodies came first (44% each); these duties were not considered among the most important obligations in progressive enterprises, ranking only fourth and sixth respectively.

While the management in progressive enterprises are typically most concerned with the qualitative functioning of production, the smooth organization of work, and the innovation of scientific advances, the management of backward enterprises are chiefly oriented towards external criteria. The latter require a great number of white-collar workers (usually 1.3 times as many as in the best enterprises) and cannot ensure high rates of scientific and technical progress nor a growth in production efficiency.

Their priorities mean that the managers of backward enterprises are easy for the administration to cope with. They avoid the risks involved in innovation, and often enjoy the firm support of higher officials. Zalipaev has offered a portrait of such 'convenient' people:

> For several years now the *kolkhoz* has been running at a loss. It does not have well-equipped workshops nor facilities for pre-school education. However, at the district level, the *kolkhoz* chairman is well thought of and is considered quite a successful manager. He has never infringed a single instruction. He has never made a serious error for the simple reason that he has never taken any risks.

Those, by contrast, who tried to introduce innovations could not help making mistakes as a consequence:

> . . . he who takes risks will succeed. Yet we often forget that this requires decisiveness and bravery. Far from everyone is capable of this. Failure threatens a loss of reputation, status and, in the end, salary. It's fine if the risk proves justified. But what if it doesn't?

Zalipaev goes on to compare the innovator with the 'convenient' director: 'Just look at his young colleague. He runs his enterprise well, but he lost out due to these reprimands and is referred to at the district level as a "difficult" person.'[8]

Innovators are troublesome for superior bodies because they demand additional effort from the latter. The officials are on a fixed salary; their position in society in no way depends on whether they allow initiative or not. (Moreover, under the present administrative system there is no way that their position can be made dependent.) The prohibition of initiative in such a situation is the rational way to behave. Furthermore, such a policy requires no effort; it is enough simply to follow instructions. A graphic illustration is provided by the fate of the famous team of innovators at the Ivanovo machine engineering plant under its director V. P. Kabaidze. This enterprise began to produce processing centres, which was an initiative not included in its plan. As a result, it reduced the planned output of outdated equipment and thereby broke the rules:

> Production expanded at the expense of the items listed in its plan. If the plan is not fulfilled, however, there are no bonuses. Kabaidze hoped that the ministry would introduce the necessary adjustments to the plan and then all would be well. But the ministry was in no hurry to reach agreement with the 'technical revolutionaries' from Ivanovo. Kabaidze's appeals went unheeded and the workforce was not allotted its bonus funds . . . Nowhere and at no time did the ministry officials speak out openly against the initiative taken by the engineers of Ivanovo. Yet their co-operation, unfortunately, only extended far enough to avoid the accusation of conservatism.[9]

When innovators find themselves among those who do not share their high valuation of innovative activities, value conflicts arise. When superior bodies are dominated by those who do not value innovation, these conflicts are inevitable and they suppress the new technical and social initiatives taken from below. It may be thought that the solution would be to install innovators in all of these official posts. The answer is not as simple as that, however, and requires additional analysis. (See Part III, below: 'The Reasons for Stagnation in Innovative Processes'.)

Progressive and backward enterprises differ not only in the value they attach to innovative activities, but also in the structure of their employees' motivations. The aim of easing their workload by adopting innovations is of little importance for progressive enterprises. In backward enterprises, however, this is one of the main motivations, and is as important as the acquisition of occupational skills is for the progressive enterprises. As Table 10 shows, the latter attach much more importance to motivations such as carrying out their occupational obligations, raising their occupational skill levels, and enriching the content of their work.

The managements of progressive and backward enterprises do not differ in all their motivations. For instance, both are equally concerned about raising their own material standards and ensuring the economic expansion of their plant. Nevertheless, it is clear that there is otherwise a substantial differentiation of structures. These reflect the quite different attitudes their respective workforces take towards innovations. In progressive enterprises, active participation in the implementation of innovations is the norm and employees do not grudge the extra time and energy spent in pursuing such activities. Such participation is an important criterion for assessing the work of a specialist and his or her status in production as a whole. Those who stint their efforts in innovation at such enterprises usually do not last long and soon change jobs. In a word, there is a favourable climate of innovation here.

This means that in the majority of cases participation in implementation is encouraged. Of the directors and chief specialists who participated in the implementation of innovations, only a minority in the progressive enterprises (21%) received no support at all. For the backward enterprises, however, this absence of support was experienced by the great majority (85%). This involved both material and non-material incentives. At the progressive enterprises, 72% of directors and chief specialists received monetary bonuses for their participation; at backward enterprises the total was a sixth of this, at 12%. The much greater value attached to innovation in progressive enterprises is shown by the more frequent acknowledgement of these activities by the workforce. Directors and chief specialists won respect and authority in the workforce for their innovations six times more often in progressive than in backward enterprises (24% compared to 4%).

In progressive enterprises, informal encouragement is given to the implementation of innovations. In backward enterprises,

Table 10 *Differences between the structure of motivations for innovative behaviour between directors of progressive and those of backward enterprises**

Reasons for engaging in innovations	*Proportion indicating motivation (%)*		*Rating*		*Difference*
	Progressive	*Backward*	*Progressive*	*Backward*	
Making one's work easier in the future	7	31	Fifth	Fourth	–4.4
Raising one's occupational skills	30	17	Fourth	Sixth	+1.8
Fulfilling one's occupational duties	40	29	Third	Fifth	+1.4
Making one's work more varied	57	44	Second	Third	+1.3

*Only those motivations where there are differences between these two categories of enterprise are included in this table.

unfortunately, encouragement much more often takes the form of ritual testimonials; employees of these enterprises were twice as likely to receive such awards.

Furthermore, the motivations for non-participation in implementation of innovations also differed significantly between progressive and backward enterprises. Both gave the number of newly employed (whether school-leavers or from other enterprises) as their first motivation, although this was 1.4 times more important for progressive enterprises (88% compared to 65%). At progressive enterprises other motivations were insignificant and did not differ greatly. The situation was different in backward enterprises, where 'too many difficulties with implementation' was also of leading importance, and nearly four times as important as in the progressive enterprises.

The next most important motivation for non-participation in implementation of innovations in backward enterprises is that 'too much time is taken up with routine everyday affairs'. This is cited 3.3 as many times as in progressive enterprises. The problem of 'muddling through' (*tekuchka*) has already been analysed in the specialist literature,[10] although not particularly in relation to this problem. Employees' efforts are concentrated mainly on solving petty, everyday problems and dealing with bottlenecks, because it is not possible to focus on work for the long term. Thus 'muddling through' does not arise from deficiencies in the psychology and behaviour of the individual, but is typical of the atmosphere of the workforce as a whole. 'Muddling through' is incompatible with a high level of activity by employees in implementation of innovations. The structure and style of management in workforces infected with *tekuchka* is not oriented towards, or adapted to, the intense implementation of innovations, or inclined towards scientific and technical progress. One of the most important reasons for 'muddling through' is the element of bureaucratization in the structure and style of management which leads to a disregard for the interests of production and to their substitution by excessive paperwork.

There are two further motivations for non-participation in implementation of innovations in backward enterprises that are entirely absent in progressive enterprises: (1) the lack of support for those who are implementing the innovations; (2) the lack of any demand that employees should innovate (both cited by 18% of respondents). These directly show the lack of a collective innovative consciousness among employees which would oblige them to take part in the implementation of innovations.

The favourable climate of innovation in progressive enterprises is a powerful social regulator of activities in the implementation of innovations. It intensifies employees' level of activity and directs it towards a more rapid and high-quality implementation of innovations. When an employee comes under the influence of such a regulator, he or she must either submit to the dominant atmosphere or change jobs.

In progressive enterprises the innovative activities of employees are supervised to ensure that only those innovations that are needed by the enterprise are implemented, and that they are fully applied and achieve a relatively complete socio-economic effect. As the data in Table 11 show, the stricter forms of supervision led to a growth in the number of implemented innovations but a decline in their quality: the majority did not yield all their potential effect. This was true whether the superior bodies supervise on their own or in conjunction with the enterprise. It was only when the enterprise itself exercised the supervision that the majority of implemented innovations were fully and completely implemented. Thus far, we can see the advantages of the favourable climate of innovation at progressive enterprises. Yet the question then arises, does this climate ease the implementation of innovations and remove the difficulties from the process of implementation?

7.3 Are there differences in the difficulties of innovation faced by progressive and backward enterprises?

As our survey showed, this favourable climate of innovation does not eliminate the difficulties linked to the passivity of employees and their unwillingness to participate in implementation of innovations. Directors at progressive enterprises indicated that 37% of innovations encountered this difficulty, as did 40% of their counterparts in backward enterprises.

Progressive enterprises implement a larger number of innovations, and moreover larger-scale innovations, than backward enterprises. Therefore the problems of implementation they face are qualitatively different. For progressive enterprises the problems arise most often because the implementation of innovations increases their employees' workloads: this was cited 1.4 times more often than in backward enterprises (35% as against 25%). The same is true of the fear of increasing their workload in the future as a motivation for non-participation: this was 1.2 times greater (30% as against 25%).

The situation is different as far as the other causes are concerned. The lack of suitable personnel who are interested in

Table 11 *The influence of various forms of supervision on the innovative activities of directors and chief specialists**

Forms of supervision	*Numbers of innovations introduced by a single director and chief specialist*	*Innovation*	
		Could be more effective (%)	*Could not be more effective (%)*
Lack of supervision	1.4	62	38
Within enterprise only	1.9	35	65
By superior administrative bodies only	2.2	69	31
Both by superior bodies and within enterprise	3.0	86	14

*Based on responses to the question: 'Who supervises your fulfilment of plans for implementation of innovations?'

implementation of innovations, for instance, was 2.7 times less important for progressive enterprises (15% compared to 41%). In the backward enterprises this was one of the most important obstacles, coming second to the concern of employees that their salaries would be reduced as a result of the innovation. In progressive enterprises the lack of personnel came last in the list.

There are differences in the qualities of employees and their motivations in progressive and backward enterprises. As a result, 2.5 times more employees in the latter feared that they would be unable to cope with their new duties (38% as against 15%). This shows both the greater skill levels of employees in progressive enterprises and their greater adaptability to constant innovation.

Implementation of innovations takes place in progressive enterprises in an atmosphere of greater trust between the different groups of employees. In all types of enterprise there is a concern that innovations will lead to a drop in salary. This was 1.3 times less marked in progressive enterprises (45% compared to 56%).

The social difficulties involved in implementation of innovations in progressive enterprises are rather less than those in backward enterprises. On the other hand, the greater scale of the innovations they introduce requires much greater economic independence. This makes certain other difficulties considerably greater in progressive enterprises: for example, the existence of outdated instructions and regulations that limit the independence of the enterprise (1.6 times more common in our study), and difficulties in dealing with district administrative bodies (3.0 times more). Difficulties connected with material resources are roughly similar for all types of enterprise.

Despite economic liberalization, many administrative instructions regulating the activities of state and private enterprises remain. The main spheres of regulation are finance and the international economic activity of the enterprises. Under implementation of innovations, progressive enterprises have serious problems with corruption in these spheres, because local and central officials often demand bribes for their services, as when they are given licences for export or are given favourable credit terms by the state, with low interest.

Progressive enterprises much more often come up against the need for reorganization. Production at such enterprises is more highly organized and therefore shortcomings in this sphere figure less frequently there (1.3 times less in our study) than in backward enterprises. This is a precondition that makes reorganization much easier. On the other hand, much more effort and time must be devoted to organizational changes at progressive enterprises. Innovations were linked to changes in the functions or duties of employees 2.9 times more often in these; additional permanently functioning subdivisions were created 1.4 times more often; additional posts for manual workers and specialists were introduced 1.2 times more often. A restructuring of the enterprise administrative system is not a common requirement in progressive enterprises, but this was still 1.8 times more often than in backward enterprises (in 7% and 4% of cases respectively).

The employees of progressive enterprises thus face at least as many, and generally more, difficulties in the implementation of innovations than backward enterprises. The favourable climate of innovation, however, and the associated higher value that employees attribute to innovative activities mean that these enterprises overcome these difficulties more successfully. Furthermore, the employees of progressive enterprises are less conscious of these difficulties. The directors and chief specialists of progressive enterprises placed the difficulties encountered in the implementation of innovations in ninth place (6%) while those in backward enterprises rated it in eighth (15%, or 2.5 times more). Employees at progressive enterprises, with their more developed innovative consciousness, have other criteria in assessing difficulties. In a favourable climate of innovation, risk and difficulties are considered a normal and indispensable part of the implementation of innovations. This aspect of their consciousness helps them to bear these difficulties much better, facilitates a more rapid psychological adaptation, and increases the efficiency of the innovative process.

The favourable climate of innovation does not eliminate difficulties but comes to terms with them. Moreover, it galvanizes employees into enthusiastically overcoming the difficulties they encounter in the implementation of innovations.

7.4 The climate of innovation as a factor in stimulating the activities of employees

In general, the directors and chief specialists at progressive enterprises perform a wider range of duties, and exercise a stricter supervision over the technology of implementation of innovations, than their counterparts in backward enterprises. This is shown by the much greater proportion of employees in progressive enterprises who are engaged in the most difficult forms of activity. This applies most of all to provision of the material and technical resources for implementation of innovations: in our study, 1.6 times as many employees were engaged here as in backward enterprises (43% as opposed to 27%). Similarly, 1.4 times as many employees were engaged in the organization and management of innovation. A particularly striking discrepancy appeared when we examined the interaction between enterprises and other organizations linked to innovation, (such as research institutes and district administrative bodies). Whilst half the directors and chief specialists in progressive enterprises were engaged in such contacts, the total was 3.7 times lower for backward enterprises. Similarly, half of the directors of progressive enterprises were training their employees in new working methods, twice as many as at backward enterprises. In progressive enterprises, the great majority of directors and chief specialists (77%) made trips elsewhere to benefit from the experience gained by other enterprises in the implementation of innovations. The figure for backward enterprises was only a half of this.

Progressive enterprises implement many more new technologies and spend several hundred times more material and financial resources than backward enterprises. The innovative activities of their directors and chief specialists are more varied in content. They have much wider contacts with research bodies and other organizations; they take more trouble in providing material and technical back-up, organization and direction for an innovation; and they are more involved in training their employees in new working methods and in making visits to other enterprises to make use of their experience in the implementation of innovations. Overall, the management of progressive enterprises engages in much larger-scale innovative activities, and spends considerably more time and effort on their implementation.

In progressive enterprises, employees also display a considerably higher level of activity and initiative in their innovative behaviour. We found there were 1.4 times as many innovators among ordinary employees in progressive enterprises, and 1.3 times as many among their directors and chief specialists. The number of innovations implemented by the director and chief specialist alone was almost twice as many. The proportion of initiators of implemented innovations among directors and chief specialists was 3.6 times higher in progressive enterprises.

The favourable climate of innovation as a whole ensures a higher level of activity at work. The following comparison was made in 1985 between the Lenin *kolkhoz*, which had a favourable climate of innovation and had implemented a great many innovations, and the neighbouring backward Kutuzov *kolkhoz*:

> On the Lenin *kolkhoz* they harvest up to three and a half times more than in the neighbouring farm . . . This is obviously the result of a different attitude to work and to the land. The chairman of the Lenin collective farm took us round the fields and building sites of his enterprise when there was a heavy rain. Everywhere we found people at work. On the Kutuzov *kolkhoz*, on a clear evening at the height of the harvest season, we could not find a single combine driver anywhere – in the field, at the office, or at home. Instead we saw machinery standing neglected by the edge of the pond. Here people work without any enthusiasm or interest.[11]

These differences in the level of activity exhibited by the employees of progressive and backward enterprises account for the difference between them in the results of their innovations.

Not only do progressive enterprises implement a greater number of innovations; they fulfil them to a higher quality. The more positive attitude of employees in progressive enterprises ensures this higher quality; this in turn means that the technology of innovation is more strictly observed, and that the specific features of each enterprise are also taken into account. Naturally, all this requires greater expenditure of time and effort by employees, but it does lead to greater success in the implementation of innovations. The proportion of unfinished innovations in backward enterprises is 1.4 times greater than in progressive ones.

In progressive enterprises, larger-scale innovations are implemented and fuller use is made of their potential. As a consequence, a greater return is received from these innovations. This finds expression in the more rapid growth of production indicators for all the main occupational groups. For rank and file employees these were 1.2 times higher; for middle-ranking managers and specialists 1.3 times higher; and for directors and chief specialists 1.5 times higher.

Overall, there are more positive social consequences of innovations at progressive enterprises. Salaries grow faster, work conditions improve, job satisfaction increases, and there is also an increase in the rights and opportunities of employees. This growth, it should be admitted, is unevenly distributed between the occupational groups. The higher-status positions and occupational groups gain more from innovations. However, it is also these groups who incur the highest social expenditure in the implementation of innovations. The proportion of rank and file employees who have to work more as a result of innovations is approximately the same for progressive and backward enterprises (14% and 13% respectively). In contrast, the proportion of middle-ranking managers and specialists is 2.1 times higher in progressive enterprises (46% compared to 22%), while for directors and chief specialists it is 2.2 times higher (29% as against 13%). These findings are set out in Table 12.

At the same time, progressive enterprises which implement more new technologies may pay a certain social price. Relations within the workforce often worsen as a result of these innovations. Relations between rank and file employees worsened 3.7 times more often in the progressive enterprises than in the backward ones in our study (11% compared to 3%). Similarly, relations between rank and file employees and middle-ranking managers and specialists were three times more likely to worsen (6% compared to 2%), and those between the middle ranks and directors and chief specialists 1.8 times more likely (11% and 6%). Only between rank and file employees and directors and chief specialists did relations improve (6% and 3%).

Table 12 *Comparison of the social consequences of innovations at progressive and backward enterprises**

Group of employees	*Salary*	*Work conditions*	*Work satisfaction*	*Rights and opportunities*
Rank and file employees	1.1	1.2	1.1	1.5
Middle-ranking managers and specialists	1.6	1.3	1.4	2.1
Directors and chief specialists	1.5	1.2	1.6	2.2

*Figures given are for progressive enterprises, taking the figure of 1.0 as the norm for backward enterprises.

The explanation for this seems to lie in the fact that the larger-scale and more complex innovations introduced at progressive enterprises require the participation of a relatively larger number of people from different groups. Greater efforts are demanded from all participants, along with closer and more intensive interaction. This seems more conducive to conflicts than the implementation of comparatively petty innovations in backward enterprises. Naturally, these conflicts are more likely to involve those working closely together (rank and file employees and middle-ranking managers and specialists) than those who meet less often in their work (rank and file employees and directors and chief specialists).

The frequency with which relations worsen as a result of innovations is comparatively small (only in 11% of cases). However, managers and researchers should pay constant attention to these situations since they are much more frequently encountered in enterprises which innovate more intensively. Consequently, this problem will become increasingly acute as the number of these enterprises increases, and may, in the long term, become one of the most important social problems arising out of changes in methods of production.

In 1992, a period of radical economic change in Russia, social tension dramatically increased with the emergence of individual farmers. Envy and aggression on the part of *kolkhoz* employees resulted in some cases in arson attacks on farmers' property. As farmers' yields increase, so social tension continues to rise.

7.5 The innovative community, a precondition for creating a favourable climate of innovation in enterprises

Since the favourable climate of innovation ensures that people become actively engaged in changing and improving methods of production, we must seek out the conditions that permit the establishment of such a climate. Analysis of progressive enterprises shows that a necessary – though by no means the only – condition for its formation is the presence of an innovative community. By this we mean a relatively stable and enduring team of people who are united by their common approval of an active striving to change and improve production methods. This group of like-minded persons regards innovative activities as a creative occupation linked to changes and improvements in production methods, and one of the higher values in life.

Enterprises that have successfully reformed their production methods usually have not a single director-innovator in charge, but a group which supports and aids him in his new undertakings. This small group serves as the nucleus for the innovative community, providing the support and approval for risk-taking innovations. The Soviet press has, in the past, often ignored their existence, but the role they play in the successful implementation of innovations is vital. In the most difficult initial period when an innovation is being adopted, this group helps the innovator to stand up for his proposal, and then ensures that it survives in a hostile or indifferent environment:

> When the chief engineer Krivosheev, and a *small group of his supporters* [author's italics], became enthusiastic about finding a technical solution for their idea, certain people thought it was futile to waste time on this unprofitable suggestion. Others silently waited for him to acknowledge defeat. What did this handful of enthusiasts do when no one else really believed that they could succeed?[12]

The answer is that they developed a non-reactive and waste-free technology for producing natural sulphur which proved economically very effective.

In such a small group, in an informal atmosphere, there is no fear of making a mistake. The primary shaping of new ideas takes place among friends and colleagues. The wilder ideas then get thrown out, while those that have a chance of success gain currency in wider circles among the specialists and manual workers of the enterprise. If such a small group constitutes a separate and independent enterprise, it is extremely receptive to innovations. The experimental enterprise directed by Khudenko, which introduced a great many innovations, in many ways fits this description.

One distinctive feature of the innovative community is that different social groups participate in the wide discussion of the new designs. As an example, we could take the construction of a hot-house orchard in the radiator workshop of the Bratsk heating appliance factory mentioned earlier:

> The idea of a hot-house orchard had been the subject of conversation in the plant for days. *For a long time, this project was discussed in the radiator workshop* [author's italics] and then it moved on to the director's study. It wasn't that no one believed in it . . . but it would mean building an extension 12 metres wide and no less than 100 metres long. There would be palm trees, and lemon bushes . . . Well-informed people had their doubts: they'll reject this project out of hand. But the head of the workshop had prepared convincing figures – apart from cement which we never had in the workshop, almost all the other materials could be obtained there by making economies. And then in the summer they began to build it . . . deadlines were drawn up for when each particular section of the factory would participate in constructing the first hot house, not only in Bratsk but in the whole Irkutsk Region[13]

When innovations are publicly discussed, their weak points are exposed and different groups of employees begin to identify with the project. Moreover, this process helps to identify the opponents of change and to take their opinions into account. In this way, certain forms of compensation may be found. The favourable climate of innovation in an enterprise is not distinguished by the lack of conflicts but by the capacity to resolve them. If a conflict emerges, the innovative community works out a compromise and does not allow it to become a destructive force which could split the workforce.

The collective taking of decisions to implement innovations is an indicator that the inter-group behaviour of employees is being regulated. It shows that there is a social norm of participation in the implementation of innovations which is characteristic of the well-established innovative community. If this community has not been established, as is the case in backward enterprises, there is no inter-group enforcement of innovative activity, which means that this task must be performed by directors and chief specialists.

If a social norm of participation does exist, employees are obliged to engage in innovative activities in spite of the expense of time and effort that they involve. If not, everything depends on the individual decision each employee takes as to whether, and how actively, he or she will participate in the implementation of innovations. This decision will be taken without group pressure and be based only on individual psychological principles. If an employee has a sufficiently strong psychological need to implement innovations, he or she will try to implement them even in such a workforce, but will generally meet with little success. The unfavourable climate of innovation at such enterprises not only fails to make its employees engage in innovation but also suppresses the activity of those who try to do so.

An innovative community is typically made up of mobile and inventive people who are able to produce, understand and implement new ideas. Obviously, such people are hard to come by. There must therefore be a conscious selection of personnel according to their attitudes to change and improvement in production methods. As a rule, this takes a comparatively long period of time, often many years. However, once a team of innovators has been built up, it is capable of accelerating the development of production many times over. Such a team will be able to find the required organizational forms of innovative activity, sometimes filling old formal structures with a new social content.

The formation of an innovating community is a natural process which begins from below. It cannot be established by decree or planning allocation – people cannot be forced to think alike and share a common striving towards a particular goal. (However, the conditions that enable such a community to arise can be established from above, as will be discussed further on.) An instructive example is the work group set up by Koltashev at the Kurgan wheel-traction factory. Over the five years of its existence, this seven-person team implemented about 100 rationalizing proposals, about 30 times more per worker than the average for Soviet industry. It also reorganized the allocation of jobs and equipment.

> Nine years ago, Koltashev had the following talk with Sasha Rudnev . . . We work different shifts, said Koltashev, but use the same machine-tool. You turn out your parts, and I turn out mine. It takes you 30–40 minutes after I knock off for you

> to re-set the machine; it's the same for me. We're in the same wage-bracket and we're equally skilled, I'd say. Let's work in batches instead. First we turn out your parts and then we do mine. Then we won't have to change the tooling or the adjustment either. There won't be any time lost. We use the same equipment and the same tables, so we'll split our wages. This was how the mini-brigade came into existence. It functioned for three years until we thought of setting up all-round specialized teams with payment by the final result.[14]

Since innovative communities emerge from below, each has its own specific history that differs from all others. Each possesses its own traditions and customs. For instance, in Koltashev's work group it is the custom to analyse the work of each member (not excluding the team-leader) at the end of the month. Successes and shortcomings are assessed, and the total earnings announced. All this is done in public by the team-leader.

Although it takes quite a long time to form an innovative community, it can be broken up very quickly. This can happen with a change of director who, as a rule, is the leader and chief innovator in such communities.

Innovative communities may also collapse if the imperfections of economic management in a given workforce mean that the implementation of an innovation leads to a sharp drop in income. This may lead to a conflict that destroys an established innovative community.

An innovative community may also be disbanded from above on the decision of superior bodies. These often resent the innovating community, and see its members as awkward characters intent on revealing the existing lethargy, and liable to provoke the opposition of the workforce by wanting too much. This was particularly common during the 'period of stagnation', when things even went as far as the legal persecution of innovators and court sentences for 'infringing financial discipline'. (A famous case was that of Khudenko, who died in prison.)

The main reason why there are very few innovative communities in Russian enterprises, however, is not that so many of them are disbanded, but that so few come into existence in the first place. The explanation is that enterprises do not perceive a need for innovations.

Furthermore, our traditional centralized and hierarchical administrative system makes it difficult to establish horizontal links between enterprises and the people who work in them. There is a strict subordination of those lower in authority which only permits such links to the extent that they facilitate the execution of orders from above. All other links are looked on as favouritism or nepotism. This gives rise to a social phenomenon that Vasiliev calls the 'shortage of sociability': 'the individual does not think about others. Each is concerned only with himself . . . It is no expression of common interests that we go to work together and speak about our work at meetings.'[15] The innovative community, by contrast, is made up of like-minded individuals who share similar values and are linked by informal relations to their work. This new type of relation, in this case in a family leasehold farm, is described by Somov:

> The Karpunin family, having been made owners of a farm and living nearby, do not distinguish between their private and business concerns. These become one and the same, and their ideas and initiative are liberated. People give up their indifference and claimant psychology. Personal interests merge with those of wider society.[16]

Before perestroika, work of this kind would have been termed 'nepotism'. It would not have been permitted, of course, in the fear that public property would suffer from the private property-owner who was chasing only personal gain.

The psychological interaction that is typical of an innovative community creates powerful non-monetary incentives to creative activity, and encourages its members to propose and implement new ideas. It becomes shameful to shirk or to reduce work to a routine activity, or not to strive towards improvement. This kind of interaction cannot arise within the centralized administrative system. It is regarded as an obstruction, since it reduces the manageability of employees and the speed and precision with which orders from above can be carried out.

If stable teams of people who are oriented towards the intensive overhaul of production methods, linked to each other by informal ties, are to come into existence, they must be able formally to organize themselves from below. In the centralized and hierarchical system of administration, organizations are only set up from above (whether they are enterprises, industries, services, research institutes etc.). In such conditions, these informal groups cannot consolidate and work normally.

At present, therefore, innovative communities mainly arise in a haphazard fashion: a director is appointed who is either an innovator, or who is willing to support and to protect the activities of innovators. The established economic and social patterns of our country tend to eliminate such directors rather than promote them. There are no constantly functioning social forces that enable innovating communities to come into being. Therefore, the only alternative is that they are artificially created from above in particular sectors of the economy where, for some reason, accelerated development is required (for example, the space and micro-biological industries). But these industries are essentially closed economic zones, which have priority in supplies, higher pay, and superior social and cultural facilities, enabling them to retain skilled and innovative personnel. Some of the old closed economic zones still exist, despite liberalization, for example chemical weapons production and R&D.

The successful implementation and rapid spread of large-scale innovations is impossible if there are not innovating communities at the majority of enterprises. This is as essential as capital investment. The most advanced modern equipment will be wasted if such a community has not been established. Either it will rust away before it has been installed, or else it will work at only half its capacity, frequently producing even less than the old equipment it replaces.

Workforces that have a favourable climate of innovation are therefore not only of great social importance, but also have a considerable economic value. Their widespread diffusion can accelerate socio-economic development and a growth in productive efficiency. Fig. 2 shows that there is a link, in the final analysis, between the significance that directors attach to innovations and the productive efficiency of their enterprises.

The value system of directors of enterprises differs substantially from that of directors at loss-making enterprises. The former put innovations first, and paperwork in fifth place. These priorities are reversed in loss-making enterprises. Therefore, a change in the values held by personnel towards giving an increased signficance to innovative activity is able, through the chain of regulators, to result in an acceleration of innovative processes in Russian enterprises. This may happen because the number of enterprises with favourable climates of innovation, where people use innovations to try to increase their occupational skills and not just to make their work easier, has increased many times over. These enterprises innovate without regard to the expense of time and effort involved, and do not avoid the complex and labour-intensive jobs. In these, it is possible to implement many large-scale innovations and ensure high rates of scientific and technical progress and a growth in productive efficiency.[17]

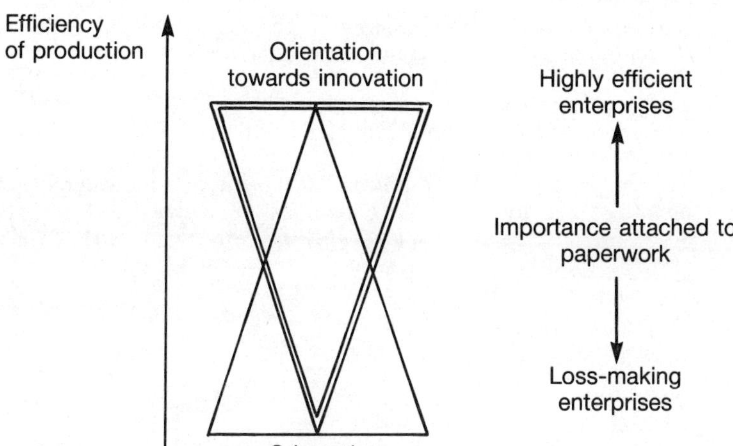

Figure 2: Differences in the system of values held by directors of highly efficient and of loss-making enterprises: highly efficient enterprises have a high orientation towards innovation and a low orientation towards paperwork, loss-making enterprises the reverse

NOTES

1 The concept of 'organizational climate' is described, for example, by E. M. Rodgers and R. Agarwala-Rodgers, *Communication in organizations*, New York, Free Press (1977; Russian trans. 1980), 85–6.
2 I. Vasiliev, *Guideposts*, Moscow, Politizdat (1988), 127.
3 A. N. Chekalin, *An economic experiment*, Moscow, Stroiizdat (1987), 263.
4 Chekalin, *An economic experiment*, 263.
5 Vasiliev, *Guideposts*, 242.
6 I. Kruglyanskaya, 'Rumours', *Izvestiya*, 5 September 1987.
7 L. Kapeliushny and B. Reznik, 'Unlike relations', *Izvestiya*, 27 August 1985.
8 V. Zalipaev, 'Who needs "accommodating" people?', *Sovetskaya rossiya*, 2 June 1985.
9 L. Gladyshev and V. Shilov, 'Initiative outside the plan', *Sovetskaya rossiya*, 13 September 1981.
10 See, for example, V. A. Skripov, 'Everyday routine', *EKO*, iv (1983).
11 A. Vasinsky and L. Ershov, 'Three sides of the same problem', *Izvestiya*, 21 August 1985.
12 V. Vukovich, 'Risk taking is a good thing', *Izvestiya*, 24 August 1985.

13 Kapeliushny and Reznik, 'Unlike relations'.
14 V. Smirnov, 'The nature of the work group', *Sovetskaya rossiya*, 13 December 1984.
15 Vasiliev, *Guideposts*, 282.
16 V. Somov, '"Farmer" means being your own boss', *Pravda*, 3 August 1988.
17 Some other factors that go towards making a climate favourable to innovative activity in Russian enterprises are analysed in L. Kosals, *Social mechanisms for the innovative process*, Novosibirsk, Nauka (1989).

8

The Lack of Economic Immunity in the Centralized Economy

8.1 Employees' assessment of the social expenditures involved in innovation

When employees in a Russian enterprise decide whether to participate in the implementation of an innovation, they first weigh up the social expenditure and results of these innovations. This, we believe, is what makes the process so different from that in market economies. There, in contrast, it is the assessment of the *economic* expenditure and results of innovations that form the basis of decision making. Therefore, according to Mansfield, the well-known specialist on problems of innovation, 'if the adoption of a technical improvement does not appear to be profitable, it will remain of potential importance until changing economic circumstances make it profitable'. If an innovation, on the other hand, promises a sufficient profit, it stands the chance of being more or less rapidly implemented. Only when the 'expected profit from the implementation of an innovation does not exceed the profit to be obtained from other investments . . . is an innovation rejected'.[1]

In a Russian enterprise, an innovation which is economically highly effective may often not be as widely introduced as it might, or may be introduced only very slowly. This is because, as we have said, its employees base their judgements on social expenditures and results rather than on economic ones.

We have already listed the social expenditure and results entailed by the implementation of innovations. The main criterion an employee applies is the effort he or she must invest in implementation of an innovation and the effect that the innovation will have on his or her status. If the efforts are small, and yet status may rise, the attitude will be positive, and vice versa.

The efforts an employee must expend in order to implement an innovation are determined by the increase in work linked to that innovation and the difficulties that are encountered in its implementation.

More than anyone else, it is the middle-ranking managers and specialists who have to work more because of an innovation. In our study, we found that the implementation of innovations added to their workload in 35% of cases, while this applied to only 20% of directors and chief specialists, and 16% of rank and file employees (these and subsequent figures are based on the expert assessment of directors and chief specialists).

One of the bottlenecks hindering change and improvement in production methods, therefore, is the position adopted by middle-ranking managers and specialists, since they have to bear the main burden of organizing work on the implementation of innovations and overcoming the difficulties of implementation.

Such difficulties occur in the overwhelming majority of cases: 86% of the total, according to the directors and chief specialists whom we interviewed. Among the main difficulties were those connected to the passivity of employees and the shortage of skilled employees with an interest in innovation (48%). (Only in 37% of innovations was this not considered a difficulty.) These difficulties arose for a variety of reasons, according to our interviewees: employees feared a reduction in their salaries (50%), more work during implementation (35%), and a future increase in their workload (26%). Other reasons cited included a shortage of people with an interest in implementation of innovations (25%), employees' fears that they would not cope with their new responsibilities (23%), and the lack of a material and moral incentive during implementation of innovations (16%).

As is clear from these figures, the main reasons for reluctance of employees to participate in the implementation of innovations was the anxiety that their socio-economic status would worsen as a result.

The directors interviewed used various methods to resolve these difficulties associated with the participation of their employees. First and foremost, they tried to convince them of the necessity and value of the innovation (74%). Second, they sought out and relied on those who took an interest in the implementation of innovations (56%). The application of positive economic incentives (wage rises, bonuses) and administrative penalties came next, and were almost equal at 12% and 11% respectively. As we can see from this list, the measures taken by directors and chief specialists in response to difficulties are hardly directed at all towards the main reasons for them. Consequently, their effectiveness is not very great.

The other difficulty in implementation of innovations mentioned by our interviewees lies in the shortage of material and technical resources (41%). When innovations were at their initial stage of implementation, enterprises were assured of only 51% of the necessary resources. The solutions employed were to use lower-quality materials already in the enterprise's possession or to obtain them semi-legally from somewhere else. In 17% of cases, the required materials were not produced by Russian industry at all. This, as we have already mentioned, is one of the basic reasons why implemented innovations are so unsatisfactory and give results that fail to maximize their potential.

The next difficulty was the worsening of relations with managers and specialists in a number of other sections of the enterprise (31%). This is often the result of conflicts which arise as the implementation of innovations is proceeding, and which occasionally spill over beyond the bounds of their enterprise. For example, Pakhailo, the chairman of the Krasnodar Region *kolkhoz* 'Kavkaz', began to measure the quantity of husked wheat not in terms of bunker weight but after threshing. This technical and organizational innovation led to a reduction of 5% and more in comparison with the existing method of calculation:

> What a row this caused! The chairman's closest aides began to view him with suspicion. He did not give a thought to the reputation of the *kolkhoz*, they complained, and was deliberately lowering their harvest indicator. We shall gain neither praise nor bonuses for doing this. Assertive controllers began to appear, often at the threshing floor: they say you're ignoring directives, and we'll punish you.[2]

The last major difficulty mentioned by the directors and chief specialists was that they themselves had to re-train and get accustomed to new ways (30%). This was a natural difficulty of implementation of innovations, linked to the non-routine and creative nature of the innovative process.

Our interviewees were hardly aware of the necessity for re-training, or the redeployment of employees made redundant as a result of the implementation of innovations – only 4% mentioned this. However, the situation is changing and this problem is becoming ever more topical following the recent break-up of the Soviet Union. So far, this issue mainly affects administrative workers, but in the future manual workers will be equally affected. The rise in unemployment was less than 1% in Russia at the end of 1992. But the main causes of the increase were as a consequence of technical innovation and rationalization of management.

We have examined the common difficulties experienced for all the different types of innovation. At the same time, the implementation of each type of innovation, and even of each individual innovation, in a given enterprise has its own specific complexities. While we cannot encompass all their variety, we shall describe several of the difficulties of implementing one of the most important organizational and administrative innovations of recent years in the Soviet economy. We are referring to the transfer of enterprises in the Agro-Industrial Complex to full cost-accounting and self-financing. These difficulties were revealed during a survey of DAA directors in 1988. Only 18% thought that the transition was going well, and without major difficulties. The rest mentioned various problems, the most common of which (68%) was the poor financial and economic state of the enterprises. Thereafter, in declining order of importance, they included: the lack of staff training in economic matters (50%); the shortage of material and technical resources (40%); the lack of initiative and entrepreneurial attitudes (36%); and the unrealistic purchase plans (34%). They gave other reasons, such as the lack of responsibility on the part of employees, the low quality of the cost-accounting system in itself, and so on, but these were rated of far less importance.

We may reduce the above list to two main types of difficulty: those concerning the system of economic relations and the economic consequences to which it gives rise, and those involving the quality and nature of human resources. Analysis of the above survey leads us to conclude that the significance of these two types of difficulty is roughly equal. The first primarily requires action by the upper levels of administrators and management. The second depends for its solution on greater activity by employees, above all by lower level management and, of course, by rank and file workers and specialists.

The implementation of innovations is therefore accompanied by the need to overcome considerable difficulties and demands great expenditures of time and energy. We must now examine what these employees gain as a result of innovations.

8.2 Assessment by employees of the social results of innovations

In a number of cases (24%), it was impossible to estimate who in particular had benefited, and which groups had gained most, since the entire enterprise had benefited from the innovation. In those cases where an estimate could be made, rank and file employees benefited most from the implementation of innovations (28% of cattle-breeders, 23% of combine and tractor drivers, and 10% of rank and file employees in general). Their work became more varied and interesting (62%), their pay increased (58%), their work conditions improved (56%), and their rights and opportunities expanded (43%).

Middle-ranking managers and specialists enjoyed relatively small gains from innovations. Overall the variety and interest of their work increased as a result of 64% of innovations, but their work conditions improved in only 34% of cases, their rights and opportunities in 27%, and their pay in just 20%. Thus, middle-ranking managers and specialists were the group which suffered most from the implementation of innovations.

Directors and chief specialists, on the other hand, were affected least of all. Innovations made little change in their work and status, with 39% of them asserting there was no change; 14% said that work had decreased, while 13% said that output indicators had improved in the branch where the innovation had been adopted. A further 8% said they drew moral satisfaction from innovation, 8% that it had become easier to manage their workforce, and 7% that their work was more interesting as a result.

The greater part of managers (not to mention ordinary employees) receive no material rewards for implementation of innovations. Of directors and chief specialists engaged in innovation, 55% received no reward whatsoever, while 33% were given a bonus. As for non-material rewards, 20% felt they had increased their authority in the workforce, while 10% felt they had done so in the eyes of their superior administrative bodies.

Innovations thus demand considerable social expenditure that can hardly be compensated for by the social results obtained. If we accept the thesis that this is the primary consideration for Russian employees in making decisions about the implementation of innovations, it is not surprising that they are passive and do not pursue the latest developments in this field.

On the other hand, however, one might surmise that enterprises, their workforces and directors would actively pursue and implement those innovations which gave significant social results. This would indeed be the case if they could not already meet these needs by turning to superior bodies. Such 'charitable' behaviour from above, however, comes at the expense of those enterprises which work (and innovate) better, which effectively reduces or removes their incentive.

The transition to a real market economy may eventually change this situation. For the present things change slowly.

8.3 Innovations and the lack of economic immunity

Employees will normally prefer those innovations that involve the minimum of social expenditure. However, certain individuals are keen to attain the maximum socio-economic results despite the social expenditure involved. These are the active innovators, who work as hard as they possibly can even when innovations threaten to worsen their position, or sometimes actually do so. Khudenko, for example, left a major post in Moscow to go to Kazakhstan and there direct an enterprise in which he could implement his idea of the collective contract. Active innovators, who make up no more than 1% of enterprise employees, simply cannot act otherwise. Like all creative people, they want to have their contribution and attainments recognized, and are often ready to fight for this acknowledgement.

However, the vast majority of employees try to limit their efforts at work and minimize the social expenditure incurred. This explains not only why innovations are so slow to be introduced and extended throughout the Russian economy, but also why many useful innovations fail to be widely adopted.

The higher the director stands in the hierarchy, the less important the role played by social expenditure in deciding to implement an innovation. At the level of ministries and other government departments, the main consideration is an assessment of the relation between economic expenditure and economic results. This is quite natural, since at this level social expenditure cannot be felt; it is produced at the level of the enterprise where the innovation is actually implemented. At these higher levels in the administration, social expenditure linked to innovations is experienced as conflicts that must be resolved by ministerial officials, or as disruptions in the work of the enterprises. They are perceived as unexpected complications, the result of poor work by the workforces and their directors, or even as sabotage.

The implementation of innovations is very difficult to direct, or even to understand, since employees are oriented not only towards current consequences but also to unforeseen future consequences. To the outside observer, the actions of employees who are passive towards, or even resist, innovation may appear illogical. As a result, they are classified as the product of conservatism, the irrational obstinacy of those who do not recognize what is to their own benefit. This seemingly illogical behaviour, however, frequently conceals a quite rational calculation based on the fear of harming one's own interests. Employees assess the consequences of innovations – those that are easily observable and those that are unforeseen – primarily in terms of their own interests. If they believe there is a danger that their position will worsen (and innovations are almost always accompanied by risk), they may exhibit passivity or react negatively.[3]

The events that happened in Kirishi illustrate the negative consequences that arise from not taking into account the social expenditure involved in innovation. It was decided to build a factory there producing paprin, a new protein and vitamin concentrate. This took the form of dried yeast, which is a natural form of this concentrate. There are almost no doubts as to its value. The factory will produce 120,000 tons per year on an area of 60 hectares, replacing the output of 150–200,000 hectares of soya beans. The addition of one ton of paprin to mixed animal feed will eventually yield an extra half-ton of pork and one-and-a-half tons of chicken meat.

The decision to build in Kirishi was taken without sufficient consideration of its effect on the environment. The town's inhabitants were not informed, and their views were not taken into account. Moreover, when the technology was devised:

> oversights arose at each stage . . . It is well known, for example, that alien proteins may provoke an allergic reaction in humans. This was tested on the digestive system and all was well. But the designers did not think to test what would happen if people inhaled these dried yeasts. It never occurred to the planners and economists to consider the psychological consequences of their decisions. Since this new type of production was based on the products of oil-refining, and demanded energy, they assumed it must be situated where these were easily available. What the local population might have to say was not a concern of the planners.[4]

The factory by-products led to an outbreak of allergic sickness and a sharp reaction among the local inhabitants. The factory was then reconstructed and a technology adopted that produced little waste and by-products. However, the local population, supported by the press and TV, continued to take a negative view of the factory and its workforce, a situation which naturally makes their work much harder and less satisfactory.

In this case, it was the town's inhabitants who bore the social expenditure of this innovation. The majority of them drew no substantial benefits whatsoever from the location of the factory on their territory, simply because oil-refining products and energy were easily available there. Had they been considered when the initial decisions were taken, it is possible that the factory would have been built somewhere else. The greater immediate economic costs would have helped to avoid a serious social conflict, not to mention the additional economic costs arising in the future from reconstruction, educational work among the population by a team of specialists, and so on.

Since the desire to minimize social expenditure means that certain economically effective innovations are not implemented, influence from above becomes essential. Some innovations will only be adopted if firm leadership from above stimulates the stalling enterprise into action. However, only a very small number of innovations can be implemented and monitored in this way: only those that give an absolute guarantee of success and attainment of a tangible result. All risky innovations must be filtered out at the stage of institutionalization; if they are adopted throughout the country, any error will prove much too costly. The loss from unsuccessful innovations would otherwise be so enormous that it would exceed the gains made from successful innovations.

The introduction of innovations from above is inevitably conservative, and yet, despite its conservatism, this approach still constantly has its failures. The number of reliable and simple innovations that could be adapted to local conditions throughout Russia without particular modification is very small, especially in agriculture. People still remember the campaign to sow maize everywhere, even as far north as the Arctic Circle. Such examples point to the centralized and regulated economy's lack of economic immunity: it has no warning system that would give the alert and limit the extension of an unsuitable innovation. Although a particular innovation may be useful in limited conditions (within a restricted territory or branch of industry), the more it is adopted or extended beyond these limits the greater the losses this innovation brings. This unhelpful extension of an innovation which is locally useful comes about when conservative superior bodies demonstrate energy and insistence in its widespread implementation (often from the best of intentions).[5]

The market economy has economic immunity which prevents the adoption of unwanted innovations. In the states that formerly constituted the Soviet Union, however, there is instead a socio-political immunity in the conservatism of leaders who restrict the propagation of innovations. Consequently, in our centralized system for adopting innovations, the more that directors and leaders are innovation-oriented, the greater the disruptions will be. The lack of economic immunity is a dangerous disease for society, comparable to the acquired immune-deficiency syndrome (AIDS) in the human body. Attempts to introduce as many innovations as possible from above may lead, in these circumstances, to significant harm as well as benefit. Of course, this does not mean that no innovations at all must be implemented. But they must be aimed at arousing the independent innovative activities of so-called entrepreneurs.

In Part III of our study we will go on to present a conception of the causes that together have led to the present critical situation as regards innovative processes in the states of the former Soviet Union.

NOTES

1 E. Mansfield, *The economics of technological change*, New York, Norton & Co. (1968), 131.

2 K. Aksenov, 'And what's in the bunker?', *Pravda*, 6 January 1986.

3 This conclusion conflicts with the assertions made in much Soviet literature on the subject, that 'workers regard the saving of labour as a result of technical progress as a progressive phenomenon', and that they 'do not fear any worsening in the socio-economic status' as a consequence. The advantages technological change offered to all have frequently been adopted as an unquestioned postulate in such texts. Such attitudes derive from an ideological norm of the superiority of the socialist system.

4 A. Pokrovsky, 'Our stumbling blocks or the psychological barriers on the path of technical innovation', *Pravda*, 16 April 1988.

5 Sahal put forward an interesting conception that may help explain the dynamics of innovative processes in Soviet society. The returns on technology, he suggested, are dependent on the time (or, more precisely, the accumulated practical experience) and scale of its diffusion. See D. Sahal, *Patterns of technological innovation*, Reading MA, Addison-Wesley (1981), 132–48.

III

The Reasons for Stagnation in Innovative Processes

9

What Holds Back Innovative Processes?

This chapter is an attempt at a more systematic presentation of the factors we have already discussed as impeding innovation in the Russian economy. But first an examination of the socio-economic pre-conditions for innovation is called for, since their lack is one of the root causes of stagnation.

We make a distinction between social and economic and organizational causes of delays in innovation. The social causes have an adverse effect on the human component in innovation, while the economic and organizational causes serve as a disincentive for innovation and modernization.

What follows is an analysis of the two groups of causes and an examination of their principal consequences in the enterprise.

9.1 An apathetic workforce and management

There are several immediate social causes that hold back innovation in the economy.

A very low level of innovative activity among the workforce

The management and the workforce seldom introduce innovations on their own initiative. There are too many apathetic and even hostile workers, and far too few inventors and innovators. As a result the number of new products, processes and other innovations is small, and the number of real breakthroughs in technology and socio-economic relations in the sphere of production is even smaller. Furthermore, the introduction of many innovations is imposed from above. This sometimes results in 'phoney innovations' designed to conceal the absence of real change. The slow tempo of production modernization, a tempo bordering on stagnation, and the fact that new machines and technologies are only marginally better than the old ones, are the immediate effects of the low rate of innovative activity.

A reluctance to meet the expenses involved

Innovators at Russian enterprises are few and far between because too many workers avoid exertion, risks, conflicts, the need to retrain, possible cuts in wages and loss of job etc. Relatively few people devote themselves to innovation on their own initiative, seeking to make their jobs more interesting and fulfilling. It is personal fulfilment rather than promotion that most innovators seek, and in their innovative activities they usually set their sights very high. They view promotion, higher pay and other material rewards solely as proof of the recognition of their contribution to progress. They are motivated by a sense of duty, not greed. Since they are a rare species, the renewal of the Russian economy is proving a slow process.

The majority of workers are self-seeking and avoid taking risks unless there is an immediate material advantage for them. They are no help to enterprises in their innovative activities.

The absence of a favourable climate at most factories and farms

The attitude of the workforce to innovation is largely negative. Rare is the enterprise where the climate is favourable for innovation; there, the work of innovators is socially approved and is seen as a useful contribution to the performance of the enterprise, and the innovators enjoy great prestige and respect among the management and the workforce. They are highly respected members of the group, and if one of them leaves his or her job this is experienced as a loss. Those who dodge innovation activities, in contrast, are frowned upon as bad comrades.

Wherever active participation in innovation has not become a social norm, innovators are treated as cranks whose airy theories only prevent others from doing a decent job of work. They are not treated as members of the group, and a sign of relief often greets their leaving the enterprise. Dodging innovations is not frowned upon. On the contrary, unless material rewards are forthcoming, it is the norm. In this stagnant atmosphere, an innovator becomes a voice in the wilderness, compelled to tread the round of bosses of various ranks, begging for a room, a tool or a helper. The management usually refuses outright, and any promise to help is apt to be promptly forgotten. What is more, initiative is punishable. The penalty for mistakes, an inevitable part of all innovation, may be more severe than for shoddy workmanship or idleness. Innovators are frequently accused of setting themselves against the collective. The end result is a stagnant social atmosphere in which any winds of change are promptly stifled and the socially acceptable norm is inaction.

This unfavourable climate often leads to occasions when an innovation needed by the enterprise fails to be implemented even though the grounds have been prepared for it: an official order has been issued, funds appropriated, equipment supplied, and specialists and managers sent abroad to acquire new skills. However, the new equipment has yet to be installed, the funds have still to be drawn from accounts, and the management blames 'objective difficulties' for its failure to launch the new product on time. The exact number of such cases can only be guessed at, for they are hushed up by publicity-shy managers fearing retribution, particularly if the equipment in question has been imported and paid for in convertible currency. If the excuse for the failure to innovate is believed, the superior authority may confine itself to a mild reprimand and even adjust the factory's production plan.

The lack of an innovating community in most enterprises

Enterprises with innovative communities encourage active participation in innovative activities. Innovation is the social norm there. These communities are self-regulating, and their members' efforts are directed toward a common goal – the implementation of innovations. The climate is one of camaraderie and mutual assistance, not only in innovative activities but also in production activities in general. Workers feel that they belong to a team, and this team spirit is of greater value to them than a better-paid job elsewhere. Yet individuality is not crushed or sacrificed to the interests of the group. Quite the contrary; individual accomplishment is praised and others are encouraged to emulate it, so there are no jealousies and intrigues. Mistakes are openly discussed to reveal their causes and to boost performance, not to apportion blame. The shop-floor activities of innovative communities are very open. Frequent meetings are held to discuss problems, and all decisions are taken collectively in a spirit of compromise. The opinions of all employees count, and there are no hidden grudges. The members of the group are well informed about new developments and know that they are part of the team. In short, such communities, even if they are small, lead a varied and interesting life.

Innovative communities have a complex inner organization. The following social roles may be identified within a successful community.

The *group leader* (preferably the director of the enterprise) gives innovation top priority. Each member of the community is given a progression of increasingly ambitious goals. The sets of individual goals must be interchangeable so that the members of the team are aware of their interdependence and understand the importance of their part of the assignment. The leader channels the interests and aspirations of the team towards a common goal, and must be capable of mobilizing and enthusing people. To do so, he or she should also be an innovator, and must work alongside the group in the factory or office, not be remote from his or her colleagues.

The *generator of ideas* is an unconventional thinker whose job is to supply a pool of fresh ideas. In this way, the innovative community insures against inertia and assures a constant stream of stimulating ideas.

The *sober critic* has to set out before the group the information and priorities it needs for a weighed and reasoned choice of each new idea. He embodies the conservatism and stability the team needs if it is not to lapse into adventurism.

The *organizer* has to find and explore ways of implementing new ideas.

The *creative executant* carries out the actual development of the new idea resulting in a prototype.

The *trouble-shooter* must be a past master of compromise.

The *conductor* of new ideas explains them to the workforce and makes a case for innovation. A similar function exists in social psychology.[1] The conductor not only explains new ideas but also collects critical comments about them, which are then taken into account by the innovative community in the development and introduction of new products, processes etc. The function is preferably fulfilled by representatives of different social groups – managers, specialists and shop-floor workers.

The *cosmopolitan*[2] is concerned with public relations: he or she brings new ideas from the outside world and registers outside reaction to the work of the innovative community.

Although one person can combine several of these functions, all of them are necessary for the innovative community to work successfully.

Another characteristic of innovative communities is their cohesion. When conflicts do arise they are strictly limited to business (for example there may be different approaches to a production problem) and are settled amicably through compromise.

An innovative community is thus a complex social organism. Such communities do not appear out of the blue. They need favourable social conditions and take a great deal of effort to build. The lack of them is one of the root causes of stagnation in the Russian economy, and their continued absence will make any acceleration of, and qualitative change in, the innovative process unlikely.

The lack of a workable system of incentives

Even if a major innovation saves an enterprise millions of roubles, the innovator's reward is a lump sum that does not usually compensate the time, effort and financial expenditure. What is more, there are no clear-cut legal guarantees that the innovator will actually get their reward.

As a result, inventing and innovating is not a sound proposition for the individual, either socially or materially. Innovators do not enjoy high social prestige, and there are no waiting lists to fill such posts. Only those who cannot help innovating (fanatics of innovation) become innovators.

All this, however, does not mean that the work of innovators is not useful to Russian society. On the contrary, probably no other country gets so much from innovators while giving them so little.

The need for permission in order to show initiative

Any move outside the daily routine must be sanctioned by superior authorities. An innovation needs scores, sometimes hundreds and even thousands, of go-aheads from various officials. Most have the right of veto and can block any initiative. What is more, they can be relied upon to do so, since this makes their daily workload easier, and does not affect their salaries. For this reason, virtually all initiatives have to be pushed through the chain of command, even though the officials involved may not necessarily be opposed to them. As a result, innovators feel compelled to look for patrons, who for their part are rarely disinterested parties. Phoney co-authorship of innovations is the most common kind of bribe for assistance that sometimes amounts to the mere performance of official duties or an agreement not to block an initiative. In this way, the innovator is always beholden to the bureaucrat.

Since 1987 innovators have been able to establish their own businesses. But private businessmen are now so dependent on the state sector that they have no real opportunity to put their ideas into practice without the support of state enterprises. The position of the innovator in the state sector is almost the same as it was in the pre-Gorbachev period.

The daily phenomenon of 'muddling through'

In the absence of any clear, long-term projects, managers concentrate on day-to-day activities, production bottlenecks and trouble-shooting. In the absence of an independent management policy a great deal of effort is wasted on a host of petty chores. As a result, innovations are introduced only by the order of a superior authority, or in situations where the problems facing an enterprise are so severe as to threaten a halt in production.

The sum total of the above factors is a lethargic workforce and an apathetic management. While it is true that a superior can prod an enterprise of this nature into innovative activity, this stimulus will be short-lived, reprimands will be quickly forgotten and everything will return to normal. Furthermore, managers will always have a good excuse for inaction: they lack the necessary prerequisites for innovation.

9.2 Objective problems of the human factor

The following objective reasons explain why the management and workforce become primarily concerned with daily production routines.

There are no economic incentives for innovation

Russian state enterprises, the greater part of all enterprises, can survive, and even grow, without innovations. Unaffected by market pressures, they are not penalized for ignoring changes in consumer demand. What is more, whenever they run into problems, such as rises in the price of raw materials or non-delivery by suppliers, they can ask a superior authority for help. On request, the corresponding ministry will provide them with extra financing from centralized funds, credit with low interest, etc. Clearly, in this situation Russian enterprises simply do not need innovations. Since they do not need innovations, they do not need innovators. Since they do not need innovators they do not need to create conditions which are favourable for them; indeed, it is often simpler to get rid of these 'busybodies' as soon as the opportunity arises.

The tradition of formally planned innovations

In the Soviet system there were assignments (state orders) for innovations, just as there were assignments for the production of traditional goods. These assignments had the power of law, and were backed up by resources, both material and financial.

As long as the innovation assignment was not in conflict with an enterprise's real needs, no problem arose. But if there was a conflict of interest, the enterprise would normally resort to phoney innovations backed up by doctored statistics.

The centralized planning mechanism tends to be successful when an 'innovation' has already been introduced elsewhere and is not a serious risk, or when it has been developed by a leading research organization and its introduction is controlled by a superior authority. The mechanism malfunctions severely, however, when an innovation is suggested from below, by an enterprise or an independent inventor without a patron. Its examination, development and implementation may then take years (or even decades), so that it becomes more economically viable to import a comparable machine or technology.

Following the breakdown of the Central Planning System, there were no innovation plans or pressure from above to implement innovations; as a result, the innovative process has sharply declined in the state sector.

There is no satisfactory material and technological provision for innovation

This is the most common excuse given by managers for delays in innovation. In practice, it often has some justification. A typical progression might be as follows. New technology cannot be introduced without an indispensable piece of machinery. One possible solution would be to order it from a local manufacturer. However, up until the early 1990s the local manufacturer had to meet the production assignments it was given by its ministry. Therefore, the next step was to ask the ministry to include the development and production of the item in question in the state order assignment. The ministry would often refuse, however, particularly if the new technology involved the use of new machines, none of them covered by the official plan, and problems then multiplied in a geometrical progression. As a result, enterprises could be discouraged from introducing even those innovations in which they were genuinely interested.

Enterprise management structures are ill-suited to innovation

Organized on several levels, the Russian economic management structure before the perestroika period was highly standardized and centralized. Enterprises were set up by branch ministries, and their internal structure had also to be approved by these ministries. All major structural changes required the sanction of a superior authority. This was a serious impediment to innovation, for most major technological innovations (not to mention managerial ones) called for structural changes in the enterprise (such as the decentralization of management, the creation of new jobs etc.).

The fact that the economy as a whole formed a hierarchical structure slowed down innovation to a considerable extent, because the greater the number of hierarchical levels, the higher the probability that an innovation would be seriously delayed at one of them.

Since enterprises were created by decree of a superior authority, innovation from below was bound to run into many problems. Many innovations would not make it from the drawing board to the shop floor without the assistance of a special development organization. In principle, such an organization should be uniquely suited to the personality of the inventor. But in the past the invention was likely to be sent to another research establishment specializing in the same field for comments and 'polishing up'. The inventor thus became dependent on competitors who had the power to delay the innovation and were unlikely to offer useful advice.

In the period 1987–92 superior bodies lost control over the activities of enterprises. Now Russian state enterprises and the enterprises of other former Soviet republics, though set up by superior bodies, are not for the most part subject to orders from above concerning their current management. The situation is the same for innovative activity. But most state enterprises are monopolies and have no fear of bankruptcy. Therefore they have no need to innovate. The effect of a decentralized state system of enterprise management, without administrative pressure for implementation of innovations, is worse than the situation in the traditional centralized economy. The present system of management has most of the old defects and some new deficiencies as well, for example extreme instability of economic ties between enterprises. This deficiency makes all business activities difficult, especially the implementation of innovations.

The two groups of factors (objective and subjective) which hold back innovation are complementary. For example, the shortage of material and technical resources needed by some enterprises for innovation was frequently a result of the very low level of innovative activity at other enterprises. Another contributory factor is that the planning and management structures are ill-suited to innovation and have difficulty in allocating the necessary resources.

These direct causes of stagnation interact together to form an obstructive mechanism to innovation in the enterprise. In turn they are determined by certain institutional causes which are not immediately obvious to the social scientist.

NOTES

1 See E. M. Rodgers and R. Agarwala-Rodgers, *Communication in organizations*, New York, Free Press (1977; Russian trans. 1980).

2 Again, see Rodgers and Agarwala-Rodgers, *Communication in organizations*.

10

Defects in Economic Institutions

10.1 Economic institutions and types of economic system

This chapter is an attempt to explain the causes of stagnation in the country's scientific, technological and socio-economic development in terms of certain defects in its economic institutions.

These three kinds of development involve a number of innovative processes taking place simultaneously throughout the country's territory and economy.[1] These processes, which are closely interdependent and interconnected, are the key to development. Unless enterprises practise innovation, there will be none in the corresponding industries, or in the economy as a whole.

First of all, since the notion of an economic institution is relatively new in our country, a closer examination of this term is called for.[2]

An economic institution is a variety of social institution. If we take the definition of 'social institution'[3] as a point of departure, we may define an 'economic institution' as a system of norms of economic behaviour assigning certain roles to individuals and groups of individuals that are designed to enable them to perform certain socially significant economic functions. Examples of such functions include planning, material and technical supply, setting of prices, provision of credit etc. We may thus speak of these institutions as controlling their respective spheres of economic life. Economic institutions bring order to economic life, assuring its stability and continuity.

In performing the roles assigned to them, individuals may

display various qualities of economic behaviour. They may perform their duties (e.g. in the implementation of innovations) with varying degrees of deviation from the norm. If their performance falls short of social expectations, we may speak of a defect (malfunction) in the economic institution.

We have already pointed out that the stagnation in innovation may be traced to certain defects in the country's economic institutions. Since innovative processes embrace, and depend on, all economic institutions, we shall now look out certain of their universal traits that lead, in the final analysis, to an atrophy of innovative activity. The remainder of this chapter is an examination of the more common of them.

Economic institutions may differ broadly depending on the degree of centralization or independence of enterprises, the employees' freedom of choice of economic behaviour, the exact spread of economic roles, the lack or presence of competition etc. In other words, the economy will function through various economic institutions in which the conditions for innovation may be either good or bad. Various forms of economic system could exist within one and the same political structure, such as liberal democracy or a totalitarian regime. In view of their different characteristics, some of them may be more congenial to innovation and innovators than others. It follows that whatever makes the economy uncongenial to innovation is a defect in its economic institutions.

The exact type of economic system is determined by the sum total of its economic institutions. Two diametrically opposed types of economic system may be visualized in Russian society: the market system and the administrative system. Both are characterized by the same set of economic functions required for the survival and continuity of the national economy: material resources have to be distributed, prices set, and goods sold in any type of economy. However, these and other functions may be performed by means of various economic institutions using a variety of techniques.

What we need to examine are some inherent features of traditional Soviet economic institutions which may either hold back or speed up innovation.

The traditional Soviet economy may be roughly defined as an 'administrative economic system'.[4] We shall now examine the inherent defects (principles of organization) that hold back innovation, and the mechanisms through which they hold back change.

10.2 Principal defects in Soviet economic institutions

At present there is a crisis of management in the Russian economy. Traditional controls no longer work following Gorbachev's perestroika and the period of transition under Yeltsin, which encouraged a sense of independence, while the emergent economic controls have yet to become effective. The reason for this is the *de facto* dependence of the workforce on the administrative system. This is true of both individuals and entire enterprises.

This contradictory situation was provoked by the defects of traditional Soviet economic institutions in the new conditions of liberalization.

The non-existence of owners (as a social stratum) in the economic sense of the term

The economic role of owner would involve a certain relationship between the means of production on the one hand and individuals and groups performing an economic activity which we might call 'good husbandry' on the other. 'Good husbandry' means that the owner has full control of the means of production which he or she is using to achieve the best economic result (such as the maximization of profit). The socio-economic status of the owner may be distinguished by the generation of income, the amount of which is a function of the owner's success; it is this income, rather than a wage or a salary, which forms the owner's livelihood.

An owner cannot be appointed, although property can be given as a gift. An owner cannot be demoted by administrative decree, although it is possible to lose property as a result of bad housekeeping. Like anyone else in society, the owner strives constantly to multiply his or her wealth. What is more, he or she is interested in the long-term, as well as the short-term, acquisition of wealth. In other words, owners have long-term economic goals. This explains their interest in innovations, and why an enterprise managed by owners is impelled towards innovation. Furthermore, an owner may even form the nucleus of the innovative community which is a *sine qua non* for a favourable innovative climate.

In summary, the existence of the economic role of owner is a prerequisite for the rapid modernization of production. The lack of this role, it follows, is an impediment to innovation, because innovation can be maintained only by stable innovative communities held together by owners.[5]

Meanwhile, in the present situation of social instability, the new Russian entrepreneurs have no long-term economic goals. With no traditions or strong legal organizations which could represent their interests effectively and guarantee social security, the economic role of owner is only now being formed.

The overshadowing of the entire functioning of the economy by ministries and other government departments

Together with the enterprises under their control, the ministries formed closed administrative systems immune to any influence from the consumer.[6]

Each government department in the economic sphere was therefore a monopoly producer of some specialized item. Wielding enormous economic power, and having at their disposal vast material resources, these departments could survive and thrive without any innovations. What is more, innovation usually threatened their status, since higher efficiency would compel them to resort to temporary production cuts, less input being needed to meet unchanged demand.

As an alternative to innovation, enterprises had a choice of at least two techniques to improve their standing with superiors. First, they could increase the output of the old product. In the past economic system, gross output figures, rather than product quality, were used to evaluate enterprises. This was possible because the performance of an enterprise was assessed by its own ministry. Thus, enterprises were immune to consumer pressure, which could otherwise be a powerful stimulus for innovations. The second method enterprises could use to improve their standing with superiors was to solve their problems by such practices as doctoring accounts to conceal reserve production capacity and then later 'milking' it.

State bodies can no longer provide immunity from the market to state enterprises. In some spheres, as in public and commercial services, state enterprises are up against strong competition. But in most parts of the Russian economy (in industry, agriculture, transport services etc.) state organizations are predominant and have no real competitors yet from the private sector. State enterprises are not controlled by superior bodies or by the market. Therefore they may survive and prosper without innovations, supporting constantly declining output by permanently rising prices.

The state's paternalism towards enterprises and individual employees

This socio-economic paternalism consisted of a system of guarantees for the continued existence and maintenance of an already achieved socio-economic status. It worked by taking from the rich and giving to the poor. Under this 'egalitarian' system enterprises in dire financial straits as a result of their own ineptitude were bailed out and did not have to innovate. Infusions of material and financial resources made it unnecessary for enterprises to introduce new products and processes in order to survive. For example, instead of mechanizing a monotonous and arduous operation, the enterprise management could simply raise workers' wages and solve all its problems at one stroke: the workers were better off and there was no need to re-tool (because in the past there were virtually no financial restrictions on state enterprises). Alternatively, enterprises in trouble could get extra breaks in their dealings with suppliers, customers, superior organizations and the state itself (for example, tax rebates, reduction of production assignments, higher prices for products of poorer quality etc.).

The system of paternalism is now breaking down. The Yeltsin transition demands a refusal of paternalism. The Supreme Soviet, on the other hand, which depended strongly on the electors and some lobbies, supported social guarantees and guarantees for state enterprises. In 1992 there was a political balance between the efforts of the government and those of the Supreme Soviet: sometimes government carried out its policy, sometimes the Supreme Soviet was successful. As a result, those social groups and enterprises that were successful in gaining advantages received state support by using force (strikes, threats to bring down the government etc.). Thus there are ways of gaining help from superior bodies, but they require more effort than in previous periods.

If the non-existence of the economic role of owner is not conducive to innovation, departmentalism and socio-economic paternalism make innovation unnecessary for survival, or even for the achievement of economic goals. Rather than preparing the ground for innovation themselves, enterprises prefer to wait for someone in a position of authority to do so, and have even been known to complain when nothing happens. This procrastination is no way to speed up progress in an area where, according to R. Foster,[7] only the attacking side wins. The end result can only be economic parasitism and total defeat in the face of economic problems. This is part of the reason why 'conservative' techniques for speeding up innovation processes have failed. Such techniques could meet with success in some areas of science, technology and the socio-economic sphere, but they are incapable of generating independent innovative activity on the shop floor, without which overall progress is impossible.

The control and manipulation of all economic activity from above

In the period before perestroika all economic life was subject to centralized planning, and every enterprise had to report periodically to a superior authority. No individual or organization was independent of the state; everybody was subordinate to somebody else; everybody was given a plan assignment from above[8] and had to report periodically on its fulfilment to a superior authority.

One of the forms of such dependence was the dependence of the innovator on the bureaucrat. The innovator could not independently implement a new idea, but was obliged to make the rounds of superiors, asking them to include his or her invention in a plan for research and development, to provide a laboratory, funds, resources etc. It goes without saying that he or she was not protected by patent law, for there was none. The innovator was reduced to the role of a supplicant, and bureaucrats were free to turn down any request with complete impunity. Since innovative activities, particularly in the early stages of development, involve certain risks, and since government departments by definition were not interested in innovation, the innovator was rarely given a fair hearing. Furthermore, such dependence on the bureaucrat was likely to be a disincentive to future innovative activities.

Given this total state control, economic agents, such as factories, banks etc., could not be defined as voluntary associations of producers set up to achieve maximum efficiency through co-operative efforts. Rather, they were structures created from above to administer economic activity and to advance the interests of the command system. This explains why until recently organizations advancing the interests of ordinary people rather than of government departments were non-existent, and why those that are now appearing are facing so many difficulties.

The changes in the current situation in Russia, following perestroika and transition, are apparent rather than real. Under the command economy individuals and organizations were directly dependent upon superior bodies, whereas now economic agents are indirectly dependent upon state bodies. The main material conditions for business activity (such as land and buildings) are under the complete control of state departments. For example, if someone has the intention to establish a restaurant, he or she has to lease a building from the municipal government or the municipal legislative authority, because there is no estate market in Russia, and almost all buildings are under state control. This is one means (there are many others) whereby the dependence of the innovator upon the bureaucrat is preserved. Such dependence is indirect, but is none the less almost as strong as the old direct dependence.

Another major consequence of this total control and manipulation of the economic sphere was the virtual absence of reserve capacity and manpower. This was the result of the natural striving by the ministries to exploit production capacity and the workforce to the full. In the name of efficiency, every acre of fallow land may be ploughed up, every square foot of the shop floor stacked up with machine-tools, and almost every nursing mother put on a tractor. The end result is not greater efficiency,[9] but necrosis of production capacity. The only reserves that enterprises had were those that they had 'salted away' and were keeping secret from the superior authorities. When the latter periodically urge factories to be more enterprising, factories merely release these secret reserves.

At the same time, major technological innovations normally require additional floor space for new equipment, additional specialists and skilled workers, and additional supplies of raw materials and parts. The absence of reserves, including sources of additional financing, is a block on normal innovative activity. Innovators, managers and specialists have to substitute by drawing from their secret reserves or 'going to the bad'; the result is a low quality of innovation with a high social and economic cost.

At present state bodies have no real power to continue their struggle towards fully utilizing production capacity and the workforce in enterprises. Instead of this struggle they maximize the profit from their management of production capacity. They have enough power to put a brake on privatization and to lease state property with large profits for officials. For example, in order to lease a building for office use in the centre of Moscow, a bribe of US $10,000 is required, according to some expert estimations. In the meantime the buildings in the centre of Moscow and St Petersburg are disintegrating, but municipal officials refuse to start the process of privatizing them. We know of another example, the attempt to establish a joint venture in Novosibirsk in 1992, when the Director of State Enterprise demanded for himself 800,000 roubles from the whole rent on production building, which amounted to 1,200,000 roubles a year. Certainly the planned joint venture for the implementation of new technology in the timber industry was not established.

The departmental structure's potential for ignoring the population's needs has brought forth a self-sustained 'zero-cycle economy'. To quote Gaidar and Yaroshenko:

> If we define all activities, the hypertrophied development of which is due to the absence or weakness of public control over the movement of resources, as 'zero-cycle branches', and if we then analyse the links between them, we shall find out that they are largely self-sufficient and their *raison d'être* is to sustain each other rather than the population at large.[10]

In this situation, the economy begins to work on its own account,[11] and the goals of all economic agents become distorted: they are seeking to maximize the use of resources and to minimize social expenditure. The enterprises are no longer producing goods: they are fulfilling a plan. Whenever they can do so without actually producing goods – which is possible through a combination of departmental paternalism and easing of controls from above – they will create imaginary production figures. One can therefore visualize a 'ghost enterprise' drawing resources from centralized stocks, then simply destroying them at a minimum of cost and effort, and covering up the operation with 'genuine' reports on the fulfilment of production targets. Such a factory might also engage in bogus innovation activities entitling it to additional resources, which it could either destroy or use for starting a black-market operation.

Another possibility, besides phoney innovation, is the introduction of relatively simple new processes involving the use of huge primary resources:

> The distinctive feature of many areas in which we are leading the world is the relative simplicity of the technologies used which as often as not involve the movement of enormous amounts of earth, rock etc. . . . Chronic shortages have made material and technical supply our most difficult problem. The more complex the production links of an enterprise, the more difficult its existence.[12]

In summary, the control of economic activity from above is an obstacle to the implementation of useful innovations for which there exists a genuine demand. It has made the innovator dependent on the bureaucrat, creating the necessity for the institutionalization of innovations. It has fostered parasitic innovations which have created 'black holes' in the economy, into which huge resources are disappearing.

Too many levels in the administrative structure

The number of levels in the administrative structure makes it exceedingly difficult to manage unconventional creative activities. In the administered economy, the minimum number of levels is two, with every organization having a superior authority. In reality there may be more, with a count of five levels in the case of the Agro-Industrial Complex: enterprise (farm), district, regional and Russian Ministry of Agriculture. The introduction of an innovation in the state sector may require the go-ahead from many levels in the hierarchy, and it may be withheld by any of them. Since each level is a block to innovation, the greater the number of levels the greater the braking power of the administrative structure.

In addition, the hierarchical organization of the economic management system has a further negative effect: promising young specialists with innovation potential are all too often promoted to managerial positions. According to Kowalewski, a Polish expert on management problems, 'the hierarchical system steals promising specialists, as a result of which they can no longer be used in their professional capacity.'[13] Innovative communities consequently lose their leaders to administrative careers.

In brief, the multi-level organization of the economic management structure does not make it receptive to innovation.

Economic agents do not have to compete for custom

In the traditional Soviet administered economy, there was no economic natural selection. As a result, managers were spared many unpleasant realities: suppliers were tied to customers; new producers appeared only by sanction of a superior authority and did not drive anyone from the market, which had already been divided up; and there were no bankruptcies because most producers did not stand to lose anything of their own. For this reason, Russian captains of industry did not have to worry about the future. Neither did they need to worry about innovation, since their survival was assured.

This does not mean, however, that the administrated system was free from all competition. Firstly, government ministries and enterprises had to compete for resources (investment, labour etc.). Since resources were not allocated according to economic criteria, they were more likely to go to a unit with a higher status in the hierarchy than to one that was actually delivering the goods. As G. Popov put it: 'those boasting the greatest resources and labour inputs, even the greatest number of Party members in the workforce, have the greatest clout.'[14] It was a case of resources attracting resources. However, this type of competition was not conductive to innovation – on the contrary, the winner could manage without innovation because his or her prosperity was assured, and it was even possible to hoard resources.

Secondly, managers had to compete for higher status in the administrative hierarchy. In the command economy, both consumer goods and production resources were distributed in accordance with a given official's status. Other conditions being equal, the higher the status, the greater the entitlement to resources, and, consequently, the brighter the prospects of the enterprise and its workforce. However, once again this form of competition did not stimulate innovation (with the possible exception of prestigious innovation projects). It was rather an obstacle to innovation, since the race was judged not by the consumer interested in a better product, but by the superior authority searching for loyal and dependable employees.

Finally, consumers had to compete for supplies against a background of chronic shortages. Far from promoting innovation, this type of competition tended to turn consumers against it because of the possibility that it might lead to a fall-off in production during the development phase.

Therefore, these three types of competition bred anarchic attitudes which were further aggravated by a phenomenon that we may describe as 'planned anarchy'. It was not 'planned' in the sense of being part of any plan, but was, in effect, the result of too much organization. It was the inevitable product of an unbalanced economy and the direct operation of the centralized planning mechanism. Secondary anarchy (i.e. non-fulfilment of plans, unmanageable enterprises, bloated administrative staffs, red tape etc.) brought about anarchy of the third order – doctoring of statistics, avoidance of reality by the upper echelons of command, the secret classification of economic data, etc.[15]

The result of all this was anarchy on a scale comparable to, and even greater than, 'production anarchy' under capitalism. For example, the factory manager was never sure of his or her planned share of resources (the ministry might re-allocate them to an enterprise standing higher on the list of priorities, or the supplier might simply fail to deliver them on time). The workforce had no way of knowing whether they would still have the same manager in a year's time or whether he or she would be promoted to a post at the ministry. Consumers standing in a queue did not know if there would be enough for everybody. Lack of stable horizontal links between enterprises and other economic agents, combined with the constant possibility of outside interference, made economic life uncertain in the extreme. Any initiative, particularly unconventional initiative of the type usually involved in innovation, involved enormous social expenditure: people had to compensate for the imperfections of the system by sheer hard work.

This state of affairs was hardly conducive to long-term motivation for production modernization and innovation in general. Lack of competition for custom, along with built-in 'planned anarchy', combined to bring about numerous imbalances in the economy: shortages in some sectors accompanied by overproduction in others. Because of these imbalances, the economy became extremely unstable and the economic links were severely obstructed, which, in turn, made innovation very difficult because any production reorganization involved the prompt creation of numerous new economic links. In a centrally planned, anarchy-ridden economy, this involved huge social expenditure, borne by everyone, from the shop-floor worker to the minister.

In conclusion, lack of competition for custom was not conducive to innovation in a command economy, while the types of competition that did exist were, in effect, obstacles to innovation.

At present there is no economic natural selection in the Russian economy, as there was in the traditional Soviet command economy. There is no longer an institution of bankruptcy; although the appropriate law has been passed it is not yet in operation and the Russian Central Bank (RCB) gives favourable credit terms to enterprises in trouble. State enterprises compete not for material resources but for financial subsidies distributed by the government and the RCB. The decay of the USSR and economic transition have resulted in unstable economic ties between enterprises – more so than in the pre-perestroika period. Therefore innovations in the state sector are fewer than they were in that period.

Private enterprises are more determined to innovate than state ones. But the most part of business energy among Russian entrepreneurs is expended on the struggle for survival and for primary accumulation of capital. Therefore, in spite of their large innovation potential, private enterprises do not innovate either.

The end result of the defects of economic institutions that we have considered is that, just as there were no forces in the traditional

Soviet economy, so there are none in the new Russian economy that can irresistibly impel enterprises towards innovation.

10.3 An ownerless economy and motives for innovative behaviour

Since problems of ownership play a special role in slowing down innovation, a closer examination is called for.

Ownership may be defined as one form of appropriation of the means of production by an economic agent (an individual or social group that make decisions important from the standpoint of economic development), combining their use, possession and disposal.[16] Ownership is a social relationship enabling the owner to exercise maximum control over the means of production. The essence of this relationship is that other agents recognize this right of the owner, and consider the means of production to be his or her property. The exercise of the right of ownership (the right to manipulate the means of production) means that the owner may undertake production or may lease, sell, give or bequeath the means of production.

The question arises whether this would be possible if the number of agents disposing of the means of production were confined to only one. In this case, would the relations of ownership be equivalent to a property relationship with all the accompanying motives including what we referred to as 'good husbandry'? In our view, the answer must be negative, because normal social relations involve a multitude of agents. It is only in these conditions that relationships of ownership can emerge, along with the economic institutions necessary to ensure their continuity. There are at least four types of such institutions:

1 Institutions for the protection of ownership providing legal protection of property and the right to own property against encroachments by non-owners.
2 Institutions enabling the exercise of property rights by owners as the organizers of the production process (the hiring of labour, the setting up of requisite organizations, the sale of finished products, the extraction of income (profit) etc.).
3 Institutions enabling (business) transactions involving property outside the production process (e.g. buying and selling of the means of production, leasing, donation etc.).
4 Institutions governing the inheritance of property.

With the help of these institutions, owners of the means of production can perform their social role, namely 'good husbandry', designed to multiply wealth (property). They can also introduce innovations without fear of being dispossessed, this security being guaranteed by ownership protection institutions.

These institutions were non-existent in the pre-perestroika Soviet economy. The official view was that the Soviet economy was based on ownership by all the people, the implication being that there was but one economic agent – the whole of Soviet society. But what sort of ownership relationship could this unique economic agent enter into, and with whom? And even this non-relationship would have to be regulated by some sort of ownership protection institution, in this case to protect the owner against pilferers and even big-time embezzlers who, logically, would have done nothing more but exercise their right of ownership!

In short, what is the use of a definition of ownership which does not contain a definition of an owner? It should be obvious that in this sense, society as a whole cannot be the owner of the means of production.

Can it be argued instead that the means of production were owned jointly by the state and its bureaucracy? The answer again is negative, because such 'owners' could be dispossessed at any moment for reasons that had absolutely no bearing on the way in which they had exercised their right of ownership. What is more, their income was in no way pegged to this exercise: they were paid a salary and entitled to fringe benefits such as the use of a special state store, an exclusive clinic etc. As soon as they were dismissed, they lost these extra benefits, which were thus part of their pay as hired workers rather than income derived from property. And, of course, there was no question of bureaucrats selling or bequeathing a plant or a factory.

Politicians do not qualify as owners for the same reasons as government employees do not.

Admittedly, officials and workers alike dispose of the means of production to some extent. But to own something and to dispose of it are two different economic roles. The role of administrator (disposer) is a very common one in Russia. So common in fact that Shmelev felt justified in stating:

> the view that the economy can and must be administered by fiat has become widespread; there is an almost religious belief in the power of the organization, accompanied by an inability

> and even refusal to see that coercion, pressure, rhetoric and prodding can achieve little in the economy.[17]

The 'administrative-command economy' (the term was coined by Shmelev) is a complex of economic institutions created to perform this function. Its fundamental distinction from the role of owner is that an administrator lacks long-term economic motivation because he or she may lose their job at any time. (This does not mean, however, that the administrators are necessarily bad workers, only that their motives are different from those of an owner.)

Before perestroika there existed a category of people – operators of 'underground' factories or restaurants and shops which nominally belonged to the state – who were rather closer to our definition of owners. We may even speak of the existence of a system of criminal ownership protected by its own institutions: corrupt government officials, Party workers, and law enforcement officers, with their own suppliers and retail outlets, illegal sources of income etc. However, black marketeers also lack sufficient long-term economic motivation, because they are not recognized as owners by society at large. They might better be termed 'shadow owners' in a 'shadow economy'.

Well-known economic innovations implemented by Gorbachev and Yeltsin's teams (such as the laws on private property instituted in 1988), started to change this situation. These economic innovations created the prerequisites for the institutionalization of the economic role of owner and the 'good husbandry' pattern of economic behaviour. However, the scale of these economic innovations is not yet sufficient for shaping stable stereotypes of such behaviour, let alone changing the social atmosphere. The innovative climate in the Russian economy has not been sufficiently affected by them.

Since there is no stratum of owners in the present Russian economy, the economic agents do not consider the means of production as their property, and therefore lack direct, long-term motivation to multiply this wealth. (There may be indirect incentives, but these are clearly insufficient to shape and support such motivation.) This means that innovators, as non-owners, tend not to care about the economic effect of an innovation because it only multiplies wealth that does not belong to them. It is here that what remains of the command system, existing in the state sector, steps in and compels them to innovate. Their natural reaction is to do so with a minimum of effort, since innovative activities, as we have seen, demand considerable social expenditure.

To the best of our knowledge, the concept of social expenditure has not been used in the Russian, any more than it was by the Soviet, social sciences, it being understood, apparently, that economic inputs alone produce the desired economic and social effects. The Soviet literature on economics available to us offers an analysis of economic inputs and results, as well as social results,[18] but no analysis of social expenditure. This approach is apparently based on the prejudiced view (not explicitly formulated by the authors) that the only costs involved in innovation are money, metal, electricity and other material resources, plus labour inputs calculated on the basis of a worker of average skill. According to this philosophy, an innovator is just another worker. This is to ignore the unconventional and creative nature of the contribution made by an innovator, which must be taken into account and remunerated.

In fact, it is impossible directly to compute an innovator's social expenditure. A more or less adequate reflection of his or her contribution is possible, in our view, only through a market of innovations. For such a market to appear, many changes will first be necessary, such as the setting up of institutions for the protection of intellectual property and patent law. Appropriate legislation has been passed, but there are no real conditions in Russia to carry it out and to protect the interests of innovator and inventor. Now in Russia the collection of taxes in the state system operates poorly. The state cannot effect the collection of the inventor's share of profits received by users of his or her invention.

Failure to take account of the workforce's striving to minimize their social expenditure has prevented Soviet economists from coming up with sufficiently convincing and full explanations, not only for the crawling pace of innovation, but for such economic phenomena as 'working to orders', when employees (including ranking officials) carry out orders that they know to be wrong or harmful without even trying to take up the matter with their superiors. It is our contention that this phenomenon is so widespread in non-market economies because a large proportion of the population are consciously weighing up the social expenditure of their economic behaviour with a view to keeping it to a minimum.

In a command economy, the exact amount of managerial power depends on the level a person occupies in the administrative hierarchy. The higher the post, the greater the power and responsibility. This would seem to imply that, broadly speaking, the striving to minimize effort (social expenditure) should be less, the higher the status of the person in the hierarchy.

10.4 The command economy in action: simulating the market and devising a strategy of development for the enterprise

We have already shown that the command economy performs the same functions as the market: it distributes resources and fixes prices. But the techniques used are poles apart.

In a market economy all indicators, such as prices, wages etc., are the result of the voluntary interaction of independent owner-agents, who compete for custom and create new markets to maximize their wealth. A system like this makes for great flexibility, diversity and differentiation of economic norms. The system therefore encourages individual enterprise and innovation, while companies are stimulated to adopt innovative strategies.

In a command economy the situation is very different. The key economic indicators are computed by bureaucrats at ministries, government departments, state committees, and other agencies. G. Popov recalls that:

> I had a feeling that the determination of an economic indicator was a very complex business, but I was proved wrong by the officials at Gosplan, the Ministry of Finance, other central economic agencies and all the ministries. They used a very simple procedure: they divided the tax and other deductions operative under the current five-year plan by the amount of planned profit, and the product was the desired indicator.[19]

It is important to point out that, even if a more complex computational procedure had been used in Popov's example, this would in no way have changed its bureaucratic nature. At first sight, these computational procedures (which, incidentally, are always based on the 'scientific method' currently in vogue) seem to be devoid of any economic or social content. A bureaucrat can easily come up with a computational technique which supplies the right answers for the powers that be, and should the results be at variance with the 'national economic interest' they can easily be adjusted. As Popov put it:

> The new economic mechanism provides for taxation of a *khozraschet* [cost-accounting] unit in favour of the ministry. One wonders what the amount of taxation should be: one per cent of the profit, or maybe ten or forty? Is ten per cent enough or too much?[20]

There are no answers to questions like this one, because the indicator is not based on any objective criterion; the ministry will exercise its seigneurial right and take as much as it needs.

In these conditions, economic indicators may have very little to do with economic expediency or common sense. Prices may be fixed at a level which does not cover costs, or the profit tax may be set at 80–90%. Even generalized indicators of economic development are not trustworthy. According to Seliunin and Khanin, who used a number of alternative computational techniques, the USSR's national income went up by a factor of six or seven between 1928 and 1985, rather than by the factor of 86 recorded by the official statistics.[21]

On closer examination, however, it becomes clear that economic indicators and the procedures of their computation are far from arbitrary. There is an iron logic here, which is the product of a bureaucratic game played according to its own rules with total disregard for the interests of actual producers. The market is simulated with the help of diverse bureaucratic procedures: conferences, board meetings, memoranda and the like. On this pseudo-market, the ministries compete for resources. The higher the social status of a ministry, the more resources it can wheedle out of the central budget, the higher the prices it is allowed to set and the lower its production target.

The enterprises haggle and bargain with their ministries over output targets, indicators and resources. In fact, according to Aven and Shironin, 'The "command economy" is gradually being displaced by a "bargaining economy" in which the relationship between lower and upper echelons is not one of subordination but one of compact or exchange.'[22] The number of resources and concessions an enterprise receives depends entirely on how much 'clout' it carries.

As in a market economy, here, too, according to Foster, 'the attacking side wins',[23] but the nature of the attacks is different. Whereas in a market economy success is a function of the speed of innovation, in a command economy it depends on one's ability to influence the allocation of resources and the setting of economic indicators. Innovators obviously do not fall into that category. On the contrary, their activities may result in temporary setbacks for their factories and, as a consequence, in their falling out of favour with the superior authorities allocating the resources and setting the indicators. As a result, their enterprise may lose its competitiveness on the pseudo-market.

One status-boosting technique is 'conspicuous innovation' (by analogy with Veblen's theory of 'conspicuous consumption').[24] Its aim is to demonstrate an organization's production potential, and examples include numerous 'projects of the century' whose real value turned out to be nil, or even worse.[25]

A *sine qua non* in any conspicuous innovation is a great deal of publicity in the local and national media and blanket exposure for people with a success story at all sorts of conferences, workshops, and the like. Without this there would be no demonstration effect and the innovation would not lead to promotion, or increase the organization's standing in the struggle for resources.

The command economy is now disintegrating in Russia. During this process the state tries to maintain control of the economy. Neither the government, nor the legislative bodies, nor any ministry has enough power to establish the economic indicators for enterprises. Superior bodies try to establish key financial parameters and international economic relations, as in states under capitalism. But at the moment the state in Russia has no power for this, because of the destruction of the old finance system and the decay of the USSR, provoked by uncontrolled frontiers with the former Soviet republics.

NOTES

1 This definition has been suggested by A. G. Kruglikov, 'The innovative conception of scientific and technical progress', *The structure of the innovative process*, Moscow, 1981.

2 In his study of economic crime, Yakovlev writes: 'This sociological study of problems involved in the combating of economic crime is based on a view of the economy as primarily one of the most important social institutions in the wider socio-political structure of society.' See A. M. Yakovlev, *The sociology of economic crime*, Moscow, Nauka (1988), 9. What makes Yakovlev's analysis especially valuable is that it is one of the first attempts in Soviet social science to apply the category of social institution to an examination of economic phenomena. What it lacks, however, is the representation of the economy as a system of economic institutions controlling economic development.

3 Among the great many definitions of 'social institution', Boskov offers the following: 'a cluster of interdependent social roles relating to a biological and/or social function'. See A. Boskoff, 'Modern sociological theory', in H. Becker and A. Boskoff (eds), *Modern Sociological Theory in Continuity and Change*. New York: Dryden Press (1957; Russian trans. 1961), 315. Like other definitions, this is adapted to the exigencies of the particular piece of research, and emphasizes one aspect of social institutions.

4 The term 'administrative economic system' is a derivation of the notion of 'administrative system' introduced by Popov. See G. K. Popov, 'From an economist's point of view', *Nauka i zhizn*, iv (1987).

5 The discussion of this highly controversial problem of ownership will be resumed in subsequent chapters of this book.

6 According to Rassokhin, the author of an insightful analysis of 'the phenomenon of ministerial self-interest', closed administrative economic systems are organized around a government department which totally controls the enterprises subordinate to it, but which also shares some common interests with them. See V. P. Rassokhin, *Mechanism for the implementation of scientific advances: politics, administration and law*, Moscow, Nauka (1985), 51–2.

7 R. Foster, *Innovation: the attacker's advantage*, New York, Summit Books (1986).

8 This may be given different names (production targets, state orders etc.). The important thing is that it has the force of law.

9 According to Popov and Shmelev: 'The 90% utilization of capacity mentioned in official statistics is a fiction. It is nowhere near the real figure of idle capacity. The utilization rate of equipment in industry seldom rises above 0.7, while the shift coefficient has dropped from 1.54 in 1960 to 1.35 in 1985. In engineering we have only 63 machinists for every 100 machine tools. In industry as a whole the ratio is even less.' See V. Popov and N. Shmelev, 'The anatomy of deficit', *Znamya*, v (1988), 169.

10 E. Gaidar and V. Yaroshenko, 'Towards an analysis of how ministries expand', *Kommunist*, v (1988), 77.

11 As Seliunin has it: 'To an ever greater extent, the economy is working solely for itself and not for the individual. Its present structure leads it to implacably reproduce a balance between capital and consumer goods that is quite unacceptable for peacetime conditions.' See V. Seliunin, 'A major reform or the bureaucracy's riposte?', *Znamya*, vii (1988), 188.

12 Gaidar and Yaroshenko, *Towards an analysis*, 76.

13 S. Kowalewski, 'Nauka o administovaniu', in *Ksiaszka i Wiedza*, Warsaw (1975; Russian trans. 1979).

14 G. Popov, 'Aims and machinery', *Znamya*, vii (1988), 171.

15 B. Semenov (pseud, B. Pinsker), 'Plan and spontaneity', *Novy mir*, xii (1987), 257.

16 This definition of ownership is taken from E. G. Yasin, 'Public property, economic incentives and cost accounting', *EKO*, xii (1984).

17 N. Shmelev, 'Loans and debts', *Novy mir*, vi (1987), 144.

18 For example, see Vilensky, H. A. ed. *Economic Evaluation of the Social Results of Implementing New Equipment*. Kiev: Naukova Dumka (1981).

19 Popov, 'Aims and machinery', 169.

20 Popov, 'Aims and machinery', 169.

21 V. Seliunin and G. Khanin, 'Deceitful figures', *Novy mir*, ii (1987).

22 P. A. Aven and V. M. Shironin, 'Management hierarchies and the distribution of resources', in *The personnel of the Agro-Industrial Complex within the system of managerial relations*, Barnaul (1987), 38.

23 See R. Foster, *Innovation.*

24 See T. Veblen, *The theory of the leisure class*, New York, Vanguard Press (1927; Russian trans. 1984).

25 The other side of this gigantomania is the hostility towards useful but small-scale innovations such as metallurgical mini-plants. When their efficiency and usefulness was proved elsewhere in the world, the USSR also began building them. Recent comment from the ministry of the metallurgical industry: 'We've had enough of these mini-plants with their mini-usefulness and maxi-headaches. Let somebody else build them.' See E. Lysaya, 'Mini-factories', *EKO*, x (1987), 116.

11

Political Institutions and Stagnation in Innovative Processes

11.1 The chain reaction of alienation

The impact of political factors on economic development has always been a favourite theme with Soviet academics. However, the period after 1985 has introduced significant adjustments to the formulation and analysis of this traditional subject.

Until recently, the problem had been formulated and analysed in the context of the need to elaborate and help to implement some of the directives issued by the Party and government. It was assumed that these directives must be implemented at all costs, in the most efficient manner. A directive could not be discussed, although it could be explained to the masses; neither could it be analysed, criticized, disagreed with or improved upon. Naturally, such directives were perceived by the population as commandments issued by an all-powerful force that demanded absolute submission.

It is true that occasionally discussions did take place, but their outcome was always a foregone conclusion. Criticism was also allowed – but only by specially appointed people in specially allocated places for strictly limited periods of time. In order to prevent accusations of electoral fraud, turnouts at elections had to be slightly less than 100% and at least one vote always had to be against the directive. The absence of open political life, together with indoctrination and manipulation of public opinion, made it easier to control society as a whole and the economy in particular. This system was immune to surprises or opposition or grass-roots activity (for what's the use of thinking and exerting oneself if one cannot change anything?). To put it differently, when the rulers are not lavish in their dialogue with the ruled, the latter distance themselves from the affairs of society and seek refuge in private life.

This sentiment is a fertile soil for apathy in the public sector and the growth of the shadow economy, black marketeering and various forms of aberrant economic behaviour. In these conditions, the economy becomes practically unmanageable and reaches a point when even an 'excellent directive' (the latest panacea for all economic ills) fails to be implemented. Of course, no one can point the finger and shout sabotage; everybody is busy doing something, but the overall result is that nothing gets done. The dismayed authorities comment that they have excellent laws and decrees which they cannot get implemented. The cure-all solution that the government resorts to is that everything must be done to carry out its directives. This approach leads to ever more directives and ever growing pressure (from above) in order to ensure their implementation. The end result is even greater alienation.

What follows is a chain reaction of alienation, and the relationship between the rulers and the ruled becomes increasingly rigid and formalized. The rulers produce ever more complex and intricate bureaucratic regulations and rules, but the mainstream of economic life increasingly by-passes official channels of administration and no number of bureaucratic dams can stop it. Shadow economic management structures begin to appear, governed by their own laws (as yet little studied),[1] and form a symbiosis with the official management structure, which becomes only the tip of the iceberg of the whole economic management system. These shadow structures spawn a number of economic institutions: criminal property ownership, relations of 'mutual exchange' etc., which regulate the economic activities of the population. These institutions have made extensive inroads into the country's economic organism, transforming the life of entire regions and economic sectors and industries, and even subordinating the official economy (examples include the Rashidov and Adylov Cotton scandals in Uzbekistan, the fish scam in the RSFSR and, more recently, a scandal involving phoney banking documents totalling more than 10 billion roubles).

These unofficial structures affect innovative processes in a variety of ways, but the overall effect is negative. On the one hand, they provide more resources for innovation and help by-pass obsolete instructions. For example, our sociological study carried out in a rural area in Siberia in 1983 revealed a mechanism which political institutions were using to neutralize opposition to innovating activities and provide unofficial protection to innovations in breach of obsolete official instructions.[2] The essence of this mechanism is that Party organizations use their political influence to overrule the opposition of economic organizations to innovations (some unofficial channels are also used).

On the whole, though, the shadow economy slows down innovation because it weakens the link between economic performance on the one hand, and incentives and material and technical supply on the other. For example, according to Kordonsky:

> New machinery and equipment are supplied, not to the foremost, highly efficient enterprises and skilled workers, but to unskilled labour and backward enterprises. In this way, the relations of mutual exchange are playing the role of 'equalizer' between social groups and economic units.[3]

The shadow administration is thus making it possible for backward enterprises to do without innovations and at the same time is making it difficult for progressive enterprises to modernize.

The chain reaction of alienation of people from the political authorities and social production is manifesting itself in social apathy and is a major component of the mechanism slowing down social progress. All new attempts by politicians to galvanize the population into more efficient work by issuing new decisions and decrees lead only to even greater apathy and the growth of the shadow economy.

This negative feedback is a natural consequence of the political system created by Stalin and his associates; the system that Khrushchev tried partly to dismantle, Brezhnev did everything to preserve. The evolutionary destruction was carried out by Gorbachev; Yeltsin broke up the Soviet Union and tried to establish the new democratic system. The system used and uses political methods of economic management dating from the time of 'war communism'. Seliunin writes:

> In 1929 the apparat put the squeeze on all forms of private entrepreneurship. Private businesses were denied bank credits, strangled with too much taxation, and charged exorbitant tariffs for transportation. The authorities nationalized or simply closed down private flour mills and terminated many leases of state-owned enterprises. In what amounted to a

revival of 'war communism', a series of energetic measures destroyed the commodity model in state industry.[4]

In such a system, in which, according to Stalin, all other organizations are but the Party's 'driving belts', the growing apathy and alienation of the masses is bound to lead to a crisis, as was the case at the time of 'war communism'. The causes of the latter were analysed by Lenin when he wrote in 1920:

> policies at the top were no longer in touch with the needs of the masses. Economic crises due to political causes ought to be resolved by political measures.[5]

Two groups of such political measures stand out. An example of the first is NEP, the New Economic Policy, which was designed to stimulate the economic activity of the population. The other is repression designed to ensure hard work and discipline. This was the course taken by Stalin's political system, which in the 1930s enacted a number of pieces of repressive labour legislation.

The 1927–8 grain procurement crisis is a good example of an economic crisis provoked by political factors. It was described by Stalin in the following terms:

> By January 1928 we had had a most severe crisis in grain procurement. Whereas by January 1927 we had succeeded in procuring 428 million poods of grain, by January 1928 grain procurement had hardly reached 300 million poods.[6]

What makes this crisis interesting for a scholar is that its liquidation was a major step towards the abolition of NEP and the destruction of market institutions in the USSR.

The crisis broke out against the background of a successful procurement campaign in the preceding year, when the volume of marketable grain had grown considerably. According to an assessment by A. Mikoyan, who was then People's Commissar for Commerce and directly involved in the supervision of the grain procurement campaign, the grain year of 1926–7 had been favourable on the whole: 'The grain procurement plan was for 675 million poods and we have actually procured 643 million, i.e. 95%.[7] The consumption of bread in town and country increased. So did grain exports – by almost 100 million roubles.'[8]

The immediate cause of the crisis was the peasant's refusal to sell grain to the state. This was due to relatively low procurement prices for grain, pegged at 40–50% and more below market prices.

Peasants began holding back grain in a bid for higher prices. Stalin blamed this on the kulaks, but added that their stocks of grain were not the biggest in the country, stating that peasants of average means owned most of the grain. Was Stalin right to blame this situation on the class enemy, or was it a product of incompetent political interference in the operation of the market mechanism?

In our view, the latter is true, as is further illustrated by the example of summer vetch, a crop grown by poor and medium peasants more than by kulaks. As the agronomist V. I. Frolov, a specialist with the People's Commissariat for Agriculture, pointed out in 1927:

> the indifferent and undifferentiated treatment of vetch as a grain crop rather than a seed material, along with uniformly low fixed prices, has done a great deal of harm. A more balanced approach to procurement, accompanied by the setting of stable or differentiated prices pegged to different uses of vetch, could have prevented last year's vetch shortage. What is more, we should not even have set a stable price for seed vetch. If we had procured only quality vetch, we would have had the necessary amount of seed material and built up considerable stocks of feed vetch for export. It's time we stopped treating seed vetch and feed vetch as one undifferentiated secondary crop. In view of its great importance as seed material, it must be excluded from the list of commodities on which fixed prices are set.[9]

Towards the end of the 1920s, state organizations accounted for 80% of industrial manufactures sold in the countryside and 90% of agricultural produce procured in this sector. While grain was bought at fixed procurement prices, prices of manufactures were steadily growing. The supply of the rural population with industrial manufactures was poor, owing to red-tape and sluggishness of supply organizations. In an article entitled 'Where are the sources of goods shortages in our co-operative?', giving a foretaste of hundreds and even thousands of similar situations in the future, E. Kosyakin, a peasant from the Ryazan *gubernia*, wrote:

> The real cause of the goods shortage at the moment is the reduction of the net supply of goods to our area . . . Although the record of several preceding years shows that 4843 roubles-worth of goods were supplied to our area, last May we received only 1988 roubles-worth of products . . . Even

herring is becoming scarce ... You can hardly claim, Comrade Kutuzov,[10] that our peasants are hoarding herring in case of war. Such items as spades, axes, roofing iron, window glass, soap, flour and hardware, so badly needed by peasant households, are also unavailable at our co-operative and Raysoyuz stores. While our peasants are clamouring for these commodities, according to the *Krest'yanskaya gazeta*, they are stocked in warehouses in Moscow and other industrial centres, and there are no plans to sell them to the rural areas that badly need them ... Our co-operative and all the peasants would like these goods to be supplied on a monthly basis strictly in accordance with our purchasing power.'[11]

Comrade Kutuzov's answer to peasant Kosyakin is also a prototype of thousands of similar replies in the years to come:[12]

As for who is responsible, I beg to disagree. The comrades are unanimous that it is the Centre that is to blame. Indeed, what a ludicrous idea that the Centre can exercise total control of the supply of goods to all the villages, towns and settlements. This is bureaucratic nonsense. Even *gubernia* authorities will be unable to do so. It is only the population itself that can supply itself with goods. This is not so difficult after all. The board of a consumer co-operative or a credit society *must* know the exact amount of salt, sugar, axes, spades, glass and other commodities that its members will need, say, for half a year in advance.[13] ... In drawing up its request the co-operative must, of course, base it on available funds, otherwise it will be just a myth. Subsequently it must obtain from the local co-operative alliance or its state supply organization a *commitment* to fill the order ... If wholesale warehouses refuse to accept the request or fail to fulfil their commitment you must make a fuss, call them to account at official meetings, bombard the local trade authorities and newspapers with complaints and so on ... In response to customer pressure, state-run wholesale trading organizations will put pressure to bear on the Centre, stocks in factory and syndicate warehouses will be discovered and finally reach the buyers, fewer goods will be sent to wrong addresses and the machine will be running smoothly. This procedure for *advance orders* has already been discussed at the Tsentrosoyuz Congress and by the government; it is now considered to be the best means of revitalizing trade and eliminating all of its

> shortcomings. *This is the only procedure* [author's italics] that can enable factories and plants to know what goods are in demand, and teach the population to take care of themselves.[14]

This policy led to high prices of agricultural produce in the open market and shortages that primarily hit the poorest rural strata and made their economic recovery more difficult.[15] The peasantry, now standing firmly on their feet and still to be instructed by Comrade Stalin that the public interest comes before private concerns, reacted in a natural and rational economic manner by withholding grain. This phenomenon increased in size as the countryside grew richer and acquired a taste for economic independence which enabled it to enter into an equal dialogue with the state procurement agencies competing for agricultural products.

The political institutions countered this market situation, which they themselves had largely provoked, by sequestering surplus grain. The Central Committee issued two directives on grain procurement in late 1927, and a third in early 1928 that was 'unlike all others in its tone and demands':

> The directive ends with a threat addressed to heads of Party organizations should they fail to effect a radical improvement in grain procurement within a short period of time.[16]

Special official representatives were sent out, with Stalin himself going to Siberia. They relied heavily on Article 107 of the RSFSR Criminal Code enacted by the VTsIK in 1926 but rarely used in the preceding period.[17] It provided for sequestration of 'surplus' grain from peasants and the distribution of 25% of this amount among poor peasants and the poorer peasants of average means. There was provision for use of military force and other repressive measures. As a result, grain procurement increased somewhat but stopped short of the previous year's level. Grain exports dropped. But the most important effect of these measures was that they served as a disincentive for peasants to increase production and undermined their trust in the economic policy of the Soviet administration. Such attitudes made more repression and a further decline in economic activity inevitable.

This repressive policy could not fail to bring about the destruction of market institutions in the USSR. The first to go were bankers, merchants, entrepreneurs of all sizes, and other independent economic agents. They were followed by institutions: joint-stock companies, brokerage firms and so on. The entire market economic culture was destroyed as a result. It was replaced by the economic culture of the administered system with its own norms and stereotypes. The stereotype of enterprising behaviour disappeared, and in the new economic culture those who had grievances were expected to complain to the competent authorities.[18] This new economic culture would block many subsequent attempts at reforming the economic management system.

Khrushchev and his associates tried to carry out reforms designed to rouse the population from its state of apathy. As Valovoi put it: 'Khrushchev, in fact, was the first to appreciate the need for urgent societal change and personally led the process of reform.'[19] However, the reforms did not prove far-reaching and consistent enough, and as a consequence they could not take root in the inhospitable soil of the administered economy, the more so as in many respects they were nothing more than 'economic appeals followed by . . . administrative reorganizations and excesses'.[20] The Brezhnev era was characterized by the search for compromise between reforms and repression. At the beginning there were more reforms; towards the end there was more repression (against dissidents, entrepreneurial directors of state enterprises etc.). The outcome was widespread apathy, the alienation of the population from the fruits of their labour, and economic stagnation.

The situation began changing and the political scene began to come alive only with perestroika. The new situation enabled the academic world and the media to take a fresh look at the link between politics and economics, the two most important social institutions, a look that involved detailed analysis of specific actions.

The experience of transition after Gorbachev shows that the new systems that are forming are inheriting in many respects the old link between politics and economics. The social basis of transition integrates the large army of the old bureaucrats, combined with the less active group reformers. The situation is not so bad because social stability in the transitional period is preserved by combining old methods of regulating with new purposes. But these old methods encourage apathy in the population, prompting social groups and enterprises to look to central bodies to decide their problems. The attempt to liberalize the international economic activity of state enterprises at the beginning of 1992 was an example of the old link between politics and economics in new conditions. This attempt provoked the export from Russia of a flood of raw materials. Then government tried to limit the international activity of enterprises by supporting an embargo on the export of some raw materials, introducing a complex bureaucratic order for giving out licences etc. And now there has appeared a large black market for raw materials exported via the new Baltic and other new states.

Since the old system is going to be very difficult to uproot, research into the impact of politics on economics (innovative processes included) should include the study of the economic agents that were dominated and shaped by the preceding period of stagnation. This is all the more necessary if we are to understand the political causes of stagnation in these processes.

11.2 The tandem of politician and administrator

Different economic systems are dominated by different economic agents. They are dominated by them in the sense that the agents take the main economic decisions, including those affecting the organization of economic institutions: decisions to change the degree of centralization, to encourage or discourage competition, to increase or reduce the number of levels in the management hierarchy, to facilitate or hinder the creation of economic organizations at the grass-roots level etc. In short, economic agents shape the economic system in their own image. (For example, driven by the profit motive, owners of the means of production set up market mechanisms that enable them to form joint-stock companies and to trade shares etc.) The traditional command economy is dominated not by property owners, but by other economic agents: administrators and politicians. These deserve closer examination because they dominate all spheres of life, including innovation.

Administrators are responsible for current management, planning, material and technical supply, incentives etc. They are usually appointed by a superior authority, although of late some of them have been elected by work collectives. Their main function is to carry out orders from superior agencies to the letter, strictly observing existing rules and regulations. Their *raison d'être* is to not be demoted and, if possible, to be promoted. They derive their income not from property ownership, but are in effect salaried civil servants whose remuneration is not determined by the 'quantity and quality of their labour', nor by the economic performance of the organizations that they manage, but by their post and rank.

The administrators are not integrated in a stratum but distributed between several groups. They occupy different posts, such as director of an enterprise or head of a sector in any ministry.

In making a decision, the administrator is primarily motivated by its impact on his or her career. Administrators have a group ethic which is the expression of their collective view of what makes a good administrator. According to this standard, the main characteristics of a good administrator are the ability to carry out orders and instructions to the letter, a reluctance to take risks, and unswerving loyalty to superiors. None of these require high professional qualifications or a great deal of initiative.

Politicians are responsible for strategic decisions. Unlike administrators, most politicians are elected. Their activity is more creative, less standardized and involves much greater responsibility. While politicians are always in the limelight, administrators normally operate behind the scenes. Politicians are motivated by the desire to amass power: it is power that makes a successful politician.

In pre-perestroika Soviet society some minor high officials (Secretaries of the Central Committee of CPSU, Head of the Supreme Soviet, Head of the KGB etc.) were politicians. After 1985 many were brought down in semi-free elections and became politicians at local and national levels. This group includes, for example, regional Soviet and Supreme Soviet people's deputies, leaders of some new political parties, leaders of social movements etc.

In decision-making the politician is primarily motivated by its impact on his or her influence. Decisions that threaten to reduce a politician's influence are rejected. Fringe benefits and other creature comforts available to a politician usually depend on post and power, (although the relationship between the two is not necessarily direct). A successful politician must be able to take advantage of the latest developments in the situation, and to grab every opportunity to enhance his or her influence. For this it is less important to be an expert in an area of science or technology (such as economic problems) than to be a judge of human nature and to know how to win supporters, particularly among people who might be of use.

A politician's influence is a function of the number and social status of his or her supporters. The greater the number of supporters, and the higher their social status, the greater a politician's influence and power. Successful politicians must also be able to use other people to achieve their ends and to put forward resounding slogans in order to mobilize people and thereby enhance their own standing. In an extreme case a politician is an adventurer capable of running great risks in order to increase his or her power. Another characteristic of a politician is the ability to sacrifice conventional morality to self-proclaimed goals.

In brief, a politician is a fighter for expanding his or her own influence, believing that the end justifies the means and that 'those who are not with us are against us'. In pursuing objectives, he or she may act in concert with those working towards useful social goals, or may be in conflict with them. For example, in order to achieve certain political goals, Lenin introduced NEP, while Stalin abolished it to attain radically different political goals.

The tandem of politician and administrator in the economy operates as a joint project to achieve the goals set by politicians. These goals formulated in the shape of political slogans may be strategic, like collectivization, industrialization, creation of the market economy etc., or they may be shorter-term aims such as the fulfilment of production plans, the successful completion of a sowing campaign, the timely repair of agricultural machinery, prevention of a miners' strike etc. (Innovations, both technical and socio-economic, were once prominent among these goals.) The salient feature is their transitory nature: old slogans are constantly being replaced by new ones. Some old slogans may even be replaced by new ones before the former are implemented. For example, the slogan 'For efficiency and quality', launched during the Brezhnev era, had to be abandoned because the necessary economic mechanism was not installed. One of the principal functions of such slogans-cum-goals, is to give an identity to a politician or a group of politicians proclaiming them. On the one hand, these slogans must reflect some pressing economic need, and on the other they must appeal to some 'higher' ideological and cultural values in order to be able to mobilize the population. This makes them 'practical utopias', and more or less successful substitutes for economic incentives in the command system.

The new Russian politicians and administrators no longer proclaim the implementation of technical innovations alongside political slogans. Only socio-economic or political changes remain as slogans. With regard to technical innovations, the officials have fixed it that such innovations will have to be implemented by the market. Since a market system is forming but does not yet exist, technical innovations have ceased to be made. The result of this policy can be seen in the contradiction between the stream of socio-economic and political change, on the one hand, and technological deterioration on the other.

The command economy itself was the handiwork of the tandem

of politician and administrator. Of course, the leading role was played by politicians who organized the activities of administrators in accordance with the slogans-cum-goals that they had launched. The principal goal was the creation of an economic system based on large-scale industrial production and all-encompassing centralized planning which ruled out even a modicum of independence from the Party and the state. Stalin and his associates named this system socialism, and in order to build such a system they abolished NEP, carried out collectivization and industrialization, and carried out pogroms in the sciences, the arts, literature, and other spheres.

Stalin set up a system of economic institutions (central planning agencies, production-branch departments) which ensured the functioning of the economy without a market, although they did imitate a market to a certain extent. In this system, politicians conferred a certain status on administrators. In some spheres, administrators were endowed with a high status, while in others their status was not as high. But there was a pattern up to the recent Yeltsin transition: the closer a sphere was to the consumer (the service sector, the light industry etc.), the lower the status of the people administering it. Conversely, the closer an activity was to the survival of the system as a whole and to its expansion (e.g. the defence industry), the higher the status of its executives. The access to resources, new technology and the like was in direct proportion to an administrator's status as conferred by politicians. It was also true, however, that the status of a sphere facing serious problems (e.g. agriculture) could deteriorate.

In the transition period the tandem of politician and administrator is breaking down. Politicians launched the slogan of creating a democracy and a market economy. To implement this slogan, many administrators from all spheres would have to lose their posts. Therefore most administrators got out of the control of politicians and started to carry on private business while remaining state officials. They combined the privileges of state posts with the freedoms of private business, blocking further liberalization. Certainly politicians will have no success in creating democracy and a market economy when they have little support from administrators. The preservation of the tandem of politicians and administrators is one of the main preconditions of transition success in Russia.

In the command system of economic institutions, the economic roles of specialist and owner were non-existent because both specialists and owners were physically destroyed. We have already covered the role of owner (see Chapter 10). Let us now consider that of specialist.

11.3 The tandem of specialist and owner

A specialist is a person who has made a trade or profession his or her lifelong vocation. Highly competent in a specific field of activity, the specialist has a definite profession which requires lengthy specialized preparation. This sociological definition is in sharp contrast to the standard Soviet definition of a specialist as a person who has received formal training and has a diploma. In the sociologist's view, a specialist does not need a diploma to be a top-notch professional. A specialist accepts a public office only to better perform his or her immediate (professional) duties. By the same token, if an official post threatens to prevent the specialist from functioning as such, it will be turned down. The characteristic feature of the social role of specialist is that this group of people are striving to attain perfection in their practical activities.

Faced with taking a decision in the economic sphere, a specialist will be motivated primarily by the desire to optimize the benefits, even if this diminishes his or her personal influence or invokes the wrath of a superior authority. Another important motive is the desire for peer recognition. Stature among his or her peers is a function of personal achievement, not rank or status in the eyes of superiors. His or her remuneration is a function of the quality of their work, while social status is also relatively independent of the centres of administrative and other powers with which specialists maintain a relationship of mutually beneficial exchange. Independence protects specialists from incompetent interference and poor assessment of their performance.

Interference from above disrupts the normal interaction between specialists, and destroys their professional ethics, but it cannot prevent the emergence of excellent individual physicians, metallurgists and other specialists. It does, however, destroy professional communities or associations of specialists which have their own criteria in assessing performance and strictly regulate professional conduct.[21] A specialist's reputation in the community is the direct result of his or her success as a professional. Societies in which professional communities enjoy relative autonomy place their trust in professionals, remunerate them well, and elevate them strictly in accordance with their real worth.

The classification of specialists under Stalin did not take place according to their worth, but according to their ideological orientation (either 'Soviet' or 'anti-Soviet'). This prompted the most unprincipled of them to make up to the authorities (the politicians and administrators) and carry out any and all instructions, including those which conflicted with their professional ethics. The grateful authorities reciprocated by helping them to do away with their rivals. The consequences of the phenomenon known as Lysenkoism are still alive, and not only in the sciences and the arts. It has spread to industry, agriculture, transport and other economic sectors. In every field, an administrator or a politician could tell a specialist where to build, when to sow, when and how much to produce in order to fulfil the plan drawn up by non-specialists. The consequences of this phenomenon may be described as de-professionalization and involve the loss of the concept of 'professional' and the sense of belonging to a professional community. Loss of professionalism leads to incidents such as Chernobyl, when specialists failed to act as professionals and carried out the commands of incompetent officials. All this is also widespread among industrial trades, where shoddy work has become the rule rather than the exception.

Now administrative control for specialists has certainly declined. But control of them by professional bodies does not exist either. Nobody knows how many years it will take to create such bodies in Russia.

Since there are no genuinely independent professional communities in Russia, there is no social base for innovative communities either. These latter are in many respects a mirror image of the former, formed on the same basis and using the same principles of organization and ethics.

Professional communities could quickly spawn innovative communities, however. For example, if university students were involved in the research work of their professors, they would have no difficulty in joining the work of the innovative community at the enterprise they are sent to after graduation. If a new job lacks such a community, the student may start creating it, drawing on expertise gained at university.

In contrast to the command economy, a market economy would be dominated not by politicians and administrators, but by an alliance of owners and specialists. The tandem of owner and specialist is capable of creating an economic system that would be very favourable to innovation. It will, however, require a number of new economic institutions which do not presently exist. Most of all, it will need the institutions of market competition. These provide the necessary objective yardstick for assessing the performance of administrators, specialists and owners, and would encourage them to be innovative.

The subordinate status of politicians and administrators in a market economy does not mean that the functions they perform are no longer needed in that system. They are still required, but only as a means of attaining objectives set by owners and specialists. One of these is the introduction of innovations. The subordination of politicians and administrators to specialists and owners would make it possible to create a system of economic and social incentives for innovations which until recently the command economy has tried to propagate by decree in the course of innovation drives.

NOTES

1 The last few years have seen a number of publications dealing with shadow management systems, their authors offering new interpretations of the administrative system in Russia. For example, two relatively independent, but at the same time interconnected, spheres may be identified in the system of administrative relations: the official sphere in which interactions are carried on within the framework of the existing administrative system, based on a statutory division of rights, duties and responsibility between administrative agents (levels in the administrative structure); and the unofficial one in which interactions are also carried on within the framework of the administrative system, but are based on mutually profitable exchange. We will refer to this latter form of interaction as 'relations of mutual exchange'. See S. G. Kordonsky, 'The problem of mutual exchange relations: their essence and role in managing production', in *The personnel of the Agro-Industrial Complex within the system of managerial relations*, Barnaul (1987), 23.

2 This is discussed further in Chapter 12.

3 Kordonsky, 'The problem of mutual exchange relations', 24–5.

4 V. Seliunin, 'The sources', *Novy mir*, xii (1987), 175.

5 In this, they differ from overproduction crises under capitalism, which have economic causes.

6 I. V. Stalin, *Collected works*, xii, Moscow, *Gospolitizdat* (1949), 10.

7 The phenomenon of 'planning fetishism' did not exist at this time, which makes the 95% fulfilment figure a genuine success.

8 At the same time agricultural exports accounted for about two-thirds of the country's export earnings. The quote and details are taken from Kutuzov, 'Don't blame it all on the central authorities', *Krest'yanskaya gazeta*, xli (1927).

9 V. I. Frolov, 'Make way for vetch . . .', *Krest'yanskaya gazeta*, xxxix (1927).

10 Kutuzov, head of the economic department of the People's Commis-

sariat of Commerce, wrote an article attributing goods shortages in rural areas to the fact that peasants were hoarding goods in case of war.

11 I. Kosyakin, 'Where are the sources of goods shortages in our co-operative?', *Krest'yanskaya gazeta*, xli (1927).

12 The freshness of style and the frankness with which he explains the causes of the phenomenon and makes suggestions about ways of combating it were rarely equalled by writers on the subject in following years.

13 This period of 'obligatory foresight' was subsequently extended to five years. This seems to be based on an assumption of considerable parapsychological powers among the common people.

14 Kutuzov, 'Don't blame it all'. Comrade Kutuzov proved to be a false prophet: in the 60 years that followed, factories and plants remained in the dark as to the real demand, although the population did learn how to take care of itself, to a degree.

15 According to Frolov: 'exorbitant market prices of vetch seed in spring, i.e. before sowing, usually lead to their shortage and, as a consequence, insufficient acreage is sown to this crop . . . Such prices not only make vetch hay more expensive, it is breaking the back of the peasant and prevents the ploughing up of shallow acreage, so necessary is the combating of hunger.' It might be added that the state naturally subsidized the poorest rural strata through 'soft' credits etc.

16 Stalin, *Collected works*, xi, 11.

17 Stalin interpreted this article of the Criminal Code as a repressive measure to be used in accordance with political expediency. 'If there are no difficulties next year and the procurement campaign proceeds smoothly, Article 107 will not be applied. And conversely, if we run up against emergencies and the capitalist elements resume their tricks, Article 107 will reappear on the stage.'

18 See the quotation from Kutuzov's article on pages 171–172. For more on the subject of the transformation of economic culture and the emergence of the culture of the administrative system, see T. I. Zaslavskaya and R. V. Ryvkina, *Sociology of economic life*, Novosibirsk, Nauka (1991), 96–227.

19 D. Valovoi, *Economics in its human dimension*, Moscow, Politizdat (1988), 8.

20 Valovoi, *Economics in its human dimension*, 81.

21 Such communities existed in pre-revolutionary Russia. According to A. Meshcherskaya (1987), unethical behaviour by a physician, lawyer etc. could be criticized in the press with a resulting loss of practice and expulsion from the association.

12

The Propagation of Innovations: Not Diffusion but Innovation Drives

This chapter is devoted to state activity in relation to the Soviet innovation system. The main difference between the latter and the national innovation systems of the USA, or Britain, or any other country with a market economy lies in the particular manner of propagating innovation, called here 'innovation drives'. This refers to the propagation of technical and socio-economic innovations under the traditional command economy within a strong state. Now that this economy is being dismantled, innovation drives in technology are seldom implemented. It is necessary to explore this history to find the roots of recent apathy in renewing technology and in creating a market system in Russia.

At present the state is attempting to create the conditions for high activity in building new business organizations which would be able to implement considerable technological innovation. Up until the end of 1993 these attempts have failed. To understand the roots of this failure we need to analyse the propagation of innovations in pre-perestroika Russia.

12.1 Orders instead of incentives

Where now many political slogans call for socio-economic modernization, in the past the call was for technological modernization. Politicians launch such slogans out of necessity, since in a command economy innovations do not filter upwards from below as a result of appropriate motivation. The biggest shortage in the command economy is the shortage of incentives, which have been supplanted by orders. Both are external stimuli designed to produce a certain response, but this is where the similarity ends. An incentive implies a free choice of the mode of economic conduct which corresponds to an individual's inner motives and needs. An order, by contrast, rules out free choice and, whatever the individual's inner motivation, he or she has only one possible line of conduct. This makes it necessary to introduce a punitive mechanism which comes into effect when any deviation from orders occurs.

In contrast, if proper incentives exist, a punitive mechanism becomes superfluous, since a motivated individual will weigh the benefits and costs of each mode of conduct and make what one might call a rational choice, that is, from the viewpoint of the individual. Faced by an order, on the other hand, a person often has to act irrationally, contrary to common sense and logic. For the individual, it does not matter that the carrying out of an order may be in the interest of the state, society or the enterprise, because he or she finds the order incongruous.

Given this incongruity, an individual has at least four possible courses of action. Outraged by the whole situation, he or she may complain to their superiors and appeal to the common sense of those who have issued the order; he or she may ignore the order and continue doing whatever they think necessary; he or she may ignore the order and do nothing; or the order may be carried out. As the example of Kosyakin, which we discussed in the last chapter, shows, there were once many people who opted for the first two strategies (known, in the official jargon, as 'adopting an activist stand in life'). Gradually, however, the command system broke them of the habit. Opposition to orders (or disregard of them) involved greater personal effort (and risk) for the administrators at no extra pay. Since doing nothing was an option without negative consequences, they become insensitive to any pressure for changes from below. In their turn, the workers being administered came to feel that all pressure from below was useless and that it was much better and safer to mind one's own business.

The product of this co-operative effort between politicians and administrators was an atmosphere of stagnation in the economy, in which any action required enormous effort. All the more so for the propagation of innovations, which involves enormous social expenditure even in situations when there are workable economic incentives. For this reason, all major innovations under the traditional command system now tend to be implemented with the help of campaigns or drives. Political initiatives in essence, innovation and modernization drives are launched by political institutions. Examples include the promotion of livestock-breeding complexes, low-till farming, combating of soil erosion, intensive farming techniques, shop structure of production management, and many, many more.

12.2 The innovation drive: a social anatomy

An innovation drive begins after the completion of its institutionalization. This essentially means that the innovator has succeeded in convincing ranking officials and specialists at various political, economic and research organizations of the usefulness and potential of the invention. The main task at this stage is to win over the largest possible number of supporters of the highest possible social status. It is desirable to win support in all of the three spheres which decide the fate of the innovation: politicians (in the pre-perestroika period, 'instructors' and secretaries of the CPSU Central Committee, district and regional Party committees); economic executives (factory managers, heads of functional departments, ranking officials at ministries, state committees and other government departments); and the academic and research officials (scientific councils of the leading research institutes, specialists and heads of branch research institutes, design bureaus etc.). The activities of the innovator at this stage recall those of a candidate for election to a desirable political post – with the difference that if successful he or she will not usually be appointed to any post. Understandably, it is extremely difficult to persuade such a vast number of people that the innovation proposed is highly effective and useful. At times this may involve obtaining hundreds of signatures when a large proportion of such officials are not making an effort to perform additional work for a fixed salary. Therefore, this stage may drag on for many years before a high-ranking politician or executive is finally convinced and pushes the innovation into production. For example, when Khudenko suggested the introduction of collective contracts in agriculture, no less a person than Khrushchev finally gave the go-ahead shortly before he was ousted.[1]

Even a recommendation and unambiguous instruction from a high-ranking official do not mean, however, that a decision on the introduction of an innovation has been made, although it does facilitate the process. All such decisions are made by collective bodies, and the more important the innovation, the more authoritative must be the official body. For example, the suggestion to resume the teaching of sociology as a discipline in the USSR dates from the 1960s. For over 20 years the idea gradually won support; a special commission was set up and specific projects worked out. The idea was supported by the CPSU Central Committee, the USSR Academy of Sciences, the USSR Ministry of Education, and other interested government departments. Finally, in 1988, a special edict by the CPSU Central Committee was issued on the promotion of sociology in the USSR, with a section specifically devoted to the teaching of sociology. Following this edict, the USSR State Committee for Education, the USSR Academy of Sciences, the Russian Federation's Ministry of Education and the Russian Federation's Council of Ministers all issued their own edicts which elaborated on the decision of the CPSU's Central Committee. For example, where the Central Committee's decision dealt with the guidelines for the organization and development of the teaching of sociology, the corresponding documents of the USSR State Committee for Education dealt with such concrete information as the number of universities and colleges in which sociology would be taught, the number of colleges which would have their own sociology departments, the number of those where only sociology courses would be read, the deadlines, and so on.

Up to perestroika, a politician, even at the highest level, would order the introduction of an innovation only after assuring him or herself that it was not only useful but also had sufficient support – or, at least, no influential enemies. The politician's social role was such that he or she could not launch a drive to disseminate even a highly promising innovation if the executives in the industry or sector in question were hostile to it.

There was ample evidence that if a politician failed to take due account of the administrators' views, decisions made at the very top were not carried out, deadlines were not observed, and inventions did not make it to the shop floor. This meant that in the tandem of the politician and the administrator, power did not lie solely with the politician. The two roles were closely inter-related. In addition to their interaction on a day-to-day basis, this manifested itself in the exchange of personnel between the political and economic governing bodies[2] and in close personal contacts. This inter-relationship meant that politician and administrator were equally responsible for the non-introduction of innovations. Attempts therefore to shift all the blame on to the bureaucrat, the little brother, are in our view not quite justified.

Now, when the tandem of politician and administrator is being destroyed, a single politician is able to order the introduction of socio-economic or political innovations despite opposition from some influential politicians or administrators. For example, in the summer of 1992 the chairman of the Central Bank of Russia, Gerashenko, made an order for mutual cancellation of debts between state enterprises, amounting to 1.5 trillion roubles, despite strong opposition from the government. And President Yeltsin put out the edict on trade for plots of land in Ramenskoe (Moscow's suburban area) in the face of great opposition from the Supreme Soviet and many agrarian officials. As a result, socio-economic and political innovations may be implemented despite strong conflicts, or they may be prevented from being implemented. In this situation, at least, nobody knows what order will go through and what order will be refused.

Naturally, an innovator's chances of victory are higher if he or she enjoys high social status. An organization, such as a research institute, a design bureau or a factory, has more chances of success than a solitary innovator or a group of enthusiasts who do not represent anyone but themselves and their own innovation. The quality of the innovation may be less important than the status of the innovator.

The tangible expression of an innovator's victory is the issuing of an order. An order is a directive document which instructs all the enterprises subordinate to a ministry or a government department to make the innovation part of the production process. An order may take the form of a circular specifically dealing with the innovation, or it may be included in a plan on the introduction of technological advances and modern technologies. The order is usually framed by the administrator, sometimes with the collaboration of the innovator. The document contains a list of enterprises that are obliged to introduce the new technology, stipulates the extent of its introduction (how many hectares of land are to be ploughed up using the new cultivation techniques, or how many tons of new product are to be manufactured), fixes deadlines (the commissioning is frequently timed to coincide with official holidays), and even enumerates the expected benefits.

After the order has been framed, it is sent to enterprises, of which there may be tens, hundreds, thousands, or even tens of thousands. The order then has to clear all the intermediate levels of management, each of which adds its own elaborations and details. For example, in the agro-industrial sector, these included Gosagroproms of the Union republics, and regional and district agro-industrial committees. In Moscow, these did not usually draft orders for individual enterprises (with the exception of industrial giants of Union subordination) but passed the order down the chain of command.

After the order has been issued, and has reached all enterprises, the next stage in the innovation drive is assistance to enterprises and pressuring them into action. At least some of the enterprises will try to refuse to implement the innovation, invoking lack of preparation or production backlogs; more often they will simply disregard the order. Pressure from above results in uncompleted innovations. Like Russian managers and researchers, Western scientists noted this result of innovation policy in a command economy. For example, as D. Slider argued: 'The predictable result of such an effort is the token or formalistic adoption of the innovation.'[3] The superiors react by bringing pressure to bear on the recalcitrants, sometimes with the help of political (i.e. Party) authority. Or again, the ministry may try to entice the enterprise into action with promises of additional supplies of raw materials, spares and parts that are in short supply, or additional funds for construction work.

For their part, enterprises start requesting additional material and financial resources, operating procedures, and specialist advice needed for the introduction of the innovation. Not infrequently, enterprises have to breach regulations in the process of introducing an innovation. This triggers the already described social mechanism for the protection of the innovator (this happens much more frequently during drives than in the normal process of innovation). This alerts the social mechanism which blocks the enterprise's innovative activity (see Fig. 3).

The operation of these mechanisms may be illustrated by the construction of an animal feed shop that had not been provided for in the plan. During a drive to promote the construction of animal feed facilities, the finance unit of the local government district executive committee uncovered a breach of financial regulations during a regular auditing of the enterprise in question. This fact was duly reported to the district branch of the Agroprombank and the district Party committee. Thereafter the bank (whose action was duly approved by the district's financial authorities) stopped financing the project, thus putting an end to this innovative activity.

The social mechanism for the protection of the innovator through unofficial channels then went into operation (as outlined in Fig. 4).

When the First Secretary of the district Party committee assured himself that there had been no *corpus delicti* in the management's action, he tried to prevent sanctions against the enterprise. However, he failed because the breach had already been reported to the regional financial authorities. Then the First Secretary

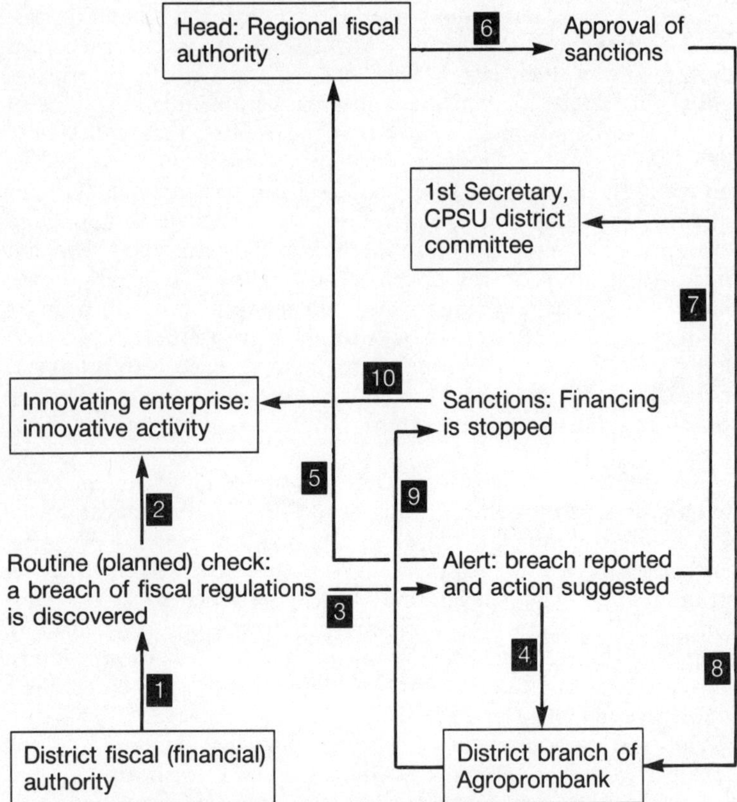

Figure 3: Social mechanism blocking innovation at enterprise level

telephoned the regional Party secretary responsible for agriculture, with whom he was on good terms, and asked him to help in seeking the revocation of the sanctions. In his turn, the regional Party committee secretary telephoned the region's banker and, having explained the situation to him, asked him to drop the sanctions. The outcome was an instruction for the district financial authority to resume the financing of the construction of the animal feed shop.

An important feature of the mechanism for the protection of innovators is its strictly unofficial character. Conducted mainly by telephone, it is an unseen, flexible, prompt, and unhampered operation which can take account of all the nuances of the situation. Unfortunately, these same characteristics also make it

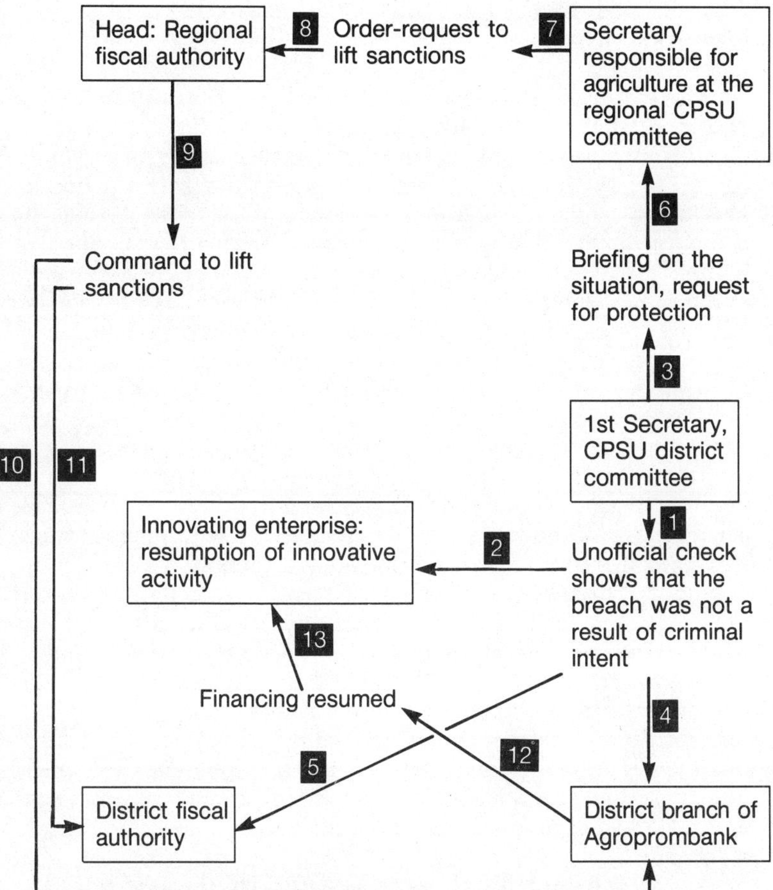

Figure 4: Social mechanism for the unofficial protection of innovating enterprises by political institutions

eminently suitable for the protection of false innovators and builders of Potemkin villages, as well as for the punishing of so-called 'mavericks' who implement useful innovations. Wherever persons lacking integrity hold office in political institutions, the great freedom of manoeuvre permitted by this mechanism may lead to total arbitrariness, or the protection of crooks and the harassment of honest people. The social conditions making such freedom and arbitrariness possible will be dealt with later, in Chapter 14, on socialist monopolism.

12.3 Planned disasters and some of the consequences of innovation drives

Another result of this unofficial protection mechanism is that it becomes dangerous to engage in innovative activities that are not part of an official drive. There is a high probability of sanctions against innovators; it is practically impossible to introduce an innovation without violating a regulation or official rule (by definition, innovation is a breach of some official instruction), or without creating problems for at least one of the many administrative bodies. The latter in itself can serve as grounds for reprisal. For this reason, no major innovations to date have come through innovation drives. They have been carried out under the tutelage of a high-ranking official prepared to provide cover to the innovators at any moment and to help them solve their problems. Loss of patronage frequently led to the failure or suspension of an innovative activity. For example, when Kazakhstan's deputy minister of agriculture withdrew his support from the experiment carried out by Khudenko, the latter, together with his associates, was put on trial and the experiment was forcibly stopped.

In order to spread, an innovation requires a 'most favoured nation' status. This means priority in the allocation of every resource and the suspension of certain official regulations standing in its way. So long as the attention of the superior authorities is concentrated on an innovation – even if this is some time after its introduction – the innovators get the necessary parts and high-quality metal, they are allowed to dispense with some paperwork, and are spared sanctions if they breach regulations contrary to the essence of the innovation. However, as soon as the central management loses interest, or its attention is diverted to other innovative activities, the old cycle repeats itself: the workforce and the low-level managers begin to stint time and effort; repressive regulations go back into effect; customers refuse to accept the new product; suppliers deliver low-quality raw materials and parts; and so on.

Consequently, the innovation which has already been successfully introduced has a difficult time surviving in an inhospitable organizational and technological environment which obviously cannot be modified by a temporary campaign. What is needed are permanent controls such as the free choice of suppliers, an orientation towards the market etc. The lack of these explains the frequent quick demise of useful innovations, as a result of which enterprises have to revert to old ways.

Such was the fate of a technique for the assembly of industrial buildings from prefabricated lightweight metal parts described by Malakhiev in 1985. The technology developed by an industrial construction combine reduced construction time and labour inputs by two-thirds and increased productivity per worker by 3.5 times in comparison with the traditional technology. However, its large-scale introduction meant problems for its superiors in Glavkrasnoyarskstroi, and, in any case, it did not improve performance in terms of gross output. What is more:

> many building organizations subordinate to the ministry and responsible for industrial construction are not prepared to use the new parts and are sometimes not capable of doing so. That is why they refused to accept them. As a result, the central directorate ordered a 66% reduction in the number of engineers and technicians employed by the combine, although the USSR Gosplan had recommended the setting up of a design bureau with a staff of 30. It was also decided to transfer one of the combine's units to another organization. This just stopped short of the combine's liquidation as an independent economic unit.[4]

At the same time, a political campaign may ensure an even more rapid and large-scale propagation of an innovation than the market. In the first 15 years of its intensive chemicalization campaign, the USSR achieved what it took the USA more than two decades to achieve, according to Y. B. Kvasha.[5] New technologies involving large volumes of relatively unsophisticated products that can be manufactured with a minimum of social expenditure may spread very rapidly.

However, the chemicalization example also shows that drives are fraught with grave consequences. There have already been many instances of poisonings from watermelons, cabbages and other fruits and vegetables containing high amounts of toxic substances. The following description gives an idea of the problems that can be caused by an innovation drive:

> The road-sides and the edges of the fields display numerous signs of liquid chemical substances seeping into the soil and making their way to the groundwater table, as well as mountains of pesticides . . . Our republic [Tadzhikistan] has unwittingly been turned into a testing ground for Soviet and imported pesticides.[6]

The ordering of innovations from above, without due regard for the wishes of enterprises, frequently means that the latter are subjected to pressure in spite of the fact that they are not really prepared to adopt the new technology or product. As Kruglikov points out:

> if such inputs as raw materials, parts and other allocated resources required for the introduction and development of an innovation, as well as the overall technological level of production, skilled engineers, technicians and workers, are in short supply or expensive, then no matter what its future potential, the innovation proves to be unworkable.[7]

There are numerous example of disregard for the real worth of an innovation. This not only leads to fiascos (as in the case of Khrushchev's 'maize campaign'[8]) but also sometimes poses a direct physical threat to people. For example, in 1986 the Soviet government decided to promote the use of natural and liquefied gas as motor fuel. By 1989, all taxis in Moscow were to be provided with gas tanks. Far from all of Moscow's taxi operators proved to be prepared for this switchover; many lacked the fire-fighting equipment required by the new, more stringent, regulations. In an article appropriately titled 'on the verge of an explosion', Blokhin wrote:

> the conversion of taxis at the rate prescribed for 1988 will inevitably lead to fires and explosions . . . The management of the Moscow transportation directorate are fully aware of this danger and it is no accident that all instructions involving the conversion of taxis to natural gas are being issued exclusively in oral form.[9]

The response of a government department to an innovation campaign is determined by the fact that the decision to launch the drive is taken by a high political authority. Since the ministry is in effect an extension of the political apparatus, it has to carry out the decision and meet the stipulated deadlines. Enterprises (or most of them), in contrast, do everything in their power to dodge the innovation, and give objective reasons for their inaction (some of the reasons are genuinely objective, others are only ostensibly so). A superior authority cannot reliably assess an enterprise's readiness for an innovation, a task which is best done by enterprises themselves. For example, in Blokhin's account of plans to convert Moscow's taxis to natural gas, employees of Moscow's taxi pool No. 7 estimated that this would cost them about 1 million roubles and require some specialized design work. The government department, however, had not asked the taxi drivers to assess their readiness for this change: they had decided it for them. Severe pressure was applied to the drivers, including threats of firing taxi pool managers and cutting the allocation of petrol if they failed to comply immediately. The author concludes:

> We pinned great hopes on the appearance of the first cars fuelled by natural gas on our roads. However, their large-scale conversion by means of outright pressure should give us cause for concern.[10]

Many other forms of pressure can be applied by the authorities – official and unofficial reprimands, cuts in supplied resources, harsher production quotas, bigger plans etc. – but all of them are designed to impose an innovation on an enterprise which is not prepared for it.

This leads to 'planned disasters'. Although they are not planned by any specific person, these are a direct consequence of the centralized planning mechanism responsible for everything, including modernization. The more sophisticated the technology, the greater its potential dangers; clearly, an accident at a nuclear power station is likely to be far more destructive in its effect than an accident at a thermal one. One effect of this phenomenon, which I have described as the economic immune-deficiency syndrome (absence of economic barriers to the propagation of uneconomic innovations), is that innovators frequently win Pyrrhic victories; innovations that are potentially useful turn out to be harmful, just like a useful medication taken in huge doses. The end result is disappointment. Those on whom the innovation has been imposed grow disgruntled with it; as such instances accumulate, people become sceptical of innovation drives and despair of their ability to change anything for the better. Another result is alienation from the superior administrative bodies. At the same time, people cannot help comparing their products with highly efficient imported products and processes.

12.4 Innovation drives and the economic immune-deficiency syndrome

Innovation drives are not proof of some deficiency in the management structure. They are the only possible means of effecting major innovations in a command economy. As we have already seen, though, the command economy suffers from many deficiencies. In addition to those we have previously discussed it has the added disadvantage of being suited to only a narrow range of innovations.[11] Since, in the absence of economic rewards, the workforce seeks to dodge innovations, it becomes necessary to resort to innovation drives. Innovation drives generate even greater resentment against innovation, which, in turn, makes it necessary to launch more drives and to increase pressure from above, creating a vicious circle of drive and resentment.

The upper and lower echelons in the chain of command use different criteria to judge innovations. Although the high-ranking politicians launching innovation drives bear greater administrative responsibility for their success or failure, they do not directly bear the social expenditure involved in the introduction of innovations. As a consequence, they think in terms of an innovation's economic benefits rather than the social expenditure involved in its introduction. In contrast, the lower echelons (factory managers, engineers, shopfloor workers) are primarily thinking in terms of social expenditure because they are not owners and bear much less responsibility for its introduction. The result is a conflict between the goals and criteria of the two groups, a conflict which is commonly resolved in the following manner.

In a command economy, the introduction of major innovations usually begins when there is a consensus among the politicians, administrators and innovators so that the innovation enjoys the necessary support. It is obvious that the weakest partner in this trio is the innovator: his or her social status is the lowest. This is quite understandable, since in a command economy innovation is the prerogative of politicians and apparatchiks, and also a means of achieving political and administrative objectives. Innovation drives can lead to changes in the social status and influence of a large group of politicians and administrators, who may be either promoted or demoted.

Innovators may also be promoted to higher posts. In principle, this is a positive development making the economy more amenable to innovation. However, the promotion of innovators to positions of responsibility in itself cannot speed up and improve the modernization of the production process to any great extent. Even if all positions of responsibility were held by innovators, and the ministries and government departments were concerned solely with scientific and technological progress, the problems would not all be solved.

Considering the need to speed up and streamline the modernization process, an administered economy managed by innovators would be no better than a command economy managed by conservatives. To begin with, all innovators have their own particular hobby horse, an area of scientific and technological progress or a pattern of organizational change which they believe to be the best and the most promising. The innovator's subjectivism is even greater than that of a disinterested conservative to whom all innovations are alike and who usually opts for sure-fire projects which will not undermine his or her position. For this reason, if innovators ran an administered economy it is unlikely that there would be a greater diversity of innovations, or that they would be better adapted to the needs of production, although the total number of new products and processes would certainly grow. Furthermore, given the apathy of the lower echelons, even the most intense innovation activity by the upper echelons is unlikely to bring about a significant increase in the number of 'nuclei of growth', without which the nature of innovation processes can hardly be modified. Finally, putting innovators in power is not likely to cure the economy of its immune-deficiency or change the propensity of the majority of the workforce to minimize the social expenditure involved in production modernization. As a result, the combined effect of enhanced innovative activity in the upper echelons may even be negative, especially if one takes into account the uncertainties and risks involved in innovation. In the final account the negative effects of an innovation may even outweigh its positive aspects.

Our contention is, therefore, that even if all the ministerial posts in the pre-perestroika period were held by inventors and innovators, and the government ministeries and departments were obliged to deal exclusively with scientific and technological progress and the streamlining of the economic mechanism, this would lead to little significant change if the administrative system remained the same. This is not surprising because the ministerial system of management could not cope with even the much simpler task of supplying the country with traditional goods, production of which does not involve great inventions and changes.

In a normally functioning administered economy run largely by conservatives, with only a handful of 'tame' innovators, the consensus among politicians, administrators and innovators is for a slow, protracted process of institutionalization of innovations which may spread over several years. It is during this stage that the administrators weed out innovations which may prove harmful to the command economy, along with those which may lead to serious economic losses if introduced on a large scale from the centre. Then they eliminate those that might considerably worsen the social status of some sections in the political and/or administrative apparat, often the people who had been responsible for the introduction of the existing, conventional technology and who are ill-equipped to replace it with a new one. Also weeded out are complex innovations involving great social expenditure (i.e. those about which the management anticipates strong opposition from below, from the workforce, specialists and middle management).

The screening of innovations from the standpoint of their social expenditure also takes place at this stage. It is the relatively simple innovations that pass the test, those which do not call for any radical measures, which involve only insignificant modifications in the production process, which are not fraught with social instabilities, mass dismissals and other headaches for the management. As Hanson and Pavitt have argued: 'Insofar as rewards are created for invention and innovation in a centrally administered economy, the system lacks the filter provided by the test of use acceptance for separating wanted from unwanted innovations.'[12] In a market economy, too, there is a selection of innovations, and many potential applications fail to materialize. However, the selection criteria and mechanism are different from those in a command economy. The main criterion is profitability. It ensures the economic efficiency of innovations and prevents the spread of inefficient ones. Innovations are introduced not by order from a ministry, nor after haggling that involves numerous clearances from officials at several levels, but voluntarily as a result of decisions taken by the owners together with administrators and specialists. Innovations are introduced only when businesses are prepared to do so because otherwise they will not be profitable.

It might be added that these decisions are only voluntary in a relative sense, since they are taken in the face of pressure from competitors. Businesses have to introduce new products or processes to avoid going bankrupt. The advantage of competition, however, is that it gives businesses greater freedom to choose the ways and means of modernizing. In a command economy, in contrast, enterprises have relatively greater freedom to participate in modernization or to avoid it, but have no freedom in choosing the ways and means of modernizing. This enables enterprises in a command economy to avoid innovation, a course of action barred to businesses in a market economy with its competitive pressures.

Many Soviet command economy institutions do not exist now: Gosagroproms of the Union republics, plans for the introduction of technological advances and modern technologies etc. What remains is the nostalgia of top officials for complete control from above, and the population's habit of subordination. This old mentality is fundamental to the economic immune-deficiency syndrome: conservation in the current Russian economy.

The immune-deficiency syndrome in a traditional command economy, with its low rate of modernization and low rate of return on those innovations that do succeed, is the result of the absence of feedback between its political and economic institutions. It is in effect the price it pays for the large-scale involvement of political institutions in economic activity, more specifically in innovation processes.

This interference of political institutions in economic activity runs counter to the basic tenets of economics.[13] For the purposes of our study, three factors are important here. Firstly, politicians set goals for enterprises which often involve the introduction of certain innovations. Secondly, executives and specialists are frequently reshuffled with the help of the nomenclature mechanism. Finally, politicians interfere in the day-to-day management of enterprises. Interference begins with the setting of goals. Ideological imperatives and cultural constraints play an important role here.

NOTES

1 This piece of information comes from V. V. Filatov, Khudenko's close associate. The idea was implemented only under Gorbachev because of Khrushchev's ousting.

2 In a study dealing with the careers of several ministers and chairmen of state committees of the USSR, Lebedev wrote that in the past over 70% of careers were linear (i.e. were made exclusively in the economic sphere) while the rest took a zig-zag form (i.e. included appointments from other spheres, primarily political). With the coming of perestroika, the percentage with linear careers dropped and the number of those with previous experience in other spheres rose: 'Top personnel from the same ministry or department account for almost half of new appointments . . . The second largest category of new appointments (over 25%) are persons who had previously held high offices in the Party.' P. Lebedev, 'What do we know about our ministers?', *Ogonek*, xxxi (1988), 7. This trend may be interpreted as the growing interdependence of the institutions of politics and economics under perestroika.

3 See D. Slider, 'Regional aspects of policy innovation in the Soviet Union', in *Politics and the Soviet system*, London, Macmillan (1989), 158.

4 M. Malakhiev, 'Ministerial obstruction', *Sovetskaya Rossiya*, 13 August 1985.

5 Y. B. Kvasha, *The time factor in socialized production*, Moscow, Statistika (1979), 11.

6 K. Atakhamov and A. Karpov, 'A dangerous vegetable', *Nedelya*, xxxiii (1988), 11.
7 A. G. Kruglikov, 'Economic analysis of the spread of scientific and technical innovations (using the example of new technologies in famous metallurgy)', in *Mathematical models and the statistical analysis of scientific and technical progress*, Moscow, VNIISI (1982), 85.
8 In the early 1960s, following his visit to the USA, Khrushchev was in favour of the idea of cultivating maize all over the USSR to solve the food problem. The Politburo of the CPSU decided to cultivate a vast maize-growing scheme, and the Central Committee of the CPSU and regional committees all carried their plenums in favour of the drive. The Agriculture Ministry put the task of cultivating the maize to most *kolkhozy* and *sovkhozy*, despite their differences in climate. The press, TV and radio transmitted programmes about successful experiences of cultivating maize and about bureaucratic attempts to block it. If someone wanted to explore the main problem in Soviet state policy under Khrushchev, they would discover it to have been maize cultivation, not the Carribean crises. Certainly there were a great many mistakes and losses made during the maize drive.
9 A. Blokhin, 'On the verge of an explosion', *Sotsialisticheskaya industriya*, 23 July 1988.
10 Blokhin, 'On the verge of an explosion'.
11 According to available data in the early 1980s only 0.6% of innovations were adopted by more than five enterprises. See Lapin, 'Social aspects of the intensification of innovations', in *Ways to improve the social mechanism of the Soviet economy's development*, Novosibirsk (1985), 85. According to our expert poll among managers of research units in 1992, the same figures applied in the early 1990s: the average number of innovations were implemented in 1–2 enterprises only. The *renumbere* innovations are implemented in more than five enterprises.
12 See P. Hanson and K. Pavitt, 'The comparative economics of research, development and innovation in East and West: a survey', *Fundamentals of pure and applied economics*, xxv (1987), 19.
13 With the coming of perestroika, the negative effects of this interference from political institutions in the economic management was openely acknowledged and became a subject of lively debate. Several publications deal with the need to separate the political and economic instruments in the running of the economy. Some attempts at such analysis were made in pre-perestroika Russia. See, for example, M. I. Piskotin, *Socialism and state administration*, Moscow, Nauka (1984), 204–8.

13

Cultural and Ideological Reasons for Stagnation

13.1 The interplay of ideology and culture in Soviet society

Human motives in production modernization are not independent variables. The motives of individuals do not lend themselves to sociological analysis; motives for the innovative behaviour of social groups, however (administrators, managers, specialists), are determined largely by the institutions of ideology and culture.

Despite rapid changes in ideology after 1985, the influence of Soviet Socialist ideology is prolonged and will continue well into the future. This ideology comprised a system of social norms reflecting Soviet society's prevalent view of socialism (both as a social and an economic system), its principal characteristics and paths of evolution, as well as an assessment of its role and place among other socio-political systems. It was closely linked with culture – that is, with the system of social norms and values ensuring the passing on of patterns of activity and behaviour from generation to generation.

Ideology played a particular role in Soviet society. It integrated and kept under supervision all other institutions of society. All deviations from 'socialist choice' in the economy, politics, culture etc. were corrected according to ideological norms. Ideology had the strongest direct influence on the culture, on the system of human values and on stereotypes of behaviour.

An examination of the interplay of these institutions from the standpoint of their influence on stagnation in innovative processes leads to the conclusion that ideological dogmatism contributed to stagnation in the economic culture, while cultural stereotypes favoured the acceptance of some ideological norms and the rejection of others.

For example, a large proportion of the Soviet population was convinced that equal incomes for different social groups was a characteristic feature of socialism. This conviction was shared by representatives of diverse social strata from workers to cabinet ministers. For example, asked by a correspondent about a fiscal system which taxes co-operatives out of the market, the then USSR Minister of Finance, Gostev, said in 1988:

> This is in effect the taxation of superprofits. We have a category of people whose incomes are too high. Such disparities are intolerable in socialist society. The exorbitant incomes of members of co-operatives have aroused the legitimate resentment of workers who put in ten hours a day and earn a wage of only 200 roubles.

Asked what he thought about co-operatives, a worker replied: 'Cooperatives are legalized blackmarketeers.'[1]

The idea of egalitarianism in the form in which it exists in today's mass economic consciousness has been transplanted from the system of socialism's ideological imperatives, and it now has a place in Russian economic culture, as one of its principal values. Latterly this idea has started to change towards acceptance of the market-economy norms – tolerance of private property, inequality of incomes etc. But these changes are on the part of the younger generation in particular. For the most part, the older generations adhere to egalitarianism, in spite of rejection of socialist slogans.

At the same time there was, and is, a cultural failure to adopt and adapt all the ideological norms of socialist ideology formulated by Marx and Engels. Thus the idea of the need to create conditions for man's all-round development in the economy was rejected, and ideas about freedom of movement and the elimination of national frontiers, and the idea of a free choice of a new job were disregarded. This shows that culture is highly selective, effectively acting as a filter through which ideological imperatives are screened. This screening is anti-innovative in essence; it is precisely those imperatives that call for enhanced innovative activity on the part of various population groups that have been filtered out. At the same time, the essentially anti-innovative slogan of egalitarianism has been widely accepted.

The slogans of modernization drives have been dictated by ideological imperatives rather than economic necessity. Therefore a close examination of the impact of ideology on innovation is called for.

13.2 The Marxist ethic and the spirit of socialism

For an innovative activity to be motivated it must be perceived by the subject as rational. No innovative activity can sustain itself without the propagation of the values of rationalism. What sort of rationalism can underlie modernization in Russia?

Let us first discuss Weber's analysis of rationalism in his book *The Protestant ethic and the spirit of capitalism.* Weber defines economic behaviour as engaging, in accordance with one's inclinations, in activities which bring one nearer to God and thus contribute to the achievement of the goal of individual salvation.[2] Economic thinking or the ethos of an economic form, is thus seen as being determined by religious considerations. Weber illustrates his point by examining the link between the modern economic ethos and the rational ethics of ascetic protestantism.[3] Western capitalism inherited certain values from ascetic Protestantism, called by Weber 'the spirit of capitalism', which constitute what is essentially a philosophy of individualist rationalism. The criterion of rationality of an action here is its correspondence or non-correspondence to one's avocation, with the individual freely deciding which economic actions correspond to his or her avocation and which do not.[4] Economic culture based on this ethic is highly mobile and innovative because it removes external constraints of individual self-expression and creativity in the economic sphere and provides consistent motivation for these two modes of behaviour.

> We find here the most fertile soil for the sort of attitude to work as a goal in itself and avocation that capitalism requires, as well as the most favourable conditions for overcoming the routine of traditionalism, the conditions shaped by religious education.[5]

Marxism as an economic ethic incorporated two forms of rationalism from the outset. The first one is collectivist rationalism, within the framework of which any action by an individual is rational if it brings society nearer to Communism, although it may be contrary to the common sense of the individual performing it.

The second form of rationalism is individualistic rationalism according to which all is rational that contributes to the free, all-round and harmonious development of the individual.

Both forms of rationalism were to be found in the Communist Manifesto, which invisaged that in the society of the future they would merge and that the free development of each would be the condition of the free development of all.

Soviet society, however, failed to combine the two forms of rationalism. It chose a collectivist rationalism[6] which inverted the original formula and proclaimed that the free development of all would be the condition for the free development of each. Collectivist rationalism imparted a specific value orientation to the economic functioning of Soviet society which we all refer to as the spirit of socialism. Its hallmark is equality achieved through the destruction of classes, the building of a society which is socially homogeneous, and the predominance of the common interest over that of the individual.

When consistently implanted in society, collectivist rationalism exhibits a total disregard of individual common sense. Rational economic behaviour in this case consists of activities which bring Communism nearer. It is noteworthy that at the first stage of Soviet society this rational behaviour was based on an ethic of ascetic socialism. The principal agents in economic life were people engaged in activities that were bringing society closer to Communism and did so with total self-denial (just as early Protestants did everything in their power to come closer to God and achieve salvation). A large proportion of them were genuinely selfless and practised asceticism in their personal life.[7] During that stage in the 1920s and the early 1930s, Soviet society was highly mobile and innovative. Of course, it paid too high a price for this.

The experience of those and subsequent years showed that the free development of all is often in conflict with the free development of each. 'Great leaps forward', supposedly performed by a 'free' population, led to the suppression of the freedom of the individual, denial of human rights, and was inevitably accompanied by massive repression and the appearance of a network of concentration camps. The policy of rapid industrialization pursued by Stalin and his associates for ideological reasons led to widespread economic conflicts in Russia with its predominantly peasant population. Yesterday's peasants were not used to the urban way of life and work in industry, and found it extremely difficult to keep up with the pace of production, strict discipline and application required by factory work. What made it especially difficult was a particular feature of the Russian national character that was largely a product of the rural way of life in tsarist Russia. A. N. Engelhardt commented on this trait:

> Unlike Germans, our workers cannot work steadily day in and day out. They work in bursts. It is their inner temperament that has been shaped by the conditions prevailing in our agriculture; owing to climatic conditions all operations must be completed within very short periods of time. It is natural that where winters are short or non-existent, and where agricultural work is going on almost throughout the year, and where there are no rapid changes in the weather, the character of agricultural work should be quite different . . . It is the conditions of our climate, though, that moulded the character of our workers, who cannot work as steadily and as carefully as the Germans do. However, when necessary they may rise to the occasion and move mountains – *if their masters succeed in infusing them with sufficient energy* [author's emphasis].[8]

It was with great difficulty that yesterday's peasants adapted themselves to the strict and uniform tempo of industrial work. This led to constant disruptions and even stoppages of the production process in industry. Armand Hammer, an American businessman who opened a pencil factory in the USSR in the late 1920s, had the following to say on the subject:

> The organization of production involved great problems. It was difficult to find skilled workers and discipline was frequently slack . . . Often the German supervisors complained that the workers were too slow and their productivity was low. And then I had the happy idea to introduce piecework . . . From then on the supervisors reported that the productivity of the Russian workers was no longer below that of the Germans and most of them even broke all German records.[9]

Disruptions in production schedules, industrial conflicts and refusals to take part in modernization were treated as political crimes in the political situation prevailing in the country in the 1920s and 1930s. They were branded as economic counter-revolution, sabotaging the Party's decisions, or as counter-attacks by class enemies. Memories of the Civil War and of foreign intervention were still fresh, and Stalin was still locked in battle with his political opponents in the Party leadership. Against this background, such ideological and political interpretation of economic conflicts by the political leaders of various stripe who headed bodies of economic administration is not surprising. The conflicts grew in number with the progress of industrialization, which involved the hiring of ever greater numbers of yesterday's peasants. For this reason, Stalin's slogan that the class struggle becomes increasingly acute as socialism makes progress was accepted by most office holders without surprise or outrage. They did not fail to notice that it was becoming increasingly difficult to work, but blamed this on sabotage by class enemies: kulak sympathizers, kulak children, the clergy, old specialists who survived the Revolution etc. These class enemies had to be crushed in the process of class struggle.

In the political situation in the 1920s and 1930s, the ideological slogan of accelerated industrialization inevitably led to massive and ever growing repression.[10]

This example shows what happens when forcible modernization has been dictated by ideological considerations and when innovations become the focus of political struggle. This situation creates feedback between political, ideological and economic institutions, with ideological imperatives triggering political campaigns. These campaigns amount to tampering with the economic mechanism with tools which are alien to it, and lead to the sort of 'mistakes' and 'excesses' which are dealt with in Stalin's article 'Dizzy with success'.[11] Attempts are made to rectify them through adjustment of the old ideological slogans and the launching of new political campaigns, which, in turn, result in economic dislocation. This pattern, which was quite common in the 1902s and 1930s, has since repeated itself, in a slightly attenuated form.

The innovations introduced during that and subsequent periods frequently clashed with common sense and economic practicability. One need only recall the collectivization in agriculture, which was accompanied by wide-scale executions, devastation and famine. The period is evocative of the time of the building of the great pyramids, with the role of the Pharaoh played by Stalin. He justified disregard of economic expediency in the following terms:

> Under capitalism large grain-producing farms strive to extract a maximum profit or, in any case, a profit close to the average rate of profit, without which they, generally speaking, cannot survive. This consideration inevitably adds to the cost of production, thus putting formidable obstacles in the way of the development of large grain-producing farms. Under the Soviet system, in contrast, large grain farms, which are state-owned enterprises, need neither maximum nor average profits

> for their development: they can do with a minimum of profit (and sometimes can temporarily do without any profit at all). This, along with the absence of absolute land rent, has created extremely favourable conditions for the development of large-scale grain-producing enterprises.[12]

Thus collectivist rationalism means disregard of common sense, differences (in opinion, taste, inclination, interest etc.) and economic expediency. It is utopian rationalism in many respects, aiming to implement innovations which are practical utopias.

There are at least two types of such utopias. The first is a fantastic project whose principal merit consists in the fact that when completed it will make the *Guinness Book of Records*. The population at large and the country's leaders will be amazed by its size, originality, fantastic usefulness and breath-taking prospects. An example of such a project can be found in Platonov's *The juvenile sea* (1987), in which one of the characters had a dream of building a dinosaur-sized super-cow which would give the proletariat rivers of milk. Other examples include the hare-brained schemes of 'plant-breeder' Lysenko, and the so-called 'project of the century', a plan to divert the Siberian rivers to the south (which has only recently been abandoned).

The second kind of utopia is the holding up of an ordinary innovation as a panacea for all economic problems (witness Stalin's slogan that 'Technology solves everything'). This panacea is forced on to society in spite of the opposition of what were once termed 'class enemies' (whose role has recently been replaced by 'conservatives').

Both kinds of utopias are still alive, although in less extreme forms. They are still used to inspire the slogans of innovation drives. For example, asked by a TV correspondent in 1988 when the USSR's entire output would be up to the world standard, the chairman of the USSR's State Committee for Standards replied: 'In four years time.'

At the same time, in spite of their utopian character, these projects are instigated in response to specific needs of society and its citizens. They are attempts at practical, rather than theoretical, utopias.

Innovations that have been implemented are thus a compromise between utopia and real human needs (which they meet only to a certain extent). For example, in the 1920s to 1930s, Novosibirsk's authorities launched a grandiose project for the construction of a 'panoramic-planetary' opera theatre. Although the building proved strikingly original and imposing from the outside, so that it became the symbol of Novosibirsk, it had bad acoustics, a stage which was impractically designed, and dressing rooms which were poorly equipped.

Ideologically, the slogans of innovation drives were based, and in many respects still are, on the imperative to 'catch up with and overtake' economically advanced capitalist countries within the shortest possible time.

It is true that, by ignoring common sense, utopian rationalism in the first stage of its development had an enormous power of renewal. It created an illusion that man can work miracles and carry out seemingly unbelievable technological and social projects. It unleashed the imagination and promoted the spirit of innovation, which, in spite of a lower literacy rate, was more developed in certain strata of the population than it is today.

Utopian rationalism also meant a conflict between the goals of society and the individual, as well as between social goals and common sense. In the context of innovation, the conflict was resolved in two ways. First, innovations were propagated because the mass of the people identified themselves with the prevailing values and with the group (society as a whole). People genuinely believed that the projects they were working on were rational, useful and conducive to the accomplishment of the goals with which they identified themselves. This blind trust was made even stronger by the charismatic leader who could not be wrong.[13] Given this absolute trust, no coercion or economic incentives are necessary to mobilize the masses to carry out even the most fantastic of projects.

However, in the absence of blind trust, when people do not believe in the rationality of what they have been called upon to do, conflicts are resolved, and innovations propagated, by the second method: with the help of force and reprisals. In this situation, individuals do not identify themselves with the predominant values of society as a whole.

It is true that, in the second case, the conflict between society's goals and common sense is played out at the level of individuals who are aware that in carrying out orders they are doing a senseless thing. When this sentiment of senselessness becomes widespread in society and encompasses its most diverse strata, we can speak of a crisis of utopian rationalism, whose very foundations begin to be seen as impediments to progress. As the overall level of education and literacy rose in Soviet society, an ever greater proportion of its citizens began combining outer submission to official dogma with an inner rejection.

The following are the most important ideological imperatives which gained the status of dogma in the USSR (a complete list would include hundreds of examples).

1 The Soviet state is a state of the whole people representing the interests of all social classes, strata and groups. Therefore, any actions of the state or its officials work to the benefit of society, and criticizing them or opposing them is anti-social.
2 State ownership of the means of production is the supreme form of ownership. State property is national property because the state represents the people and society. All other forms of ownership of the means of production (private individual, co-operative) are subsidiary forms standing at a lower level of social evolution. That is why it is justifiable that economic, legal and other conditions enjoyed by workers in these spheres should be worse than the rights enjoyed by employees of state enterprises.
3 Centralization in the economy and other spheres is in society's interest; it ensures a proper combination of individual, group and society's interests, which always have priority. For these reasons, it is commands by superior authorities that advance society's interests, rather than spontaneous moves from below.
4 Socialist society and its economy can and must develop according to a unified national plan which has the force of law and reflects society's needs. Therefore, any initiative from the grass-roots must be examined, and approved or rejected, by the top, and then directed into the appropriate planning channel. (This dogma can also be interpreted as meaning that there can be no socially useful activity outside officially approved organizations.)
5 Labour under socialism has a directly social character. No market is needed to make it socially acceptable.
6 Economic competition is destructive; it makes the economy uncontrollable and hampers the achievement of socially useful goals.
7 Collectivism is a positive phenomenon; the collective is always right and the individual is obliged to submit to its dictates.
8 Equality is always just, while inequality is always unjust. Therefore, one of our society's principal goals is social homogeneity.
9 Big organizations are more efficient and productive than small ones.
10 Since socialism is a superior social system, it is not beset by the economic and social problems exclusive to capitalism. Among these are political, economic and other crises, inflation, organized crime, poverty, drug addiction, corruption, ethnic conflicts, stagnation in scientific and technological progress, etc.

At the same time, outward submission is characteristic of one section of the population only. Other sections have made all the ideological imperatives completely their own and rely on dogmas to classify all activities as 'socialist' or 'unsocialist'. Dogmas are thus used as grounds for the banning of certain forms of practical activity.

Prior to perestroika, these and other ideas were not debated or called into question, the more so that some of them have not, to this day, been formulated in an explicit form. Nevertheless, they have been espoused by millions upon millions of people (leaders, engineers, physicians and workers) as self-evident truths. Actions or pronouncements running counter to them produced an immediate negative reaction and outrage on the part, not only of official ideologues, but also 'ordinary' citizens, even if those actions and pronouncements were not against the law. For example, it has been alleged that entrepreneurs are making too much money for themselves and spreading inequality and injustice in society. Local authorities (and sometimes higher-level authorities) may respond to these allegations by persecuting private firms, raising taxes even if they have not breached any regulations.

The consequences of socialist dogma are thus a means of stamping out the incipient nuclei of social progress. The overcoming of dogmatism was one of the central features in the concept of perestroika. As Mikhail Gorbachev said: 'the most important thing for society as a whole is to overcome dogmatic thinking because it afflicts politicians, writers and researchers alike'.[14] Leaders of CPSU, close to Gorbachev, regarded socialist ideological norms as reasons for the existence of institutions which blocked societal progress and resulted in stagnation:

> In retrospect it is clear that too much effort has been spent to achieve something that served as a theoretical justification for complacency and outward well-being, and which led to stagnation of the country's socio-economic and political development. We must resolutely get rid of this heritage. If we want to draw philosophical and moral lessons for the future this must be done thoroughly.[15]

The ideological norms provided theoretical grounds and moral foundation for the Soviet economy's total dependence on the tandem of politician and administrator, the liquidation of the social role of owner, the ministerial organization of economic management, direct centralized planning, and many other things that shackled Soviet society for decades. Years of ideological suppression of any transforming or innovative activity by means of a system of prohibitions and repression have resulted in a relative surplus of motivation and a shortage of outward stimuli.

In this situation few people, and fewer innovators, have found self-fulfilment. 'Every day I come across talented people who have not made their mark. The sight of them is unbearable. Without self-fulfilment a person cannot be happy. His or her life becomes a torment for themselves and for those close to them.'[16] As a result society has accumulated enormous potential energy which cannot be used constructively and therefore finds an outlet in aberrant behaviour, such as drunkenness, hooliganism, criminal entrepreneurship, black-marketeering etc. Other negative phenomena, such as tampering with statistics, faked 'innovation', and so on help to perpetuate stagnation.

Now most Russians refute the old socialist ideology, though it is preserved in the subconscious. The population needs a new ideology to fill the vacuum left by socialist values. If this absence of common beliefs, of an integrated ideology, continues, it seems unlikely that the majority of the population will create their own individual purposes and values.

The irony of reform in Russia lies in the need for the integrated socialist ideology to decay before the country could begin to take steps towards a market economy, because a strong anti-market ideology like Sovietism, in which most people had no knowledge of the market system, would stop all the potential economic changes. But without the kind of concordance in the reform programme provided by an integrated ideology, economic transition is impossible. Unfortunately, reform in Russia began with the destruction of the ideology and, with its destruction, of the Communist Party. This destruction provoked the breakdown of the Soviet political system and of the USSR. Therefore the 'Chinese variant' of reform was impossible in Russia.

Furthermore, it is necessary to formulate common ideological principles to be followed by both the authorities and the population. An example of such a principle is the so-called 'presumption of competence', which means that everything that is not explicitly forbidden is allowed.[17] These principles must then be enshrined in corresponding legislation. This must be done openly and publicly, with due account taken of the views and interests of various social strata. The ridding of Russian society of dogmatism must in our view be aimed at shedding the utopian elements of collectivist rationalism and moving toward individualistic rationalism. This means that the institutions which limit the economic freedom of the individual (and his or her freedom in general) and hamper this self-fulfilment must be abolished. On the other hand, it calls for the creation of specific institutions which enable people to act as free economic agents.

13.3 Stagnating culture and the climate favourable for innovation

Culture assures continuity of values and norms of society. It is society's 'social memory.'[18] In terms of the impact on innovation processes, two types of culture may be distinguished: a culture of innovation and a culture of stagnation. The first type of culture encourages people to modernize and to innovate. The second kind of culture, in contrast, encourages apathy and passivity.

The degree of a culture's innovativeness is largely dependent on the degree of its susceptibility to cultural innovations. Borrowing from an article by Arutyunov, we can classify these into three types: innovations which emerge spontaneously in a given culture; innovations which arise naturally under the stimulus of impulses; and borrowed innovations.[19] If the evolution of culture is based mainly on spontaneous innovations, its hallmark is the striving of people in all spheres of activity to be high achievers. Achievement is noted and encouraged by means of both material and moral incentives. It is respected and emulated. This type of culture is tolerant of differences in opinion and of unconventional behaviour. It is highly appreciative of new, original ideas because it understands their power to transform society. And it sets itself challenging goals, although it may lack all the prerequisites for their achievement. Confronted with problems, it discusses their essence and does not merely bow to authority. In short, this type of culture is 'innovation-friendly'.

Cultures that evolve naturally as a result of innovations stimulated by outside impulses are not likely to stagnate. An example is the economic culture of Japan, a country that has kept itself open to technological advances made abroad.[20] Borrowed technology serves as an impetus to rapid growth and accelerates the modernization process. However, this is only possible when a country has its own social base for development, and when its workforce does not stint on the time and effort required for production modernization, but want to be high achievers.

A culture that is based primarily on borrowed innovations and cultural achievements, however, is a culture of stagnation. It discourages differences of opinion and unconventional forms of behaviour. Its slogan is 'don't stick your neck out'. It has no mechanisms for the encouragement and selection of new values and behavioural patterns. What is more, it suppresses them with the help of special social control mechanisms. The accomplishments of others are not admired and emulated, they arouse jealousy and the desire to put successful people 'in their place'.[21]

The hallmark of a culture of stagnation is routine which is not conducive to the development of the individual's full potential.

Another characteristic of a culture of stagnation is that people do not like, and are not prepared, to take risks, and do everything possible to avoid them. Those who run even small risks are branded as adventurers. They are condemned even more harshly than those who are passive or hide-bound.

A major feature of a culture in stagnation is its orientation towards the best foreign examples and authorities, and a reluctance to appreciate its own accomplishments. Such cultures get most of their technological advances and innovations from outside, laying little store by their own, home-grown, ideas because they do not appreciate their power to transform society. One effect of the borrowing of ready-made innovations (be they machines or theoretical concepts) is that the link between innovations and new ideas becomes masked in the process. Foreign innovations are frequently attributed solely to a developed material base, while the origins of this developed material base are never explored. In stagnating cultures, new ideas are treated as the cheapest of commodities, cheaper even than unskilled manual labour.

Economic culture in the states of the former Soviet Union displays many features of a non-innovative culture in stagnation. This is largely due to the extensive use of new imported technologies. It is much easier to introduce a tested innovation developed by somebody else than to start the process from scratch on one's own. What is more, the latter course is risky, needs approval from many superior authorities, and is not likely to increase one's income. Imported innovations, in contrast, are almost certain of success, and also hold the added promise of highly remunerative trips abroad.

Over-emphasis on the use of foreign technology may also lead to the copying of obsolete products and processes, chronic dependence on foreign science and technology, and other negative social effects. In line with the adage that 'no prophet is accepted in his own country', a sort of science and technology inferiority complex has developed. The results of the national R&D effort gain acceptance in this country only after gaining recognition abroad. The few examples of breakthroughs of truly international importance are exceptions confirming the rule.

Another manifestation of this inferiority complex is the striking indifference to national accomplishments and researchers, unless, of course, the latter are recognized authorities in prestigious fields of science and technology. The fact that bureaucrats stonewall innovators is thus aggravated by non-recognition.

Another effect of the habit of importing foreign technology is that economic administrators of various rank are completely unaware of the time and effort that go into research and development, and are thus incapable of appreciating the work of a scientist, a researcher or an inventor. What is more, they are scornful of domestic science and technology which do not bring immediate economic benefits or other practical results. This in turn adds to the national inferiority complex.

Stagnating economic culture has also affected the sphere of education. The institutions of family and the educational process do not orient people towards independent creative activities. Upbringing within the family does not emphasize independence; Russian children remain materially and psychologically dependent on their parents up to, and beyond, the age of 30. Child labour is prohibited up to the age of 16. At present, some schoolchildren sell newspapers, clean cars and even start their own businesses, sometimes earning more than their teachers. But there are to date not enough young workers to include this factor as a norm in Russian economic culture. Schools and universities are less concerned with the fostering of independent thinking and creativity, than with passing on a considerable body of knowledge to students. School and university students have virtually no opportunity to choose courses or teachers. Self-government by university students, let alone by school students, is rudimentary and is often shackled by academic councils, student research societies, and other organizational forms imposed from above. School and university graduates know very little about the practical aspects of industrial R&D when they are first employed.

That Soviet economic culture has not been innovation-minded is also due to the fact that it absorbed much of Russia's peasant commune culture, with its emphasis on egalitarianism and assistance to the weak.

For all these reasons, the prevalent cultural mechanism has generated only a small number of people who could be described as 'potential super-innovators', and large numbers of those who evade risk and fight shy of innovation. Existing cultural patterns have thus served as a brake on modernization in Russia. They have slowed it down through the minds of the people, who are indifferent to innovation and innovators. This has resulted in a stagnant social atmosphere unfavourable to innovation and fatal for the few innovators that do exist.

NOTES

1 A. Bossart, 'An iron curtain of a tax', *Ogonek*, xxix (1988), 4.

2 Innovative behaviour, which is a component of economic behaviour, can be treated in a similar way.

3 M. Weber, *The protestant ethic and the spirit of capitalism*, New York, Scribner (1952; Russian trans. 1972).

4 This approach is somewhat simplified (choice is never absolutely free) but is sufficient for the purposes of our analysis.

5 Weber, *The protestant ethic*, 33.

6 The term 'chose' here is provisional. No one consciously chose which type of rationalism to adopt or debated (let alone voted on) this issue. Simply, those values closer to a society with the strong traditions of the Russian peasants' commune were the ones that took root.

7 The main character in Bek's novel *A New Appointment*, People's Commissar Anisimov, is an example of such an ascetic: he headed an enterprise worth millions and possessed just one suit of clothes.

8 A. N. Engelhardt, *From the village: 12 letters*, Moscow, Mysl (1987), 153. Both the Stakhanovite movement and the widespread practice of rushed work are easier to understand in this light. The seeds fell on fertile cultural soil.

9 A. Hammer, *Autobiography*, New York, Putnam & Sons (1987; Russian trans. 1988), 108.

10 The normal pace of industrialization (spreading over several decades in the case of industrially advanced countries), or even a somewhat rapid pace, would not have led to such political tensions and massive repression. However, it would have run counter to the slogan of catching up with and overtaking developed countries within the shortest possible time.

11 Stalin's forcible collectivisation of peasants into *kholkozy* in the 1930s provoked great social tension and armed uprisings against the policy. In response, Stalin wrote the article 'Dizzy with success', in which he accused local authorities and Party organizations of mistakes and excesses in carrying out Party directives, which were in themselves beneficial.

12 I. V. Stalin, *Collected works*, xi, Moscow, Gospolitizdat (1949), 192–3.

13 This brings to mind the phrase from Engelhardt which we have already quoted: 'if the master succeeds in infusing them with sufficient energy'. 'The master' indeed knew how.

14 M. S. Gorbachev, *Through democratization to a new type of socialism*, Moscow, Politizdat (1988), 23.

15 A. Yakovlev, 'Attaining a qualitatively new state of Soviet society and the social sciences', *Kommunist*, viii (1987), 5.

16 A. Radov, 'Inventors and bureaucrats', *Ogonek*, xviii (1988), 2.

17 Y. Tikhomirov, 'Permitted if not forbidden', *Khozaistvo i pravo*, vi (1988), 10.

18 See R. Ryvkina, 'Economic culture as the social memory of society', *EKO*, 1 (1989).

19 This classification is borrowed from S. A. Arutyunov, *Innovation in the culture of an ethnic group*, Moscow, Nauka (1985), 33. Without changing its essence, we have somewhat modified the terminology. Arutyunov distinguishes between (1) spontaneous transformation; (2) stimulated transformation; and (3) borrowing.

20 Moritani, an expert on scientific and technological progress, wrote of Japan: 'It owes its might to the fact that like a foster parent it has been setting "foundlings" from other countries on their feet.' At the same time he noted: 'It is true that Japanese corporations have started emphasizing the importance of creativity: creativity is finally in great demand.' M. Moritani, *Advanced technology: the Japanese contribution*, Tokyo, Simul Press (1983; Russian trans. 1986), 129.

21 In a typical comment, Shmelev writes: 'I am convinced that the principal sin of the command economy is the intense and blind jealousy of a successful neighbour. This has become, at practically every level, a formidable obstacle to the ideas and practice of perestroika. Until we do something about it, the success of perestroika will be open to question.' N. Shmelev, 'New alarms', *Novy mir*, iv (1988), 175.

14

The Prime Cause of Stagnation: Socialist Monopolism[1]

This chapter is an attempt to analyse the phenomenon of socialist monopolism as the root cause of stagnation in the innovative processes in Russia. This phenomenon does not result from a distortion or deformation of any original idea. It has taken shape in the course of the application of socialist principles in Russia and is a product of one of socialism's variants (hence *socialist* monopolism).

A vast economic literature on monopoly has grown up since the 19th century. Most of these texts regard the problem in the context of a market economy and political democracy. At first sight, looking at the question of monopolism in the context of a totalitarian society theoretically controlled completely by the state is wrong. And indeed it would be, if freedom, public life and competition had not existed at all in Soviet society. But even in a state-controlled society like that of the former USSR, some forms of individual and group autonomies from the system existed, and some version of competition operated too. Therefore it is possible to put the question, considering the ways of state control and the ways of the population's escape from state supervision to a private life.

Socialist monopolism brought about, and kept alive, certain defects in the institutions of politics, ideology, economy and culture which have slowed down the rate of modernization. Socialist monopolism is a feature shared by these institutions. It is therefore a systemic malady of society affecting all of its spheres. Although it manifests itself in a variety of forms, they also have some common characteristics.

14.1 The essence and emergence of socialist monopolism

Monopolism may be defined as exclusive control by one decision-maker of a sphere of activity: politics, ideology, economy, science, literature, the arts etc.

The monopolist's predominant position gives him or her absolute power and complete freedom of action in the attainment of goals. Any means may be used to achieve this end, because there are no forces opposing him or her in society. Common sense and economic expediency may be disregarded; white may be declared black and black white, with no fear of being exposed as a liar.

Socialist monopolism is fundamentally different from capitalist monopolism primarily in its scope. Whereas, under capitalism, monopolism may affect only some of the economic sectors, parts of the country or social spheres, socialist monopolism is total and all-inclusive. A capitalist monopoly is a product of competition. Socialist monopolism, in contrast, is a product of the elimination of competition, and rules out all open (i.e. legal) competition against the monopolist. Unlike a monopoly under socialism, a capitalist monopoly is constantly threatened by the loss of its monopoly status. Finally, socialist monopolism is state monopolism, in which the monopolies are part of the state apparatus.

Every sphere of social life has its own monopolist. In the economy, it is the production-branch ministry or department; in science, it is the Academy of Sciences and the leading research institutes; in the arts, it is the creative unions; in public health, it is the Ministry of Health; and so on. At the same time, under socialism all of these monopolists are dependent on politicians. Politicians reign supreme over all other monopolists and integrate them into one single whole. In their ruling and integrating activities, they themselves are primarily guided by ideological criteria of what constitutes socialism and what does not. All developments and phenomena in every sphere of social life are assessed primarily from this standpoint, and those that are judged to correspond to socialism are encouraged, whereas those that are felt to be contrary to socialism are suppressed by political, administrative, judicial, and other means. In this way the socialist uniformity of society is enforced, and society is purged of everything that in the view of politicians does not accord with socialism.

To put it differently, under socialist monopolism all social institutions are totally dependent on the institutions of ideology and politics, because politicians guided by ideological criteria (and administrators carrying out their decisions) can interfere in the activities of any other institution, be it the economy, the sciences, the law or literature.

In this set-up, politicians at the top formulate objectives for all other institutions. The latter are not fulfilling some useful social function, but are tackling specific political tasks. For example, agriculture (or, to be more precise, the AIC) is not producing food and raw materials to meet the needs of the population and society: it is implementing the food programme drawn up on the instruction of political institutions, and collective and state farms are working to implement plans formulated by order of political bodies. By the same token, the press is not an institution giving expression to the interests, opinions and will of various social groups. It does not reflect the collective consciousness, ways of life, plans and suggestions of diverse groups of the population, but is the sum total of publications that are called on to educate the masses, propagandize the latest political decisions, and serve as a safety valve in case of friction between the administrative apparatus and the population at large.

Thus, under socialist monopolism, social institutions are not the sum total of naturally arising social norms and people performing various social roles in accordance with these norms to fulfil meaningful social functions. They are instead extensions of the institutions of ideology and politics working to attain various objectives set by them.

Of course, each social institution has its own social norms and social roles, but all of them are strictly controlled (and some of them are formulated) by politicians. The most important are controlled directly, while others are controlled indirectly. For example, politicians abolished the role of owner from the economy for purely ideological reasons (and also because it would have hindered political interference). This led to the destruction of the economic culture that had grown up on the basis of this role. Part of this culture was the combination of norms and behavioural stereotypes that form the widely accepted concept of 'good husbandry'. The economic institutions through which this role manifested itself (market institutions, laws protecting property etc.) were also largely destroyed.

In addition, politicians assign tasks to all social institutions and distribute social statuses within them. They offer every support to certain groups of functionaries and give them monopoly status, while at the same time depriving others of their support. The social sciences are a good example. The dependence of science, and scholarship in general, on ideology and politics is such that it is no longer an institution promoting culture and its development, but a sum total of people and organizations propagandizing politicians' decisions, elaborating upon them, applying cosmetic repairs to the original ideological tenets, and transmitting them to students (through the intermediary of teachers). God forbid that they interfere with decision-making or understand its workings! As a consequence of playing this role, the social sciences, which have no independent social status, have not evolved their own position on the problems they are concerned with. They merely echo the government apparatus in a supposedly more scientific form. As a result, they cannot be critical of decisions affecting the economy, culture, and other spheres.[2] Lacking a position of their own, the social sciences cannot come up with a critique of erroneous decisions or counter them with constructive and thoroughly prepared projects.

The overall effect is that the quality of decision-making has frequently been lower than could be expected given the country's intellectual potential, which has unfortunately lain virtually unused by decision-makers in the past; this was one of the main reasons for the stagnation of the Brezhnev era. As Yakovlev noted: 'we entered the 1980s not only with the grave shortcomings and miscalculations that are now widely recognized, but also with a theoretical consciousness that was largely of the 1930s vintage, when our society was at a relatively early stage of its development.' He therefore has every reason to ask: 'Haven't the ideas of "anti-marketeers", which were more like political accusations, turned out to be a brake on the economy? It was supposed that the academic and research community was engaged in a scientific debate, but in reality disregard for objectivity reigned supreme, both in theory and in practice.'[3]

Of course, these ideas did lead to economic stagnation, but one cannot help wondering how the anti-marketeers came into existence in the first place. They are largely the product of a practice whereby politicians proclaim a scientific school to be the only correct one or 'truly Marxist-Leninist', thus giving it a monopoly status and handing it *carte blanche* to massacre its opponents (explained as a manifestation of the class struggle in science). This automatically ruled out the emergence of new schools in the social sciences, because the truly 'Marxist-Leninist' form of social science already existed.

These ideological 'blows below the belt', especially considering that the victim could not hit back, slowed down progress in areas in which the USSR had been the pioneer. Examples include the mathematical techniques of economic research pioneered in 1939 by the Nobel Prize winning academic L. V. Kantorovich, the path-breaking research by the economists Kondratiev, and Chayanov, and the work of sociologists Sorokin and Gurvich.[4] Unfortunately, the technique of ideological 'blows below the belt' as a substitute for genuine debate in the social sciences was still alive not so long ago, and acted as an impediment to new ideas. For example, this was the technique used by V. Y. Elmeev, a professor at St Petersburg University to throw political accusations at economic sociology, a new development in the social sciences. In an article in *Vestnik LGU*, he claimed that economic sociology was a bourgeois science, which the Soviet people did not need because they already had political economy.

Under socialist monopolism, social institutions have structures that are designed to facilitate, to the greatest extent possible, interference by the institutions of ideology and politics. These are hierarchical structures in which the lower levels are completely subordinate to the higher ones. Organizations at the lower levels have been set up to perform various technical functions of elaborating and transmitting commands from above. They are not voluntary associations of people, designed to meet individual and social needs. All exchanges (horizontal exchanges) must be sanctioned by a superior authority. Any other relationships will be branded as 'shadow activities'. The apex of this hierarchy is the monopolist or supreme administrator, who is in immediate contact with his or her political counterpart, from whom in turn, he or she receives instructions. It is an administrative system, and relations within it are administrative relations involving the marshalling of human and material resources. This is the way our economy, our sciences, our education system, our public health, all operated in the past. This multitude of administrative systems has been created to carry out the commands of the institutions of ideology and politics as quickly and as faithfully as possible, rather than to produce metal, bake bread, treat patients, teach schoolchildren, or sew garments. If the administrative systems do these things, they do so as a by-product. We owe them a debt of gratitude because in principle they could dispense with these activities altogether; they certainly have the power to do so.

Total interference by the institutions of politics and ideology in the functioning of any social institution had received a theoretical base (from academic disciplines that were as stagnant as they were servile) in the principle of unity between the Party's ideological, political and economic work.[5] It had been argued that this principle creates cohesion in Soviet society and enables all of its spheres to function in accordance with the same ideological imperatives. This provided a spurious academic credibility for the institutions of ideology and politics that had eliminated all trace of competition and competitiveness in Soviet society and created monopolization of every sphere of life.

Stalin and his associates[6] were mostly responsible for this. Between the end of the Civil War and the late 1920s, Soviet society displayed some elements of pluralism. It had several economic structures (economic pluralism); there were different opinions within the Party concerning how to start building socialism (elements of political pluralism); a great diversity of opinions, styles, schools and movements existed in the sciences, arts and literature (cultural pluralism). Clearly, that particular society was not totally controlled from above. It was self-administered to the extent that it was pluralistic, and, as a consequence, it resisted direct interference by politicians.

This prevented Stalin from achieving his ends. For example, in the late 1920s, there were 25 million peasant households in agriculture selling a sizeable proportion of their produce in the open market. In order to carry out rapid industrialization (at the expense of the peasants) Stalin had to supply the urban population with food (mostly grain products) at fixed prices. This policy was based on political and ideological considerations and led to a wide disparity between the prices of manufactured and agricultural products. The peasants reacted by cutting their deliveries of grain to the open market, leading to the so-called 'procurement crisis'. The authorities countered this by resorting to harsh administrative measures and to repression. In order to avoid a repetition, market institutions in the countryside were abolished, owners as a social group were destroyed, and peasants were forcibly driven into collective farms. The latter were not co-operatives (i.e. voluntary associations of producers) but administrative units supervising agricultural activity. It goes without saying that all competition, including that between procurement agencies, was abolished. Describing the most important measures taken to put an end to the procurement crisis, Stalin pointed out that: 'We had to put our procurement organizations under the control of Party organizations, to stop them competing with each other and to oblige them to pursue a Soviet policy of prices'.[7] These measures enabled Stalin to get all the food he needed for his rapid industrialization drive practically without opposition.

The elements of pluralism in society described above were eliminated in the late 1920s and 1930s, when complete uniformity and unity were achieved. Stalin physically destroyed his political opponents and gained a monopoly of political power. In his book *United Ranks*, the historian S. L. Dmitrenko gave this strict

Stalinist interpretation of the role of the Komsomol in the struggle against the opposition:

> The preservation and strengthening of the Party's unity really involved clashes with various opposition movements and groups which were trying to divert it from the Leninist road, frustrate the fulfilment of its creative plans, and restore capitalism.[8]

The seizure of unchallenged political power enabled Stalin to dismantle market institutions in the economy, destroy those who embodied the corresponding economic roles, assert the rule of Lysenko in science, destroy representatives of all except 'Marxist-Leninist' schools in the sciences, and ensure that socialist realism became the only accepted school in the arts.

As a result, the 1930s saw the emergence of a socio-political system in which all institutions were characterized by socialist monopolism. This evolved solely as a result of directives from the institutions of ideology and politics. All unsanctioned initiatives were discouraged. The effect of monopolism on all spheres was an ever greater standardization and uniformity in public life, and eventually the rule of orthodoxy. Monopolism suppressed dissidence and all unorthodox thinking.

The principal negative effect of monopolism is the perpetuation of the existing state of things and the blocking of progress, accompanied by active opposition to all attempts to change the existing order and to find alternative ways of life. It is now time to examine some specific forms and features of the socialist monopolism which still permeates every major sphere of Russian life in order the better to understand the mechanism by which it is slowing down innovation.

14.2 Principal forms and features of socialist monopolism

There are four principle forms of socialist monopolism.

1 The monopolism of office holders stems from the high status of an individual in an activity or organization. It may find expression in 'soft' forms such as respect for rank, or 'hard' forms such as the personality cult. It is based on a monopoly on power and on the abuse of power.

2 The monopolism of a group of people, which may not officially be constituted as an organization but is made monolithic as a result of close personal (unofficial) contacts between its members. Such groups may form larger clusters on the basis of close informal ties, as a result of which their power and influence become even greater. They may control the economic and social life of entire regions, with dire consequences for their development. As Dodolev observed, 'the consequences of this "social cataclysm" for one of the leading republics with a population of 19 million [in this case, Uzbekistan] have been devastating. Boundless greed and a sweat-shop system of labour enabled criminal elements to become millionaires.'[9]
3 The monopolism of an organization may come about because it performs some special function that cannot be performed by any other organization. For example, a single industrial facility may account for the production of the bulk of a commodity in the country, or one of its regions. The monopoly of a single producer makes the market highly unstable and dependent on the state of affairs in just one organization. The entire economy can be sensitive to accidents, negligence and other unforeseen circumstances within that organization.
4 The monopolism of ministries and other government departments.

These four forms of socialist monopolism do not exist in isolation, but are closely interconnected. For example, the monopoly of a government department leads to the monopoly of organizations. This is reflected in drives against overlapping in R&D, and against dissipation of resources on the setting up of several small enterprises instead of one big one, and so on. In a number of regions, powerful mafias co-exist with departmental monopolies, and enjoy protection in Moscow.

A number of common features make socialist monopoly a definable social phenomenon.

The monopolist was assured of a guaranteed existence and the preservation of achieved social status irrespective of actual performance

Even if a government department has not met its production targets, as a result of which there are shortages throughout the country and soaring production costs, there is no threat to it, for there is no competitor to drive it out of the market by producing more products of better quality and at a lower cost. What is more, everything will be done to bail it out and thus encourage poor performance.

The impossibility of bankruptcies and the guaranteed sale of output in the broad sense of the word (i.e. goods, services, works of art etc.), irrespective of quality and quantity, made the monopolist immune to the vagaries of the market and censure by superiors. Even if a department or organization produced large quantities of output for which there was no demand, this had no serious effect on its position: it will not be deprived of its headquarters in the centre of Moscow; Gosplan will continue to allocate funds; it will never be declared bankrupt. Of course, overproduction did have negative effects for the monopolist, too. However, under socialist monopolism, in contrast to market economies, it posed no threat to its continued existence.

Another instrument guaranteeing the survival of the monopolist was the institution of 'mandatory purchase'. The ordinary consumer came across it whenever he or she wanted to buy an item that was in short supply and could only do so by also taking other items that might not be needed at all. In the production sphere, this meant that suppliers were rigidly tied to customers; in the public health sector, it meant that residents in an area could use clinics in that area only; and so on throughout every field of society. In short, the customer had no freedom of choice.

It is noteworthy that this practice had been legitimized by the sciences. For many years, the Soviet political economy conducted intensive research into the concept that labour under socialism has a directly socialized nature. The concept is still to be found in most manuals on the political economy of socialism. In practical terms, this means that if a government agency had drawn up plans for the production of so many tons or items of a commodity, the entire output was 'accepted'; by society (naturally without any market mechanism.) What the customers or consumers thought about the quality of the commodity in question made no difference, because labour inputs into its production had already been 'accepted' by society before it reached the shelves of a warehouse or shop. Once the production quota had been fulfilled, the producer felt free to report that the production target had been met, entitling him or her to cash bonuses, honorary citations, government decorations and promotions. If customers and consumers refused to buy these fruits of directly socialized labour, so much the worse for them – no substitute product had been provided for in the plans, and there is nobody to manufacture it because there was only one, monopoly, producer. When customers or consumers balked and rejected low-quality products, they were the ones who were punished, by depriving themselves of a commodity without at the same time penalizing the producer.

In this way monopolism bred inequality between producer and consumer, wastage of resources and huge inventories of goods that nobody needed.

Socialist monopolism was constantly creating a favourable socio-economic environment for itself

This means that the all-powerful monopolist was adapting the environment to its needs. The relationships being shaped by the monopolist were with (a) administrative bodies; (b) customers and consumers; (c) regulatory agencies; (d) superior authorities defining its socio-economic targets (in the case of an organization, this was the corresponding government department; in the case of a department, it was Gosplan, the State Standards Commission and the Ministry of Finance; and (e) the public.

Examples of how these relationships were shaped to suit the monopolist include disregard by a department for decisions and decrees of central bodies, or interpretations of them according to its own needs. A case in point was the project for the diversion of Siberian rivers to the south which the USSR Ministry for Water Resources began implementing in spite of the resolution of the 27th CPSU Congress (1986) ratifying only an in-depth feasibility study.

The monopolist thus drew up the rules regulating its relationship with the economic environment. This entailed doing everything possible to make others perform as many of its functions as possible: occupants of government housing were thus expected to maintain and repair it;[10] purchasers of durable goods were expected to assemble and install complex household appliances themselves; buyers of shoddy products were expected to repair the defects themselves; and so on.

It is only natural that monopolists drew up the rules according to which they operate so as to gain a maximum of advantages for themselves and created a maximum of disadvantages for the customer. The system was constructed so that the customer had no way of putting pressure on them.

Not only did monopolists write their own rules, they also sought to control all information concerning their operations. In order to conceal from central authorities or regulatory agencies their mistakes, miscalculations, activities damaging the environment, and other things which were deemed to be unsuitable for publication, they resorted to the subterfuge of official secrets (a form of state secret). They did everything in their power to classify all information, to stamp every document with an inscription stating 'for official use only' or 'confidential'. Even specialists might be denied access to information that they needed for the performance of their duties.

In this system, the institution of censorship becomes extremely useful. All materials circulated in more than ten copies were subject to a multi-tiered procedure of censorship. Although censorship had been rationalized by a variety of ideological formulas, its main purpose was to ensure an easy life for monopolists of various stripe, since disclosure of the information kept secret might mean extra work for the monopolist.

Monopolism was inimical to openness and glasnost. It had reduced the number of persons who had access to trustworthy information about the life of society to a handful. It had thus brought about considerable social inequalities in terms of access to information. As society evolves, information becomes increasingly valuable. What is more, lack of information in closed societies leads to the doctoring of statistics and the thriving of myths.[11] Under socialist monopolism, there was no one either to debunk or to verify a myth.

Under socialist monopolism, monopolists totally controlled their internal environments

This meant that lower-level organizations and their workforces were totally dependent on the central agencies, which had the right of virtually unlimited interference in their activities. The centre also controlled links between subordinates and their links with outside organizations.

This total control was possible in general because under socialist monopolism organizations were created or dismantled solely by decree from above. The prerogative of the apparat to set up new organizations was the main prerequisite for the continued existence of monopolism. This prerogative protected monopolists from possible grass-roots competition or initiatives. It had sharply reduced or, to be more precise, almost precluded large-scale legal entrepreneurial activities because new social initiatives, the development and application of fundamentally new products and processes, and other entrepreneurial activities were impossible without new organizations. Under monopolism, unorganized activities had no chance of success.

Under monopolism, heads of organizations and their structural units are also appointed from above. Even if they are elected, the elections were purely *pro-forma*. Their outcome was a foregone conclusion because only one candidate was fielded.

The above characteristics of monopolism can be observed both in the productive and non-productive spheres. Everyday life under monopolism abounded in situations in which consumers bought shoddy articles instead of the real thing, and in the words of the prominent satirist Zhvanetsky, 'are happy that it has not also been taken away from them'. Tikhonov had the following to say on the subject:

> The Ministry of Water Resources gets billions of roubles from a rich and generous uncle; that is, the state. Subsequently it decides which projects in which parts of the country are going to be more profitable for it. It then acts as its own acceptance committee, its own banker, and its own jury awarding prizes and government decorations. It then hands over the reclaimed land to a state or collective farm. Since 'you don't look a gift horse in the mouth', they accept it, plough it up, bring in the harvest, and suddenly discover that the soil is too saline, or waterlogged.[12]

These and similar situations were not the result of a conspiracy of bureaucrats, or a lack of understanding of economic problems by leaders of government departments. They were the natural and inevitable product of the special status of the monopolist's enormous power.

Monopolism means that there are no alternatives. Society is moving along the only possible line of development, which has been formulated *in camera* by persons unknown, approved by other persons unknown, and leading to places unknown. It has never been publicly discussed, criticized or called into question. The credo of the gullible, it will be undeviatingly adhered to until the time when a new general line is formulated by persons unknown. For this reason, monopolism means a constant struggle against heresy and deviation, and an unceasing battle against grass-root initiatives which may threaten the existing order of things.

Monopolism is fertile soil for red tape and bureaucrats because it is underpinned by unlimited power, unchallenged decision-making, and a lack of responsibility for these decisions and their consequences. Monopolism breeds abuses of power, because there are no social forces opposing it.

Reigning supreme in its own sphere, the monopolist naturally rules by decree. Since the monopolist did not own the means of production at its disposal (and was thus free of economic responsibility and the threat of bankruptcy), it might exercise virtually total control of the factories, plants, state and collective farms in its realm. In some respects the monopolist was bigger than the owner, in that it was totally free from economic responsibility for its decisions. In other respects it was smaller; for example, it had no right to sell a factory. Nevertheless, the monopolist had almost unlimited economic power, and as long as it could issue absolute orders to the workforce and organizations subordinate to it, the operation relied on such 'administrative' methods. Prices, tariffs, levels of tax on profits, and other economic norms were set and even changed according to the monopolist's whim, for there was no one to oppose it.

Economic targets and indicators calculated by government departments, and imposed by them on their subordinates, are additional instruments of running a command economy. The monopolist could change them practically at a moment's notice. The social essence of prices, tariffs etc. was identical to the social essence of the arbitrary hiring and dismissal of labour, or the secondment of workers and engineers from factories in the town to do agricultural work in the countryside, and so on. Prices and other economic regulators were not dictated by production needs or contractual free-market relations: they were the product of bureaucratic games[13] played by monopolists between themselves, on the one hand, and between them and politicians, on the other. Under socialist monopolism, the promotion of 'economic methods of management' (the concept used by Gorbachev in the early perestroika period) is in effect the extension of the same policy in a slightly modified form. Although the total dependence of people and organizations on the monopolist remains unchanged, it has assumed more refined forms. In some respects, this new form of dependence offers even greater benefits to the monopolist. Firstly, it was not so overt, because commands had been replaced by 'state orders' (presently replaced by state possession of controlling blocks of shareholdings). Secondly, it has given the monopolist even greater freedom of movement, because the old forms of state enterprise dependence on the superior authorities have remained largely unchanged (their administrative subordination to ministries and departments has not been abolished although it has noticeably declined).

It is the giants of industry that may benefit from economic targets under socialist monopolism. This explains their claims that they could do without the ministries. They would benefit even under the old system if they were freed from supervision and patronage from above. They need little assistance, and outside control is always a nuisance. But would society as a whole, and consumers in particular, benefit in the process? We do not think so. It is primarily enterprises enjoying monopoly status (we are not speaking of private firms and the handful of enterprises with particularly enterprising managers) that claim not to need their ministries and other administrative bodies. Naturally, administrative control sometimes makes them heed the demands of the consumers whom they would otherwise have completely ignored. In a situation where several enterprises have monopolized a range of products, the mere lifting of controls from above has resulted in an even worse economic stagnation – a fall in output, lower quality standards and higher prices.

Of course, this is not to say that economic independence should not be granted to enterprises, or economic methods of management promoted. But we must first carefully examine the possible consequences of these moves and their possible negative impact on Russian society. We must also remember that the same measures may produce different results in different socio-economic conditions. In our view, the granting of greater economic freedom to enterprises (which only major monopolists could take advantage of in the old system) must follow, or be introduced simultaneously with, an overhaul of the system of socialist monopolism.

Monopolism needs institutions which act as safety valves for the latent tensions and resentment of a mass of people who can neither fulfil themselves nor openly protest. Criticism of such institutions has a dual purpose: it boosts the image of the monopolist and diverts resentments and aggression towards scapegoats. During the stagnation era, dissidents were used as scapegoats; before them, there were 'foreign spies'. Nowadays, the bureaucracy are increasingly used as scapegoats. The continued existence of the scapegoat institution guarantees the survival of socialist monopolism because it channels the people's energies towards weeding out those responsible for shortcomings and setbacks; the fight agains these 'enemies' justifies the existence of 'temporary problems'. The institutionalization of scapegoats has largely contributed to the growing disunity of various population strata and groups.

Under socialist monopolism, this disunity had another strong foundation: namely centralized government, as a result of which vertical links between superiors and subordinates were much stronger than horizontal ones. The fact that everybody had a superior, and all lack independent social status and freedom of choice, made it almost impossible for people to form free and voluntary associations without some kind of approval from above. Consequently, all organizations were set up by the authorities. In the few instances when they were established from below this requiries enormous pressure, and needed the approval of the authorities, who then appointed the heads of all such organizations.[14] As a consequence, under socialist monopolism most organizations were not voluntary and cohesive associations of like-minded persons working toward common objectives, but randomly assembled groups of people. Any common interest they do share is, as often as not, extra-mural. Not surprisingly, these randomly-assembled workforces usually display a proclivity to quarrels, jealousies, indifference and self-seeking.

Thus it is practically impossible under socialist monopolism to create the innovative communities which are the necessary social prerequisite for rapid and intensive modernization. The setting up of free associations is an indispensable condition for unleashing individual activity and enterprise. Enterprising behaviour in the economy largely consists of the ability to establish such voluntary associations quickly to develop and apply new technologies, to start new businesses, and to initiate other creative economic endeavours.

The main function and the characteristic feature of an entrepreneur is his or her ability quickly to form innovative communities: i.e. voluntary associations of people for the performance of a socially useful function or the meeting of a new social need. Thus, entrepreneurial activity may be defined as a creative group activity aimed at the setting up of enterprises (businesses) filling a new need.[15] The economic role of an entrepreneur implies the capacity to form organized innovative communities and to run risks involved in the application of innovations. No market institution can function without it. Under socialist monopolism (with its tandem of politician and administrator) the entrepreneur's counterpart is the organizing activity of political institutions and administrators. This administrative (bureaucratic) entrepreneurship takes the form of commands and innovation drives and, in contrast to its counterpart, does not need a market.

In our view, it is individual and group entrepreneurship that is best adapted to the diffusion of innovations from below. Individuals and groups acting as professional entrepreneurs will need to develop specialized skills fundamentally different from those of administrations or politicians.

Another by-product of socialist monopolism is the vagueness of social norms and loss of professionalism. For instance, research workers often had to serve as propagandists, and Party workers interfere in the activities of economic, cultural and scientific organizations. Depriving all social groups of independent social status, socialist monopolism obliterated significant differences between different social roles. This led to incompetent outside interference in, and incompetent evaluation of, the work of professionals (of whom precious few are left).

Furthermore, widespread interference in the functioning of the judiciary means that legal norms also become vague. Since nobody knows exactly what is permitted and what is forbidden, all major or contentious issues are resolved with the help of the 'big stick'. Socialist monopolism has the capacity to emasculate any right enshrined in the constitution, any laws, government decrees or other pieces of legislation. This is possible because under socialist monopolism every monopolist is a law unto himself, able to ignore the laws enacted by the central government, which become little more than declarations.

But the most negative effect of socialist monopolism is the enormous power that enables monopolists to tip the social balance in their own favour, bringing about a situation of chronic inequality. Its manifestation in the economy is the continuing 'non-equivalence of exchange' due to inequalities of distribution and power concentrated in the hands of industrial giants. For example, after the advocates of the interests of the peasantry were routed in the 1920–30s, the political influence of this social group became negligible. Agriculture moved to the bottom of the list for budget allocations and began to be viewed as having one of the lowest priorities. The effects of this development included changes in pricing policy, the introduction of feudal forms of labour organization, and so on.

Socialist monopolism in the economy and other spheres leads to chronic instability due to the political inequality of different economic agents. Furthermore, disadvantaged economic agents cannot speak up for themselves or work towards the improvement of their condition. They have neither the resources nor the political means to do so because sacrosanct ideological concepts rate them as second-class citizens. It was virtually impossible to champion the interests of the peasantry during forced industrialization, when 'the objective economic law of priority growth of the production of the means of production'[16] was in operation. Only 'kulaks', 'kulak sympathizers', 'clerics', 'obscurantists', 'enemies of socialism' – in short, 'enemies of the people' – could defend 'the peasant paradise' and the 'idiocy of rural life' while the country was building up its industrial and defence potential. Since these economic agents are discriminated against and cannot stand up for themselves, their status remains low, as well as their priority in the allocation of resources. Economic imbalances due to this situation cannot be corrected.

A recent example of political pressure by strong agents is the story of Gaidar's attempt radically to cut military expenses. The Russian government had a plan early in 1992 to reduce the annual military budget by 70%. The military-industrial lobby in the Supreme Soviet, together with some political organizations like the Civilian Union (headed by Volsky and Rutskov), put pressure on the government with threats to discharge it and restore the USSR frontiers of 1985. The latter would mean that the army and military-industrial complex would receive additional funding because reconstruction of the USSR would require a period of local wars with former USSR republics and an increase in military expenses. As a result Gaidar stated in November 1992 that the military state order in 1993 would be almost the same as it was in 1992.

Socialist monopolism creates vast 'stagnation zones' in which there can be no progress for decades. They are the last to be financed and supplied, and their prices and wages are low in comparison with other spheres. As a result, they deteriorate quickly, as their machinery, equipment, buildings and other assets are run down. They lose skilled labour to other sectors; their management techniques and work practices are obsolete; their morale is low; innovations are non-existent. The prime examples are the agricultural and consumer sectors, education and culture: spheres which directly affect living standards. The politically divided population cannot stand up to the well-organized and powerful military-industrial complex, or other departmental groups with extra political influence, such as the former USSR Ministry of Agricultural Reclamation.

No matter what efforts are made to isolate them, these stagnation zones are not islands cut off from the rest of the economy. No policy designed to set up 'domestic colonies' can assure their absolute isolation, and syphon off resources and manpower from them in order to attain some strategic supergoals. Since they perform socially significant functions (for example, agriculture supplies food to the population and raw materials to industry), once these stagnation zones reach a state of total decay they become an obstacle in the way of the country's economic development. Agriculture and the consumer sector have become a ball and chain attached to the legs of the Russian economy. Eventually, a day of reckoning must come, when material and human resources begin to pour into previously neglected areas of the economy and the architects of earlier policy are criticized. However, the effects of any new measures are doomed to be short-lived, since the primary assets, the production and social infrastructures, are run down. Because the prestige of the stagnation zones has been so low, skilled and ambitious personnel have found more promising employment in other spheres. Stagnation zones therefore cannot be revived with infusions of technology alone. Even if they succeed in attracting young labour, it will take them many years before they acquire the necessary skills and restore past values and habits of work.

In summary, socialist monopolism had created zones of stagnation which in turn had brought about economic imbalances, the most notorious of which were shortages, in Russia.

14.3 Monopolies and shortages

The power of monopolists stems from their unique position as the performers of an important task[17] set by the political leadership, a task which is also socially significant. This enables them to blackmail the political leadership and society as a whole. If the task is sufficiently important, monopolists can get practically anything they need by way of resources and financing. If they do not get their way, they may 'cut off the flow of oxygen', and the important task will not be fulfilled. Once resources and funds have been allocated, the monopolist can spend, utilize or waste them as it sees fit: dig foundation ditches, build factories, produce obsolete and unwanted products, and so on. As long as the monopolist is fulfilling the task set by the political authorities more or less normally, it is not accountable to anybody *de facto*,[18] even if it may be accountable to some authority *de jure*. Being the sole producer, it can always create a shortage at no extra cost or effort to itself. Consequently, when the entire range of products was manufactured by monopolies there was a shortage of everything (with, of course, a few exceptions).[19]

To create this sort of situation, it was not necessary for an enterprise to be the monopoly producer of an item. This end was also achieved when each customer was tied to just one supplier (or, to put it differently, if just one government department monopolized a particular function). Basically, in order to enhance its standing and to win additional funds and privileges, the monopolist needs to create a shortage, but not so large a shortage as to invite political reprisal. These additional resources enable the monopolist to set up new organizations, create jobs, increase wages, enhance its own prestige and representation in political bodies, and so on. This in turn enables it to obtain even more resources, and the process continues *ad infinitum.*

The result was a special relationship between the monopolist and its customers, ranging from individual consumers to political institutions. The essence of this relationship was controlled shortages (deficit). If a shortage exceeded a socially normal level and became an obstacle in the attainment of important goals, then politicians, who were the supreme distributors of resources, channelled them towards this bottleneck in order to reduce the shortage to a socially normal level.[20]

Therefore, in order to increase their social standing and their position on the list of priorities, monopolies need only stimulate shortages. This phenomenon of social blackmail means that in the competition for resources the winner is the enterprise whose product is more scarce and, as a consequence, whose economic performance is the worst! Each monopolist has sufficient power to cut output[21] or sacrifice product quality (which amounts to the same thing); to narrow the range of products; to delay delivery; to provide fewer services; to raise prices; and so on, until the shortage of the product reaches the socially normal level.[22] This 'wonderland economy' has a powerful inner tendency towards stagnation (this may be described as the 'law of constantly growing shortages'). The economic parameters that are not regulated at all, or do not readily lend themselves to regulation (e.g. product quality), follow a consistently deteriorating trend. People become increasingly alienated from the fruits of their labours, and increasingly sparing of their time and effort, while the monopolist shields them from consumer pressure which allows them to take liberties. Naturally, there can be no question of innovation in this situation.

14.4 Monopolies and innovation

Monopolists under socialism do not need innovations because they do not fear competition. There simply are no competitors. The monopolists are powerful enough to achieve their goals without innovating because they can afford to ignore the consumer. What is more, the application of innovations, particularly large-scale and highly efficient ones, may worsen a monopoly's standing because many of them involve temporary cuts in production and the use of resources. This makes it weaker in the competition for resources and makes the introduction of economically efficient innovations, which involve dramatic changes in production technology and management techniques, very unattractive. In this 'wonderland' economy, the attacking side usually loses and the winner is the enterprise that turns out masses of simple products, changing their labels and continually raising their prices.

Since monopolies do not need to innovate, they do not create the economic and social institutions necessary for the rapid diffusion of innovations. The few innovations that they apply are propagated with the help of drives or on a day-by-day basis (it being understood that modernization has been demanded by the political authorities). Should they decide to innovate on their own initiative, they will have to shift for themselves. Of course, if they are on good terms with their superiors the latter might bail them out.

It must be remembered that none of the social and economic institutions affecting economic life is prone to innovation. The centralized economic planning system, with its annual five-year and other plans, was essentially anti-innovative and rules out innovation from below. The system of material and technical supply in which requests for resources were filled over a period of one or two years; the system of performance evaluation in terms of the percentage of the fulfilment of the plan; the system of incentives for management and salaried specialists based on the same mechanism; and the nomenclature mechanism of personnel apointment – all these and other institutions (which provide the monopolist with a maximum concentration of power) completely ruled out the possibility of normal innovative activity at grass-roots level. Given these enormous social obstacles, the few innovations from below which do succeed owe their success not to these institutions but to extraordinary efforts by individual managers and work collectives. Indeed, success is achieved *despite* these institutions.

All innovations in the Soviet economy, therefore, with the exception of innovation campaigns, owed their success to conscientious managers and workers – to the human factor, rather than to some abstract mechanism. 'Unofficial' innovations under socialist monopolism are brought about not by economic or social mechanisms (which actually hinder innovations) but by psychological ones. For this reason, the rate of modernization depends strongly on the human factor. Low worker morale and alienation of the workforce from the fruits of its labours and from the administrative system, have dire consequences for the number of innovations actually applied.

We have already described the subservience of people and

organizations to monopolists. The plight of the innovator who is totally dependent on the bureaucrat is particularly unenviable. The bureaucrat controls the means of production, the finances, and the workforce. The innovating body (be it an enterprise or a group of enthusiasts) cannot get these from independent sources, for there are none under socialist monopolism. As a result, the innovator is compelled to seek support and protection from the bureaucrat. This institutionalization of innovations is a product of socialist monopolism. The innovator, who is dependent on the monopolist, cannot make an independent decision and start applying the innovation; even if this process is begun, it will still be necessary to ask for funds and resources. Since the monopolist is bound to avoid the risks and minimize social expenditures, most such requests will be turned down.

Alternatively, the innovator may be advised, 'Why don't you fight the bureaucrat, complain to the press or to the authorities?' In our view, this approach will not work because it is not the business of innovators to improve the work of the apparat; their job is to develop and apply innovations. It is not their business to ask favours from incompetent officials. Nor should the work of the upper echelons of the apparat be shifted on to the shoulders of innovators, who have absolutely no means of prodding work-shy officials into action. The struggle of innovators against the bureaucracy can only increase the dependence of the former on the latter, because even if an innovator is granted the necessary resources, he or she thereby becomes a debtor of the bureaucrat who 'met them halfway' and 'helped' them, even though not obliged to do so.

This means that the institutionalization stage of innovations must be eliminated, making the innovator independent of the bureaucrat and, if possible, disengaging them altogether. Innovators must be protected against the bureaucracy, and must not be used as pawns in the games played by the apparat. In brief, innovators must have an independent social and economic status.

This cannot be achieved within the system of socialist monopolism, under which no one has the right to start their own business, and no one is free from interference and instructions as to what to produce and at what price to sell the product. The system of socialist monopolism inevitably eliminates the economic role of owner, because property ownership institutions would protect the producer from this interference. No one has the right to give orders to owners. Even if somebody tried to order them about, the owners, strong in their constitutionally upheld, independent social status, would ignore the commands. Direct interference with the owner's activities would be illegal; interferers would be sued in court and would have to pay indemnities. It is clear that the existence of institutions upholding the independent role of property owners would curb the power of monopolists.

Furthermore, these institutions would undermine their monopoly status because potential competitors would drive them out of the market with better or cheaper products.

Socialist monopolism cannot exist if there are many owners of the means of production. A system based on administrative relations is incompatible with a system of pluralism based on property ownership relations, and including the role of owner. The destruction in the 1930s of elements of pluralism (NEP was its counterpart in the economic sphere) meant the destruction of property ownership relationships in the economy. This removed all the obstacles that prevented various monopolists from interfering in the activities of enterprises, which, together with innovators, became dependent on the bureaucracy.

The destruction of elements of pluralism prompted economic agents to minimize their inputs of time and effort in production modernization. Since neither managers, specialists nor workers owned property, and did not contribute any funds toward production modernization, their inputs were purely social. Since innovations created only problems for the workers, they did their utmost to reduce them to a bare minimum and applied only those innovations that they were obliged to. This led to stagnation in this sphere. Innovations could then only be applied by means of innovation drives sponsored by the authorities. Promoters of such drives usually put themselves out to ensure the propagation of innovations, and even went so far as to protect innovators who were in breach of existing regulations. At the same time, though, promoters of such campaigns have few objective criteria (e.g. the exact number of enterprises to be involved in the campaign, what sort of enterprises, the rate of propagation etc.) to guide them in the implementation of an innovation drive. This is due to the phenomenon which we describe as the economic immune-deficiency syndrome, which in its turn is due to the destruction of pluralism. Since practically the entire workforce seeks to minimize its social expenditure and avoid innovating activities, the upper echelons of command, which do not have the complete picture, tend to go to extremes and insist that innovations be applied even by enterprises that are not really ready to do so. As a result, individual enterprises and society as a whole may sustain economic losses.

To conclude, socialist monopolism is a formidable obstacle in the way of innovation. It keeps alive old deficiencies in all institutions regulating modernization and breeds new ones. It destroys the role of owner in the economy; it makes innovation unattractive to enterprises; it makes innovators dependent on bureaucrats; it makes innovation drives the preferred means of modernization; it nurtures stagnation in culture (which is not appreciative of innovation and encourages the economy of time and effort in this sphere); and it prevents the criticism of ideological dogmas and thus contributes to their preservation. That is why it might be called is the root cause of stagnation in innovation in Russia today.

Gorbachev's perestroika and the Yeltsin–Gaidar transition altered socialist monopolism, but did not eliminate it. The latter has transformed it into a post-socialist monopolism. This has some specific features. The main one is that the single agent in every sphere divides into several powerful groups uncontrolled by Moscow's authorities. Most of these powerful groups were formed under perestroika and even during the pre-Gorbachev era. For example, the 'Gasprom' concern was formed under Gorbachev and the Russian Ministry of Fuel Resources, and both supervised it under fuel production. Other specific features of post-socialist monopolism have a non-totalitarian and non-comprehensive character, and though the influence of the new monopolies is very strong, it takes other forms and uses other means. Like the old agents, the new monopolies use blackmail over orders to Moscow's authorities and the public. If in the past branch ministries provoked shortages in order to obtain financial and material resources, so now directors of large state enterprises and leaders of trades unions initiate strikes to obtain funds or to receive political and economic preferences. All this leads to deficiencies of independent private activities and to preservation of the dependence of innovators on bureaucrats. All this provokes economic instability and puts obstacles in the way of innovations. In spite of such obstacles, some inventors and innovators continue to carry out their inventions and innovations with the support of new (for Russia) economic conditions and new opportunities.

NOTES

1 *Translator's note*: this term has been coined by the author to denote the system's propensity to monopolize all spheres of life.

2 It is no wonder that wrong decisions were primarily criticized by the relatively independent general public, from whom most writers and commentators originated.

3 A. Yakovlev, 'Attaining a qualitatively new state of Soviet society and the social sciences', *Kommunist*, viii (1987), 8.
4 Entire schools of sociology grew around the research of Sorokin and Gurvich, in the USA and France, respectively.
5 Different authors have come up with different names for this concept. For example, V. E. Boikov, *The main condition for success: on the unity of ideological, organizing and economic activities*, Moscow, Politizdat (1988), refers to it as the principle of unity of ideological, organizational and economic activity in the system of political leadership of Soviet society. Terminological differences, however, do not change the substance of the concept, because all authors agree that interference by political institutions in various spheres of life is the cornerstone of the socialist system.
6 We owe to Stalin the ideological principle of organization according to which all institutions are but 'the Party's driving belts'. In our view, the principle of unity between the ideological, political and economic work of the Party is a more or less direct extension of this. Since organizations are only 'driving belts', they are anything but voluntary associations.
7 I. V. Stalin, *Collected works*, xi, Moscow, Gospolitizdat (1949), 14.
8 S. L. Dmitrenko, *United ranks: the Komsomol in the struggle against Trotskyism*, Moscow, Molodaya Gvardiya (1987), 194.
9 E. Dodolev, '... and one night', *Smena*, xv (1988), 18.
10 A ranking official with the Moscow housing department commented: 'Several speakers concluded their statement with the following idea: the main task of housing organizations and enterprises is to properly exploit and conserve the housing fund. One is tempted to add: and to provide a maximum of facilities and services to the population. But the speakers did not say so. Why? It turned out that their lifelong ambition is to place the onus of repairs and maintenance on to the occupants of housing.' M. Buzhevich, 'Stolen time', *Pravda*, 8 January 1987.
11 One of the principal functions of a myth is to make the public proud of the accomplishments in the myth-maker's sphere of life. This makes the workforce easier to control and reconciles consumers to 'minor shortcomings' and 'temporary problems'.
12 V. Tikhonov, 'So that the nation can feed itself ...', *Literaturnaya gazeta*, 3 August 1988.
13 These 'games' are administrative-political rather than economic in nature.
14 The Yeltsin–Gaidar economic transformation has somewhat changed this situation. Now everyone has an opportunity to create a private firm. However, the procedure of registering a firm has been transformed by officials into a process of receiving permission to establish an organization. Therefore the dependence of enterprises on state bodies, though changed, has been preserved.
15 This definition of entrepreneurial activity is closest to its 'narrow' interpretation by Schumpeter, who considered innovation to be the distinctive feature of the entrepreneur. For various interpretations of

the concepts of entrepreneur and entrepreneurship, see C. E. Black, 'Russian and Soviet entrepreneurship in a comparative context', in *Entrepreneurship in imperial Russia and the Soviet Union*, Princeton, Princeton U. Press (1983). This collection of essays, edited by G. Guroff and F. V. Carstensen, also contains an analysis of entrepreneurship specifically in Russia and the USSR.

16 Under socialist monopolism, 'objective laws' reflect rather subjective interests. These 'laws' are the result of quoting 'classics' out of context. See, for example, Solnyshkov's article 'When the bureaucrat is above the law, or his/her interests are protected by the main economic law of socialism', *Smena*, xv (1988). This details the benefits accruing from this law to the bureaucratic apparatus.

17 As we have already pointed out, the further the task is from the needs of the population and the closer it is to such strategic areas as defence, foreign trade etc., the more important it becomes.

18 Unless, of course, the politicians lose patience, as has been the case with the diversion of the Siberian rivers to the south.

19 It would be more precise to say that there was an almost permanent shortage of virtually everything. The authorities might succeed in eliminating a shortage in one area, but it was bound to develop in another. There were usually several geographical areas suffering from a shortage of the same product. It was a case of itinerant shortages (the 'law of the conservation of shortages').

20 Of course, everyone strove to weaken this dependence. For example, enterprises and official departments set up their own 'subsistence economies' and engaged in 'shadow' economic activities. The population engage in subsistence farming, seek protection, pilfer, perform mutual services and even reduce consumption.

21 This parameter is the easiest to control, which is why it is the one to be primarily manipulated.

22 The situation of people and organizations unable for some reason to do so (for example, some people are too high-minded to produce shady articles) is unenviable, since they lose out to competitors. Besides, there are 'objective differences' between industrial sectors. For example, extracting industries are at a disadvantage in comparison with manufacturing because they are not as free to manipulate product quality and price. The situation in agriculture in the late 1920s was similarly unenviable, because the political leadership created a gap between the prices of manufactured goods and agricultural produce.

Conclusion

There are no more five-year plans for the introduction of the achievements of science into enterprises. The drives on maize extension and modern methods of steel casting have passed away. It is even permitted now to set up private firms for implementing R&D results, and to earn money by selling one's own ideas.

However, in reality the innovative process in Russia has slowed down. As a matter of fact the actual need for innovations has never established itself within the enterprises. Russian society has not yet got rid of its economic immune-deficiency syndrome. No natural economic selection necessitates innovative activity. The state enterprises (still in the majority) are able to retain the position they have achieved, demanding and obtaining money from the state to solve their problems. A well-functioning innovation system is not a vital necessity for them.[1]

Therefore, any new innovation system corresponding to market economy conditions is still in the embryonic stage. Moreover, Russia is still choosing the path it will follow for its development. Until this choice is made, one cannot expect the formation of a new innovation system, because the country is facing more important tasks of political and economic self-determination.

Nevertheless, it is possible to draw general outlines of the emerging new innovation system in Russia. Its main features are as follows.

1 Several independent research firms have appeared and a relatively small number of research divisions within the enterprises have been organized. The research firms are being established at present by state research institutes, by individual inventors and by

innovators. They are also being set up at the cost of privatization of state institutes' property. The demand for industrial R&D of the majority of newly created privatized firms is low. Therefore it is possible to anticipate that in the long run most of them will either be integrated as research divisions by large private enterprises, or will change the profile of their activity, or will be closed.

2 There is uncertainty over the position of the owner of R&D results. In Russian state institutes a number of R&D results have accumulated which previously belonged to the state and were of no economic value to individuals. Nowadays, on the contrary, the ownership of these inventions and techniques is not determined: it belongs to neither the state, nor the institutes' administration, nor their personnel, nor their direct authors. Any attempt to determine an owner officially and to conduct the privatization of R&D on this basis is sure to provoke serious conflicts and to hold back the practical use of the innovations for a long time.

3 There is no control over the adoption of R&D results in the form of functioning patent legislation or intellectual property protection. The flow of innovations streams unchecked from state institutes into private research firms. R&D results are being adopted free of charge (sometimes simply stolen) and are being sold at a profit. Although some necessary legislative acts on intellectual property are being developed at present, and attempts are being made to introduce patent legislation, still these approved norms will remain inefficient in practice for some time. To make up a legal market for innovations is not beneficial to anybody for the time-being: neither to the authors themselves, nor to the administration of the institutes, nor to the managers in industry. Those innovations that are in demand are being realized by their authors (often jointly with the administration of the institute) via private firms without any regulation whatsoever. A black market for innovations is developing as a result. It may gradually transform itself into a legal one on condition that the state does enforce constraints and also that laws are adopted which would reflect the interests of the main participants of the innovative processes.

4 The extreme decentralization of the information on R&D results has led to low accessibility for potential consumers. The command economy was characterized by hypercentralization of information on current R&D, and this information was concentrated in branch ministries and head institutes. Now the state system of economic management via branch ministries is being broken: the Union ministries are liquidated, and the Russian ministries have rather weak links with enterprises and research units. As a result the centralized information system is destroyed.

Therefore data on R&D results can be obtained only from the institutes that are developing them. The specialized market organizations which would accumulate the information on R&D already released or being developed are not available yet in Russia.

The deficiencies of the innovation system that is now forming in Russia are the consequences of the incomplete transition to the market. As a matter of fact, despite the liquidation of the CPSU and of a number of other old structures the real power and control of the economy are still in the hands of the representatives of the former nomenclature clans, informally united with each other. These representatives are the directors of state enterprises, former functionaries of Party committees, executive committees of the Soviets, economic ministries and departments, former KGB collaborators, MVD officials who have entered now into the new authorities and founded a lot of quasi-private firms dependent on the state. As a result, the old nomenclature clans, in their majority, have retained a real power in the country and above all in the regions of Russia. Such a process of adaptation of the former Soviet élite to the new conditions has created relatively stable structures of economic and political power and made it possible to avoid chaos in the country. However, it has also delayed many vitally important changes, first among them the setting up of a normal institution of private property and privatization of state enterprises. The predominance of the old nomenclature makes it very difficult for independent entrepreneurs to found new firms, to obtain land and buildings on lease or to sell their products. It is clear that these difficulties are still more complicated for the innovator than for the common entrepreneur involved in organizing traditional production.

At the same time, under the conditions of stability preserved in the country over several years, a stable multi-party democracy, market economy and efficient national innovation system ensuring the dynamic development of the country may gradually be set up in Russia. This could be the best conclusion to the Communist experiment in Russia, started by history over 70 years ago.

NOTES

1 One can find a useful analysis of different national innovation systems in a large comparative study recently carried out in 15 countries in which various criteria of well-functioning innovation systems are discussed. See R. Nelson, 'National innovation systems: a retrospective study', in *Research and development in the transition to a market economy*, eds. S. Glaziev and C. M. Schneider.

Bibliography

1 Articles and books in Russian

Abalkin, L. M. 'The new economic thinking, a need of the day', *Nauka i zhizn*, vii (1988)

Ainshtein, V. 'Wanted: engineer with a school-leaving certificate', *Sovetskaya Rossiya*, 1 April 1986

Aksenov, K. 'And what's in the bunker?', *Pravda*, 6 January 1986

Alekseev, G. M. *The movement of inventors and rationalizers in the USSR*, Moscow, Mysl (1983)

Alekseev, N. I. *Economic experiment: social aspects*, Moscow, Mysl (1987)

Arutyunov, S. A. *Innovation in the culture of an ethnic group*, Moscow, Nauka (1985)

Atakhanov, K., and Karpov, A. 'A dangerous vegetable', *Nedelya*, xxxiii (1988)

Aven, P. A., and Shironin, V. M. 'Management hierarchies and the distribution of resources', in *The personnel of the Agro-Industrial Complex within the system of managerial relations*, Barnaul, Institute for Economics and Industrial Engineering, AS USSR (Siberian branch) (1987)

Bazhutin, G. 'The taste for novelty', *Sotsialisticheskaya industriya*, 23 August 1985

Barkova, E. A. 'Statistics of the quality of personnel in agriculture', *Social problems in improving the use made of trained staff in Siberia's agriculture*, Novosibirsk, Institute for Economics in Agriculture, All-Union Academy of Agriculture (Siberian branch) (1984)

Bek, A. 'A new appointment', *Znamya*, xi, xii (1987)

Blokhin, A. 'On the verge of an explosion', *Sotsialisticheskaya industriya*, 23 July 1988

Bogomolov, O. 'The socialist market', *Moscow News*, xxx (1987)
Boikov, V. E. *The main condition for success: on the unity of ideological, organizing and economic activities*, Moscow, Politizdat (1988)
Bossart, A. 'An iron curtain of a tax', *Ogonek*, xxix (1988)
Buzhevich, M. 'Stolen time', *Pravda*, 8 January 1987
Chekalin, A. N. *An economic experiment*, Moscow, Stroiizdat (1987)
Chernichenko, Y. D. *Good husbandry*, Moscow, Sovetsky pisatel' (1984)
Chernov, A. 'Model of hope', *Ogonek*, xxxi (1988)
Chernyi, L. B. 'On the problem of classifying large blocks of data according to qualitative indicators', in *Application of factorial and classificatory analysis for making a typology of social phenomena*, Novosibirsk, Institute of Economics and Industrial Production (1976)
Chesnokov, S. V. *Determination analysis of socio-economic data*, Moscow, Nauka (1982)
Dmitrenko, S. L. *United ranks: the Komsomol in the struggle against Trotskyism*, Moscow, Molodaya Gvardiya (1987)
Dodolev, E. '. . . and one night', *Smena*, xv (1988)
Dominov, V. M. *The implementation of scientific advances in the Agro-Industrial Complex*, Kishinev, Institute for Agro-Industrial Complex Problems, All-Union Academy of Agriculture (Moldavian branch) (1983)
Dozortsev, V. A. *Legislation and scientific and technical progress*, Moscow, Yuridicheskaya literatura (1978)
Dudinstev, V. 'Not by bread alone', *Novy mir*, x–xii (1966)
Dzhavadov, G. A., ed. *Management using scientific and technical progress*, Moscow, Ekonomika (1978)
Emelyanov, A. M., ed. *Scientific and technical progress and the efficiency of production: for those employed in agriculture*, Moscow, Ekonomika (1982)
Engelhardt, A. N. *From the village: 12 letters*, Moscow, Mysl (1987)
Eremeev, B. I. *Socio-economic issues in technical creativity in the USSR*, Moscow, Mysl (1967)
Ermakov, P. I. 'Science and production', *Sovetskaya Rossiya* (1978)
Ermishin, P. G. *Scientific and technical progress in agriculture*, Kiev-Odessa, Vyshaya shkola (1981)
Fedorov, Y., and Fufryansky, N. 'Accelerating the reconstruction of our railways', *Izvestiya*, 4 April 1988
Fofanov, V. P. *Economic consciousness and economic relations*, Novosibirsk, Nauka (1979)
Frolov, V. I. 'Make way for vetch . . .', *Krest'yanskaya gazeta*, xxxix (1927)
Gaidar, E., and Yaroshenko, V. 'Towards an analysis of how ministries expand', *Kommunist*, (1988).
Gareev, R. 'Is it possible to eliminate turnover among trained staff?', *Izvestiya*, 21 August 1985
Gatovsky, L. M. *Economic issues in scientific and technical progress*, Moscow, Nauka, (1971)

Gladyshev, L., and Shilov, V. 'Initiative outside the plan', *Sovetskaya Rossiya*, 13 September 1981

Gorbachev, M. S. 'The fundamental issue in the Party's economic policy', *Pravda*, 12 June 1985

——*Through democratization to a new type of socialism*, Moscow, Politizdat (1988)

Gvishiani, D. M., ed. *Problems of administrative innovations and economic experimentation*: republican conference of theorists and practitioners, Tallin, All-Union Council of Scientific and Technical Associations (1981)

Handbook for collective farm chairmen, Moscow, Kolos (1980)

Inventions and rationalization proposals: main indicators, Moscow, working paper of Russian Society for Inventors (1992)

Kapeliushny, L., and Reznik, B. 'Unlike relations', *Izvestiya*, 27 August 1985

Kapustin, E. I., and Voeikov, N. I., ed. *Scientific and technical progress and the creativity of the masses*, Moscow, Profizdat (1986)

Klemyshev, P. A., ed. *Scientific and technical potential of the food programme*, Moscow, Nauka (1985)

Kordonsky, S. G. 'The problem of mutual exchange relations: their essence and role in managing production', in *The personnel of the Agro-Industrial Complex within the system of managerial relations*, Barnaul, Institute for Economics and Industrial Engineering AS USSR (Siberian branch) (1987)

Kosals, L. *Social mechanism for the innovative processes*, Novosibirsk, Nauka (1989)

Kosyakin, I. 'Where are the sources of goods shortages in our co-operative?' *Krest'yanskaya gazeta*, xli (1927)

Kozlovich, A. 'The technology of "non-management"', *Literaturnaya gazeta*, 23 August 1985

Krevnevich, V. V., and Usenin, V. I., ed., *The working class in the scientific and technical revolution*, Moscow, Nauka, (1979)

Kruglikov, A. G. 'Economic analysis of the spread of scientific and technical innovations (using the example of new technologies in ferrous metallurgy)', in *Mathematical models and the statistical analysis of scientific and technical progress*, Moscow, VNIISI (1982)

——'The innovative conception of scientific and technical progress', in *The structure of the innovative process*, Moscow, All-Union Institute for System Analysis, AS USSR (1981)

Kruglinsky, M. 'A sore point', *Izvestiya*, 22 December 1986

Kruglyanskaya, I. 'Rumours', *Izvestiya*, 5 September 1987

Kushlin, V. I. *Production management in the future*, Moscow, Mysl, (1981)

Kutuzov, 'Don't blame it all on the central authorities', *Krest'yanskaya gazeta*, xli (1927)

——'What is imported into and exported from the village from abroad', *Krest'yanskaya gazeta*, xxxix (1927)

Kutyrev, B. P. *On the way to the collective workteam*, Novosibirsk, Nauka (1988)

Kvasha, Y. B. *The time factor in socialized production*, Moscow, Statistika (1979)

Lapin, N. I. 'Social aspects of the intensification of innovations', in *Ways to improve the social machinery of the Soviet economy's development*, Novosibirsk, Institute for Economics and Industrial Engineering, AS USSR (Siberian branch) (1985)

Lapin, N. I., ed. *Social factors of innovations in organizational systems*: conference proceedings, Moscow (1980)

——*Structure of the innovative process*: conference proceedings, Moscow (1981)

——*Innovative processes*: seminar proceedings, Moscow (1982)

Lapin, N. I., Prigozhin, A. I., Sazonov, B. V., and Tolstoy, V. S. 'Innovations in organizations', in *The structure of the innovative process*, Moscow, All-Union Institute for System Analysis, AS USSR (1981)

Lebedev, P. 'What do we know about our ministers?', *Ogonek*, xxxi (1988)

Lebedev, R. L. and Poleshchuk, G. M. 'About the attitude of the manager to the launching of new products', in Proceedings of the Siberian branch of the AS USSR: Economics and Applied Sociology series, Issue 3 (1984)

Lebedev, V. G., ed. *Management using scientific and technical progress under developed socialism*, Moscow, Mysl (1984)

Leiman, I. I. *The sciences as a social institution*, Leningrad, Nauka (1971)

Lenin, V. I. 'Concerning compromises', in *Complete collected works*, xl, Moscow, Gospolitizdat (1963)

——'Speech on the replacement of requisitioning by the tax in kind', in *Complete collected works*, xliii, Moscow, Gospolitizdat (1963)

Leskov, S. 'Leaders of defence branches in Russia and Ukraine are pushing the politicians closer to each other', *Izvestiya*, 15 January 1993

——'Prime minister troubled by the fate of science', *Izvestiya*, 20 January 1993

Lysaya, E. 'Mini-factories', *EKO*, x (1987)

Maiminas, E. Z. 'On the formation of economic machinery', *Economics and mathematical methods*, xviii/3 (1982)

Malakhiev, M. 'Ministerial obstruction', *Sovetskaya Rossiya*, 13 August 1985

Marx and Engels, 'The communist manifesto', in *Works*, Moscow, Politizdat (1955)

Maximova, N. 'Brigades at the parting of the ways', *EKO*, viii (1985)

Mikoyan, A. 'On the grain-procurement campaign', *Krest'yanskaya gazeta*, xxxix (1927)

Muchnik, V. S., and Golland, E. B. *Economic problems of contemporary scientific and technical progress*, Novosibirsk, Nauka (1984)

Musaev, A. M. *Unity of political and organizational work, the Leninist principle of rule by the Party*, Moscow, Politizdat (1981)

Ovcharenko, G. 'The right to take a decision', *Pravda*, 10 August 1985

Palterovich, D. 'Does socialism need competition?' *Moscow News*, xi (1987)

Parygin, B. D., ed. *Socio-psychological problems of scientific and technical progress*, Leningrad, Nauka (1982)

Pavlov, V. N., and Dementev, N. P. 'Technological progress and the property of optimism', in *The interconnections between scientific and technical progress and economic development*, Novosibirsk, Institute for Economics and Industrial Engineering, AS USSR (Siberian branch) (1987)

Persianov, R. M. *Socio-economic problems of technical creativity in developed socialist society*, Leningrad, Leningrad University (1977)

Piskotin, M. I. *Socialism and state administration*, Moscow, Nauka, (1984)

Platonov, A. *The juvenile sea*, Moscow, Izvestiya (1989)

Platonov, A., and Pilnyak, B. 'Che-Che-O: Regional organizational-philosophical studies', *Sel'skaya molodezh*, vii (1987)

Pokrovsky, A. 'Our stumbling blocks or the psychological barriers on the path of technical innovation', *Pravda*, 16 April 1988

Popkova, M. [pseud. L. Piyasheva] 'Who bakes better pies?' *Novy mir*, v (1987)

Popov, G. 'Aims and machinery', *Znamya*, vii (1988)

Popov, G. K. 'From an economist's point of view', *Nauka i zhizn*, iv (1987).

—— 'A time for practical steps: the search for the optimal economic machinery', *Moscow News*, xxxv (1987)

Popov, V. A. *The formation of the socio-economic structure of the Japanese village*, Moscow, Nauka (1987)

Popov, V. D. *Economic consciousness: its essence, formation and role in socialist society*, Moscow, Mysl, (1981)

Popov, V., and Shmelev, N. 'The anatomy of deficit', *Znamya*, v (1988)

Potapovskaya, G. 'Honesty in disfavour', *Sel'skaya molodezh*, xi (1986)

Prigozhin, A. I. *Issues in the study of innovations in organizational systems*, Moscow, All-Union Institute for System Analysis, AS USSR (1980)

Radov, A. 'Who should be called to account for the missing billions of roubles?', *Sovetskaya Rossiya*, 15 October 1985

——'Inventors and bureaucrats', *Ogonek*, xviii (1988)

Rassokhin, V. P. 'How to solve the problem of non-implementation', *Khozaistvo i pravo*, (1978)

——*Mechanism for the implementation of scientific advances: politics, administration and law*, Moscow, Nauka (1985)

Ring, M. P. *The cost-accounting system for creating and implementing new equipment: legal issues*, Moscow, Nauka (1985)

Rostovtsev, P. S. '"Spot-stripe" algorithms in the analysis of right-angle matrices', in *The analysis of non-quantifiable information in sociological research*, Moscow, Nauka (1985)

Rozenbaum, Y. A. *The formation of administrative personnel*, Moscow, Nauka (1982)

Rumyantsev, O. G. 'On the independent movement of public initiatives (informal associations and their role in restructuring public life in the USSR)', Preprint of report, Moscow, Institute of Economy of the World Socialist System (1988)

Runchev, M. S., ed. *Management using scientific and technical progress in agriculture*, Moscow, Ekonomika (1982).

Ryvkina, R. V. *The rural population's way of life*, Novosibirsk, Nauka (1979)

——'Administrative groups: activities, behaviour and interaction', in Izvestiya Siberian section of AS USSR: Economics and Applied Sociology Series, Issue 3(1985)

——'Sociology and the management of social processes', *EKO*, ix (1986)

Ryvkina, R. V., Kosals, E. V., Kosals, L. Y., and Narukov, G. A. 'Changes in the working activities and attitudes to work in the team contract', (Preprint), Novosibirsk, Institute for Economics and Industrial Engineering, AS USSR (Siberian branch) (1985)

Ryvkina, R. V., and Kosals, L. Y. 'The role of social machinery in accelerating the socio-economic development of society', in Izvestiya Siberian section of AS USSR: Economics and Applied Sociology Series, iii (1986)

Salutsky, A. 'The weak and the strong', *Nash sovremennik*, ix (1987)

Santo, B. 'Ways of implementing technical innovations', *EKO*, xi (1983)

Savostyanov, V. 'Is a coup threatening us?' *Vecherniya Moskva*, 18 November 1992

Sazonov, B. V. 'The activities approach to innovations', *Social factors of innovations in organizational systems*: Conference proceedings, Moscow (1980)

Science and production combines in agriculture, Moscow, Kolos (1984)

Scientific-technical progress in RSFSR in 1990: statistics manual, Moscow, Republican Informational-editing Centre, State Committee of RSFSR on Statistics (1991)

Seliunin, V. 'A major reform or the bureaucracy's riposte?', *Znamya*, vii (1988)

——'The sources', *Novy mir*, v (1988)

Seliunin, V., and Khanin, G. 'Deceitful figures', *Novy mir*, ii (1987)

Semenov, B. (pseud. B. Pinsker) 'Plan and spontaneity', *Novy mir*, xii (1987)

Shmelev, N. 'Loans and debts', *Novy mir*, vi (1987)

——'New alarms', *Novy mir*, iv (1988)

Shokhin, A. N. 'Social aspects of the struggle with unearned incomes', in *Social aspects of the redistribution policy*, Moscow, Nauka (1984)

Shvets, V. 'The economy's autopilot', *Sovetskaya Rossiya*, 14 June 1988

Skripov, V. A. 'Everyday routine', *EKO*, iv (1983)

Smirnov, V. 'The nature of the brigade', *Sovetskaya Rossiya*, 13 December 1984

Sokolov, V. 'Gang rule', *Literaturnaya gazeta*, 17 August 1988

Solnyshkov, Y. 'When the bureaucrat is above the law . . .', *Smena*, xv (1988)

Solodovnikov, P. 'Letter to the editor', *Sovetskaya Rossiya*, 12 December 1987

Somov, V. '"Farmer" means being your own boss', *Pravda*, 3 August 1988

Stalin, I. V. 'First results of the procurements campaign and the further tasks of the Party: to all organizations of the VKP (B)', *Collected works*, xi, Moscow, Gospolitizdat (1949)

——'On the work of the combined April plenum of the Central Committee and Central Control Commission: report to the activists of the VPK (B)'s Moscow organization, 13 April 1929', *Collected works*, xi, Moscow, Gospolitizdat (1949)

——'On the alliance between the workers and the peasants and about state farms: from speech on 11 July 1928 to the Central Committee plenum, 4–12 July 1928', *Collected works*, xi, Moscow, Gospolitizdat (1949)

'Statistical data on criminalty in Russia', *Rossiyskaya gazeta*, 5 February 1993

Tatarnikova, N. M. 'The problem of halting turnover in trained staff in the enterprises of the Agro-Industrial Complex', in *Improving economic relations in the APK*, Novosibirsk, Academy of Agricultural Sciences (Siberian branch) (1987)

The economy of the Novosibirsk region for 1981–5: statistical yearbook, Novosibirsk (1987)

The work of a director, Moscow, Ekonomika (1977)

Tikhomirov, Y. 'Permitted, if not forbidden', *Khozaistvo i pravo*, vi (1988)

Tikhonov, V. 'So that the nation can feed itself . . .', *Literaturnaya gazeta*, 3 August 1988

Tiurin, E. I. 'Innovating and cost-accounting', *Sovetskaya Rossiya*, 12 December 1987

Tolstykh, B. V. 'A difficult transition', *NTR*, xiii (1988)

Valovoi, D. *Economics in its human dimension*, Moscow, Politizdat (1988)

Vasiliev, I. *Guideposts*, Moscow, Politizdat (1988)

Vasinsky, A., and Ershov, L. 'Three sides of the same problem', *Izvestiya*, 21 August 1985

Vilenskiy, M. A., ed. *Economic evaluation of the social results of implementing new equipment*, Kiev, Naukova Dumka (1981)

Vooglaid, V., Iohansoo, K., *et al. Problems of innovation and experimentation*: seminar proceedings, Tallin, Commission for Economic Experiments of Committee on Management (Estonian Council of Scientific and Technical Associations) (1981)

Vukovich, V. 'Risk-taking is a good thing', *Izvestiya*, 24 August 1985

Wages at state farms and other state agricultural enterprises: handbook, Moscow, Rossel'khozizdat (1985)

Yakovlev, A. 'Attaining a qualitatively new state of Soviet society and the social sciences', *Kommunist*, viii (1987)

Yakovlev, A. M. *The sociology of economic crime*, Moscow, Nauka (1988)
Yasin, E. G. 'Public property, economic incentives and cost accounting', *EKO*, xii (1984)
Yushchenko, A. 'A coward in the field cannot be his own master', *Komsomolskaya pravda*, 14 April 1988
Zalipaev, V. 'Who needs "accommodating" people?', *Sovetskaya Rossiya*, 2 June 1985
Zaslavskaya, T. I. 'Economic behaviour and economic development', *EKO*, iii, (1980)
——'Economics through the prism of sociology', *EKO*, x (1985)
Zaslavskaya, T. I., and Ryvkina, R. V. 'On the subject of economic sociology', Proceedings of the Siberian branch of the AS USSR: Economics and Applied Sociology Series, No. 1, Issue 1 (1984)
——*Sociology of economic life: studies in the theory*, Novosibirsk, Nauka (1991)
Zinoviev, A. 'Prokopov's invention', *Izvestiya*, 15 February 1988

2 Works quoted in Russian translation

Becker, H., and Boskoff, A., ed. *Modern sociological theory in continuity and change*, New York, Dryden Press (1957; Russian trans. 1961)
Foster, R. *Innovation: the attacker's advantage*, New York, Summit Books (1986; Russian trans. 1987)
Hammer, A. *Autobiography*, New York, Putnam & Sons (1987; Russian trans. 1988)
Kalisiak, J. *Badane efectywnosci ekonomicznej postepu techniczno-organizacyjnego*, Warsaw, Paustn. wyd-no naukowe (1973; Russian trans. 1976)
Kowalewski, S. 'Nauka o administovaniu', in *Ksiaszka i Wiedza*, Warsaw (1975; Russian trans. 1979)
Kuhn, T. S. *The structure of scientific revolutions*, Chicago, U. Chicago Press (1970; Russian trans. 1976)
Mansfield, E. *The economics of technological change*, New York, Norton & Co. (1968; Russian trans. 1970)
Martino, J. P. *Technological forecasting for decision-making*, New York, Elsevier (1972; Russian trans. 1977)
Moritani, M. *Advanced technology: the Japanese contribution*, Tokyo, Simul Press (1983; Russian trans. 1986)
Rodgers, E. M., and Agarwala-Rodgers, R. *Communication in organizations*, New York, Free Press (1977; Russian trans. 1980)
Sahal, D. *Patterns of technological innovation*, Reading, MA, Addison-Wesley (1981; Russian trans. 1985)
Veblen, T. *The theory of the leisure class: an economic study of institutions*, New York, Vanguard Press (1927; Russian trans. 1984)
Weber, M., *The protestant ethic and the spirit of capitalism*, New York, Scribner (1952; Russian trans. 1972)

3 Works in other languages

Abbot, L. F. *Social aspects of innovation and industrial technology: a survey of research*, Department of Industry, CFIT, Paper no. 1 (1976)

Aram, I. D. Innovation via R&D underground.' *Research management*, xvi/6 (1973)

Black, C. E. 'Russian and Soviet enterpreneurship in a comparative context', in *Entrepreneurship in imperial Russia and the Soviet Union*, ed. Guroff and Carstensen, Princeton, NJ, Princeton U. Press (1983)

Guroff, G., and Carstensen, F. V., ed. *Entrepreneurship in imperial Russia and the Soviet Union*, Princeton, NJ, Princeton U. Press (1983)

Fliegel, F. C., Kivlin, J. E., and Sekhon, G. S. 'A cross-cultural comparison of farmers' perception of innovations as related to adoptions behavior', *Rural sociology*, xxxiii (1968)

Fusfield, H. I., and Langlois, R. N., ed. *Understanding R&D productivity*, Oxford, Pergamon (1982; Russian trans. 1986)

Goldman, M. I. *Gorbachev's challenge: economic reform in the age of high technology*, New York, W. W. Norton & Co. (1987)

Gürtler, J. and Schmalholz, H. '*Innovationsaktivitäten im verarbeitenden Gewerbe*', *IFO-Schnelldeinst*, xxxv/20 (1982)

Hagen, E. E. *On the theory of social change*, Homewood, Dorsey Press (1962)

Hanson, P., and Pavitt, K. 'The comparative economics of research development and innovation in East and West: a survey', in *Fundamentals of pure and applied economics*, xxv (1987)

Myers, S., and Marquis, D. G. *Successful industrial innovations: a study of factors underlying innovation in selected firms*, Washington, DC, National Science Foundation (1969)

Nelson, R. 'National innovation systems: a retrospective study', in *Research and development management in the transition to a market economy*, ed. S. Glaziev, and C. M. Schneider, Laxenburg International Institute for Applied System Analysis (1993)

Olson, M. 'The logic of collective action in Soviet-type societies', *Journal of Soviet nationalities*, i/2 (1990)

Robbins, S. P. *Organizational behavior: concepts, controversies and applications*, New Jersey, Prentice-Hall (1986)

Roman, D. D., and Puett, J. F. Jr *International business and technological innovation*, New York, Elsevier Science Publishing (1983)

Schleh, E. *Management by results*, New York, McGraw-Hill (1961)

Schmookler, J. 'Economic sources of inventive activity', *Journal of Economic History*, xxii (1962)

Schumacher, E. F. *Small is beautiful: a study of economics as if people mattered*, London, Blond & Briggs (1975)

Slider, D. 'Regional aspects of policy innovation in the Soviet Union', in *Politics and the Soviet system*, ed. T. F. Remington, London, Macmillan (1989)

Zaltman, G., Duncan, R., and Holbek, J. *Innovations and organizations*, New York, J. Wiley & Co. (1973)